THE COMPLETE BOOK OF SCRIPT-WRITING

J. Michael Straczynski

Writer's Digest Books

Cincinnati, Ohio

The Complete Book of Scriptwriting. Copyright 1982 by J. Michael Straczynski. Printed and bound in the United States of America. All rights reserved. No part of this book may be reproduced in any form or by any electronic or mechanical means including information storage and retrieval systems without permission in writing from the publisher, except by a reviewer who may quote brief passages in a review. Published by Writer's Digest Books, 9933 Alliance Road, Cincinnati, Ohio 45242. First edition.

Library of Congress Cataloging in Publication Data

Straczynski, J. Michael, 1954-
    The complete book of scriptwriting.
    Includes index.
    1. Playwriting. 2. Television authorship.
    3. Radio authorship. 4. Moving-picture authorship.
    I. Title.
PN1661.S75   808.2   82-2050
ISBN 0-89879-078-6   AACR2

Book design by Barron Krody.

TELEVISION
RADIO
MOTION PICTURES
THE STAGE PLAY

THE COMPLETE HANDBOOK OF SCRIPTWRITING

Dedication

To Norman Corwin, friend and mentor, and to Harlan Ellison, who together have demonstrated that it is possible to sell without selling out. Two men whose integrity, courage, honor and fierce dedication to their craft have inspired an entire generation of writers, scripters, and other apprentice sorcerers.

Acknowledgments

The author would like to take this opportunity to express his gratitude to the following persons, who have contributed greatly, in one way or another, to the present work: Lee Hansen, for introducing me to the marvelous world of radiodrama; Richard Kim, for showing the way; Dan McLeod, Chairman of the Creative Writing Department at San Diego State University, for providing a class and letting me play in it; Carol Cartaino, Senior Editor at Writer's Digest Books, without whose persistence and encouragement this book would not exist; Mark Orwoll, John Dobry, Sandy Richardson and Michael Fine, for friendship given above and beyond the call of common sense; and finally, most importantly, to Kathryn Drennan, for countless hours spent reading and critiquing this and many other manuscripts, for her constant support, and for her very presence, without which this writer's life would be infinitely poorer.

Contents

American playwrights. An anatomy of current American theater from a playwright's perspective: little, experimental, community, legitimate, and showcase theaters. A pressing need for new writers. The five benefits of playwriting.

Don't be afraid. That simple; don't let them scare you. There's nothing they can do to you. . . . A writer always writes. That's what he's for. And if they won't let you write one kind of thing, if they chop you off at the pockets in the market place, then go to another market place. And if they close off all the bazaars, then by God go and work with your hands till you *can* write, because the talent is always there. But the first time you say, "Oh, Christ, they'll kill me!" then you're done. Because the chief commodity a writer has to sell is his courage. And if he has none, he is more than a coward. He is a sellout and a fink and a heretic, because writing is a holy chore.

—Harlan Ellison, from his
anthology, *Dangerous Visions*

Preface

Some time ago, I was teaching a seminar on scriptwriting sponsored by a San Diego-based community theater. The students came from all walks of life. There were housewives and college students, mechanics and poets, retirees and a few people who couldn't have been more than eighteen. There were members of the local *literati*, who read their scripts aloud to one another and did little else with them. There were those who had never *seen* a script; those who had tried desperately for years to sell their ideas to the motion picture and television industry; and those with fragile talents and delicate sensibilities, to whom criticism or rejection is the creative equivalent of a diagnosis of terminal cancer. Finally, there were the dreamers, the craftspeople, the prophets and the illuminators of the eccentricities of the human condition—for whom a place in the scriptwriting universe is always reserved, but to whom the practice of professional scriptwriting was as great and unfathomable as the Dead Sea scrolls.

Not a few of them had been discouraged by brief and unsuccessful forays into telescripting and screenwriting, but the clear majority didn't even know where to *begin*.

In other lectures, informal talks and seminars, I've encountered the same feelings of depression and frustration and creative isolation.

This book is for those people.

At the same time, I suppose you could say I'm writing this for my own benefit. You see, when I first became involved in screenwriting, I had *no* idea what I was doing. Eventually I began to make some headway, most of it by trial and error. It wasn't easy. (For the record, it's never easy.) But it can be done—if you know what you're doing, or if you're willing to fall on your face enough times to *learn* what it is you should be doing.

That's the second reason I'm writing this book. I wanted to write the kind of book I wish somebody had written when I first started out in the business.

Here are the simple facts:

On the one hand, there are thousands of writers—experienced or inexperienced—who recognize in scriptwriting both a challenge and a need. They have the talent, the drive, and the persistence, but like the people I met in my seminar, just don't know where to begin.

On the other hand, there are producers in every medium who are engaged in a constant search for new talent. Consider this:

- Producers and studio executives at all three commercial networks and at several independent production companies sponsor contests, programs, scholarships, and internships designed to attract new talent.
- Professional and community theaters across the United States actively pursue new plays for staged readings, and workshop and mainstage productions.
- Radiodrama producers and directors, riding herd on a medium undergoing its biggest growth in nearly three decades, are practically desperate for writers who understand the all-but-lost science of radiodrama scripting.
- Many of the major motion picture studios have writers' programs that encourage scriptwriters to work at the studio and learn first-hand what the filmmaking process is all about.
- The rapidly expanding videodisc, videocassette, cable, and communications-satellite industries are opening up whole new worlds of opportunity for scriptwriters across the country.

The need is there, on both sides: the need to write, and the need to produce a variety of programs for a rapidly growing marketplace. It is the purpose of this book to help bridge the gap between these two sides. In so doing, we will examine the techniques of writing for, and selling to, television, radio, motion pictures and live theater.

Questions, Questions

But it's impossible to sell scripts without an agent, and you can't get an agent until you've sold something!

Wrong on both counts. You can become an active, selling scriptwriter without an agent. In fact, that's the primary emphasis of this book. I've written for television, completed a motion picture screenplay under contract, had plays produced and published in book form, and sold a dozen or so radiodramas *all* without an agent. This book will tell you how to get around the absence of an agent.

Agents are, however, very useful. I now have one myself, and have gotten more deals as a consequence. This book not only will help you find an agent, but give you examples of standard contracts, and put to rest the notion that you can't get an agent if you're unproduced and unpublished.

But I can't even get my script in the front door at a movie studio or a television network.

No problem. We'll examine the techniques for tracking down a producer and getting him to look at your script with the intent of purchasing it. It's a simple, step-by-step process that comes complete with release forms, standard contracts, a schedule of minimum fees, and a list of production companies and studios.

But I've never even seen a script!

In the following pages, you'll find samples of every kind of script currently in use in every medium, along with the specific typographical format required for each of them. One- and two-column scripts, videotape scripts, film scripts, radio scripts and play scripts—they're all included.

We'll examine everything from the physical packaging of your script to the marketing process. We'll look at the creative end as well, including directions on plotting, characterization, pacing, camera angles, blocking directions, dialogue and so forth.

But I'm unfamiliar with the terminology.

Every reference is carefully explained; glossaries of film and video terminologies are included.

The appendices also contain information on the Writers Guild of America, West; and a list of agents and producers.

In addition, each chapter examines the history of each medium, explaining in detail how the market came to be the way it currently is, and how a writer might best capitalize on that arrangement.

Summary

The whole function of this book is best conveyed by the way the chapters are structured: They individually cover the art, the craft, and the marketing process involved in the medium under discussion. We'll look at the creative aspects of scriptwriting, the process whereby creative ideas are transformed into the written page, and the procedures involved in getting someone to purchase and produce your script.

We will not gloss over any of these media. There are pitfalls in any profession; we will put up a red flag to warn the unwary, and explain the best techniques for getting out of a trap should you fall into one. We'll also take a sidelong glance at some of the little shortcuts and sneaky things that can make a beginning scriptwriter's life just a little easier.

There is, however, one thing this book will not do, and will not even attempt. It will not teach talent or persistence. You've either got those two essential elements, or you don't. There's no middle ground.

You see, this book is directed toward a certain kind of writer, the type best described by Mignon McLaughlin when she said, "Anyone can write. The trouble with writers is that they can't do anything else." Which is not to say that writers are incapable of doing anything else, like changing tires or extracting troublesome molars. It's just that writing is the only thing they can do for an extended period of time without chewing on the furniture or checking in for therapy. It makes them happy. It fills a need, whether that need be a longing for self-expression, or a quest for immortality through the written word.

Dilettantes, curiosity-seekers and literary sightseers are encouraged to apply elsewhere.

I am of the personal belief that there is something unique about writers that prepares them from birth and propels them throughout their lives toward this most remarkable of professions. Most of these writers are unstoppable. Throw as many obstacles in their way as you like, and still they persevere toward their goal, often with nothing more than a vague idea of what that goal might be. Nothing, not even the most severe of rejections, can impede the progress of such a writer.

If, however, this book can prove to be of some small aid to just one writer in his or her progress toward professional scriptwriting, it will have been an unqualified success.

J. Michael Straczynski
Los Angeles
October 14, 1981

The writer is a special angel or in league with the devil, depending on your view. The writer is a prophet or a colicky infant. But either way, the writer is to be indulged, spoiled, cultivated—especially if he is a comedy writer, since there are never more than fifty good ones on earth at any one time. Everything begins with words on a page. Good scripts make good (television) shows. You must pray for good writers as fervently as for salvation. If it ain't on the page, it ain't on the stage.

—Bob Shanks
The Cool Fire

1.
TELEVISION

Consider it.

At this writing, approximately 72.9 million households—98 percent of *all* households in the United States—possess at least one television set. The average family of four spends 61 hours per week in front of the television. Incredibly, this has taken place within the relatively brief span of 42 years. (May 1, 1939, signalled the first daily television schedule by RCA/ NBC.) Television has become an undeniable and awesome force in the day-to-day lives of Americans across the nation. It entertains us, diverts our collective attention from the problems that plague us, and even— from time to time—educates us.

Television . . . the ultimate magician. With its phosphor-dot sleight-of-hand, it can drown the passions of a distraught society under a tidal wave of sitcom-generated laughter or, with equal power, stop a war, incite a nation to action, or bring low a President.

It is, in short, not only a powerful medium, but a *pervasive* one. Between the commercial and noncommercial networks, independent stations, local cable stations and superstations, it's nearly impossible to turn on your television any time of the day or night without finding *something* on the tube.

But for all its power, it is vital to remember that television is a *business*, and as such it is responsive to the many laws by which any business runs, including and especially the law of supply and demand. Anyone wanting to provide 24 hours of television programming has got to start out with 24 hours' worth of scripts. And this constant need goes on, day after day, year after year. For this reason, television has been called the Great Devourer: It eats through a tremendous amount of material. In fact, someone once calculated that between 1939 and the present, the three commercial networks *alone* have used nearly 40 million pages of scripting to produce their daily programs. And that only includes material that was actually aired—it does *not* take into account the large number of pilots, special programs, and other bits of programming that never make it to actual broadcast. Neither does it include the pages used in rough or preliminary drafts, or drafts discarded entirely in favor of new ideas (but which the writer is generally paid for anyway).

The work is there. The need for quality scriptwriting is there. But before we can discuss the steps involved in writing and selling a television script, it behooves us to take a look at the history of television as a business—where it came from, and where it's going. Only with a full understanding of what television is can an aspiring scriptwriter begin to fill the needs of the Great Devourer.

A Television Chronology

Technically, television dates back to 1915, when Guglielmo Marconi, who in 1894 had transmitted the first radio signals, predicted the rise of "visible telephones." He saw these as devices that would transmit pictures over the air or through wires for great distances. This was the first credible prediction from a member of the scientific community; others, however, had long speculated on the transmission of visual images. Even Mark Twain, in 1886, wrote in his journal that he foresaw a day when "portraits and pictures *transferred by light* accompany everything. The phonograph goes to church, conducts family worship, teaches foreign languages, pops the question, etc."

In 1923, Marconi's words were borne out when Russian-born American physicist Vladimir Zworykin applied for a patent on his latest invention—the iconoscope camera tube, an early predecessor of today's cathode-ray tube. The application was complicated by the fact that competing designs and other legal maneuvers were taking place at the same time, all in the interest of being the first patented television receiver. The litigations continued for more than a decade. It was not until January 1, 1939—eight years after the first experimental television signal was broadcast—that the United States Patent Office granted Zworykin a patent for his iconoscope camera tube.

During Zworykin's litigation, progress in television technology, based loosely on his work, continued at full throttle. In 1927, the first television program was transmitted by wire from Washington, D.C., to New York City, an event heralded as final proof that commercial broadcasting was technologically feasible. After that, matters moved forward even faster. Radio's National Broadcasting Company—and its parent company, RCA—quickly realized the potential value of television, and on October

30, 1931, NBC was granted permission to open an experimental television station, W2XBS-New York, which soon began broadcasting from the Empire State Building on an irregular basis.

On May 1, 1939, NBC initiated the first daily schedule of television programming. In that year, NBC provided 601 hours of programming, and became the first broadcaster to use telephone wires as a relay between points of transmission.

During this same time period, the Columbia Broadcasting System (CBS) jumped into the fray with its own television stations. NBC was always one step ahead of CBS, however, because of its greater physical resources: NBC radio consisted of *two* actual radio networks, the Red and Blue Radio Networks, which gave NBC a wider range of technical support and expertise.

In time, however, this dual networking by NBC became more of a liability than an asset, particularly when in 1941 the FCC decided that "No license shall be issued to a station affiliated with a network organization maintaining more than one network." The FCC felt such an operation constituted a monopoly not in the public's better interests. Within the year, NBC incorporated its Blue network—116 radio stations—and put it up for sale asking $8 million, which was met by Edward J. Noble, founder of the Life Savers candy company. Eventually, this new network became the American Broadcasting Company (ABC)—a name originally owned by Radio Station WOL-Washington, which sold the rights to the name for $10,000.

Between 1941 and 1945, the FCC began mandating certain standards for television broadcasting. Transmitting standards were set at 30 single frames per second, each frame consisting of 525 individual lines. Sound was to be transmitted along certain designated FM frequencies. In addition, the FCC allocated 13 VHF (very high frequency) channels for use by commercial television. (One of these channels was later taken back for use by two-way radio, leaving us with the currently available channels 2 through 13.) At the time of this decision—July 2, 1945—there were only about 16,500 television receivers in the United States.

It was not until April 19, 1948, that ABC began broadcasting television programs through its recently acquired affiliate, WFIL-Philadelphia. Several additional affiliates were picked up in record time, and executives at ABC saw nothing but continued growth in the days to come, a prediction which turned out to be true—for about six months. On October 4, the FCC struck a heavy blow to ABC by putting a freeze on television licensing—the process by which affiliates are added to a network. This move effectively left ABC in the cold while the FCC pondered what to do about the television stations that had been eliminated by turning back one channel to radio. As a relative newcomer, ABC had far fewer stations in its organization than either NBC or CBS, both of which had almost a decade's head start. CBS and NBC were able to sit back quietly in comfort, confident that ABC's days were numbered.

Oddly enough, ABC found salvation through an only distantly related legal decision. Under the Sherman Anti-Trust Act, Paramount Pictures was ordered in 1949 to divest itself of its theater operations, and to create a separate corporation for it having no connection to its film operations. (For further details on the impact created by this landmark decision, see the chapter on screenwriting.) Leonard H. Goldenson, head of the newly formed United Paramount Theatres, decided upon a merger with ABC, a decision approved by the FCC on February 9, 1952. Less than two months later, the FCC also lifted its freeze on station licensing through a decision allowing new stations to have access to the UHF (ultra-high frequencies) channels. Seventy such channels were established (14 through 83) for commercial use, a decision not particularly popular with broadcasters because there were few television receivers equipped to receive UHF transmissions. It would, in fact, be many years before there were enough properly equipped sets available to the public for UHF broadcasting to be profitable. Even today, UHF stations generally fare worse in the ratings than VHF stations, because of the frequently inferior picture reception, and because—as some have been wont to say—it takes "the fingers of a lock-pick to tune in a UHF station."

The 1950s became a landmark in television history. ABC, which had until then been referred to as "fourth in a three-network race," was finally on sufficient financial footing to realistically challenge the superiority of CBS and NBC, even though it would take nearly 20 years for ABC to creep up toward the number one spot. The fifties also saw the official introduction of commercial color television, although color signals had been broadcast on an experimental basis as early as 1940. The FCC reversed a previous decision and approved RCA's "color compatible" system, which allowed color programs to be received on black-and-white sets without distortion; the CBS system the FCC first approved did little to compensate for this difficulty.

In addition to the decade's technological advances, the fifties also marked a subtle change in the operation and structure of the three networks. During the first twenty years of television, the medium was one vast experiment. Innovation—particularly on the part of CBS and, later, ABC—was encouraged and rewarded. Because of television's newness, there were no hard-and-fast guidelines that spelled out what you could not do. Exciting ideas popped up every day, as producers, performers, writers and directors asked themselves "What if . . . ?" Television was a toy, a magic box . . . a game whose rules changed with the sweep of the second hand or a new line during a live performance. This emphasis on innovation led performers like Ernie Kovacs to push the artistic potential of television to its very limits—often with surrealistic consequences. It gave Milton Berle a forum to revive vaudeville and imbue it with a sense of immediacy and vibrancy to electronically bridge the previously huge gulf whose borders are defined by the footlights of a stage and the first row of seats.

A roll-call of shows created during these ten years, often referred to as the Golden Age of Television, reads like a veritable Who's Who of the medium: Your Show of Shows, with Sid Caesar; Beany and Cecil; The U.S. Steel Hour; The Colgate Comedy Hour, with Donald O'Connor; Kukla, Fran and Ollie; Make Room For Daddy, with Danny Thomas; The Honeymooners; Lassie; This Is Your Life; Sgt. Bilko, with Phil Silvers; The Ed Sullivan Show; Playhouse 90; and, toward the end of the decade, Rod Serling's The Twilight Zone.

In producing these programs, television culled its artists from radio and the stage, enlisting such performers as Jack Benny, Groucho Marx, Ed Wynn, Edward R. Murrow, Perry Como and Jack Palance. During these years, artistic license was a given, a factor assumed from the very beginning. One of the most valued commodities on the market was the writer. Writers who could produce quality programming were put in charge of whole series, with a wide range of artistic control. Anthology series like Playhouse 90 and The U.S. Steel Hour highlighted the power of the written word (if only because the technology and budgets of the day left them with little in the way of grandiose visual effects), and let the writers explore a different topic each week, examining social issues and the human condition as deeply as was possible within the carefully defined parameters of what was socially acceptable on television.

But it was in defining what was socially acceptable that these writers ended up in conflict with the networks. Yes, it was a time when television writers—originally looked upon by their contemporaries in film and live theater as little more than video vaudevillians—were becoming respectable figures with viewers taking the same attitude that we now take when we say we are going to see an Edward Albee play or a Neil Simon film. The writers were being noticed.

In an interview, Rod Serling is quoted as having said, "I don't suppose anything ever made writers so famous so fast as that so-called Golden Age. Names like Reginald Rose and Paddy Chayevsky and Tad Masel and mine became household words overnight."

Television writers were solicited from other media, pampered, and given their own shows. But when it came time to determine what was socially acceptable the networks were absolutely rigid, often absurdly so. Not even Serling was above their machinations, as he discovered during the production of his script Noon on Doomsday, when he was forbidden by the network censors to identify a Jew as a Jew.

There were other such examples of peculiar censorship. When Lucille Ball became pregnant during the run of I Love Lucy, she and the rest of the cast were forbidden to use the word *pregnant* in any of the scripts, even though by the eighth month she obviously was. They could say she was "in the family way," but *not* pregnant.

Sex was a constant target for network censors. Even married couples were forbidden to be shown in the same bed; only single beds were allowed. Further, if a man and a woman *were* shown in bed—usually sitting and talking—both actors had to keep at least one foot on the floor. In a scene from a dramatic program that called for the simulation of a Catholic mass, the censors did not allow a reference to "the Virgin Mary," because the term *virgin* was blatantly unacceptable.

Another classic example of network censorship for the alleged good of the public came during the production of *Thunder on Sycamore Street*, by Reginald Rose. The story revolved around the conflict caused by a black family moving into an all-white neighborhood. The censors felt the tensions such a program would stir up were too extreme. As a consequence, the script was rewritten—over Rose's clearly stated opposition—to portray an ex-convict and his family moving into a middle-class neighborhood.

In some instances, however, the hectic nature of live television—where actors who were "dead" accidentally got up and walked away on camera, and Jackie Gleason broke his leg in front of millions of viewers—actually played into the hands of writers while remaining a constant headache to producers and network executives.

Martin Manulis, producer of *Playhouse 90*, once summarized the situation nicely. "Sponsors and network brass never got around to reading the script until a couple of weeks before it went on. They would scream from New York, 'You can't do that!' I would tell them that we were so far into rehearsal that either we did that script or they had ninety minutes of blank air."

Later on, he said, "You do the show, you watch it on the monitors for the East; you go home and watch the replay on (kinescope) for the West Coast, you cut your throat and go to bed."

In all fairness to the networks, they were frequently under fire from advertisers, sponsors who underwrote entire series. For example: During the production of a Chevrolet-sponsored western series, the sponsors requested that a line containing the words "ford a stream" be deleted. Their argument was that they didn't want to plug the competition (an unfounded fear, in all likelihood), or get a big laugh at a highly inappropriate moment (which could be reasonably argued, I suppose).

At about the same time, *Playhouse 90* was producing a drama featuring actor Charles Bickford as the captain of an 1850 whaling ship. One scene called for the character to shave with a straight razor. Unfortunately, the sponsor for that particular program was a manufacturer of electric shavers, who insisted that if the character shaved, he *must* use an electric shaver. The fact that such devices did not *exist* in the 1800s was considered superfluous. Needless to say, the scene was dropped.

It was in an effort to finally eliminate this tremendous influence of advertisers on television content that the practice of one sponsor underwriting an entire series was eventually discontinued. It was hoped this would allow greater creative freedom; unfortunately, as per-minute costs to advertisers for television time rose in this new arrangement, their power did not diminish. The threat of removing one's advertising to this day remains an imposing and impressive ultimatum.

During this time television also became more compartmentalized, more regimented. No longer could a writer/producer concern himself only with what he thought would make good drama. With greater resources and budgets, and a more heated contest for ratings—and the advertising dollars they brought—networks became less willing to gamble on the creative predilections of any one person. Suddenly, "experts" began popping up out of the catacombs of corporate structure. There were vice presidents of specials, vice presidents of development, vice presidents of programs for either coast, vice presidents of business affairs, vice presidents of comedy, vice presidents of dramatic programming, and so on, each vice president bringing with him a cadre of advisors whose purpose was to monitor the pulsebeat of the viewing public and react accordingly, sailing with the wind of popular opinion wherever possible—sometimes at the cost of creative credibility.

This trend continued on through the sixties and seventies and into the present, the severity of the problem depending on whether a network is in a high or low ratings cycle. It is a truism of television that the lower-rated networks are often more willing to experiment with new concepts. If they're already in last place, then they really have little to lose, whereas a number one network is afraid of jeopardizing its comfortable status. As a consequence, the network offering innovative programming generally begins edging up on the established network, sometimes even passing it; however, once the number three network has improved its position, it too becomes less willing to try new things. In television, creative innovation leads to corporate consolidation, which results in creative innovation at *another* network.

All this led to another development that also has a direct effect on television writers. The chain of events runs something like this: Between the early 1960s and the present, television continued to expand its range of influence, as well as to further refine the quality of its programming. This led to a perception of television as an indispensable commodity. More and more people were watching television, and expecting more *from* television, in terms of quality *and* quantity. All of this led to an ever-increasing demand for scripts capable of being produced quickly and efficiently.

This constant, extreme need put writers—virtually for the first time—in a position of power, from which they could begin to bargain for better rates of pay, guarantees of minimum wages and residuals—set by writers and the studios through negotiation—and a variety of other benefits heretofore unavailable.

Through this process, television scriptwriters have become the highest-paid practitioners of the literary profession in history. Not only are the financial rewards considerable, there is a certain status attached to telescripting. There is also, admittedly, a certain thrill inherent in knowing that your work is being given life by professional actors, directors and support personnel, and that a potential audience of millions of people will be watching something you wrote in the solitude of your home or office. Television writing is heady stuff, and its attractiveness has led to the creation of television writing curricula as an addition to the creative writing and telecommunications departments at colleges throughout the nation. Nearly every writer, no matter what genre provides the bulk of his income or reputation, at least toys with the idea of writing a television script "just so I can have the money to write what I *really* want to write, you understand."

Nowhere is this more true than in Hollywood, where some days it seems like *everyone* is writing a television script. Waiters, waitresses, gas station attendants, theater ushers, salespersons—it doesn't matter what they're doing for a living; most of them will tell you it's just temporary until they finish their script and sell it. As a rule, it's their first script, and it's rarely past the outline stage. Maybe it's something about the air that causes this, or the water, or the everyday evidence that Hollywood is the home of the Industry, a word always capitalized in speech and spoken with something akin to reverence. Go to a party anywhere around the Los Angeles area, and you'll quickly find that you can't swing a cat without hitting somebody who's got a script "in development."

At that same party, you're likely to find many people interested in telescripting who don't understand that salable television scripts don't suddenly materialize out of thin air as the result of good intentions or wishful thinking. To have an idea is not enough, no matter how good that idea might be. I don't even *know* how many times I've been approached at social gatherings, and heard, "You know, I've got a lot of really great ideas for television scripts—but what do I do with them?" or "There's so much garbage on television, so much that's already been done. I can do a lot better, if somebody would just give me the chance," or even, "Sure, I could do better than most of these other guys at writing. I just don't have the time to write them myself. Would you be willing to do it for me? Naturally, we'll share the writing credit." There are many variations on this theme.

And they are all wrong. Wrong, wrong, wrong, wrong, *wrong!* They lead only to heartbreak. There is only one way into telescripting, and that's through work, and the most essential element: the script.

The Art of Telescripting

Peculiar as this may sound, writing for television is one of the easiest, and one of the most difficult forms of scriptwriting around. It is easy in that there are many factors predetermined for you, including the length of the script, the number of acts, the range of topics, and often the types of characters you'll be dealing with. Before you ever sit down behind the typewriter, the schematic for your literary creation has already been set down; your task is to plug your own ideas into that context, which for some writers is where the process becomes quite difficult. You've got to work with characters invented by someone other than yourself (in most cases), structure the events in your plot around commercials and other artificial timing devices, and limit yourself in the number of sets and the types of situations you can develop into story lines.

The first and most obvious step that needs to be taken is to decide *what type* of television script you want to write. This is important because each type has its own specific set of rules. The different kinds of television programs are generally broken down as follows:

Episodic comedy—30 minutes long, consisting either of two acts, a teaser followed by two acts, or two acts followed by a tag. Usual length: 26 pages on film, 42 on tape. A teaser is a brief, opening segment, usually running no more than 2 minutes, that introduces the characters and the action to follow. A tag is generally the same length; it ends the program, wrapping up the action into a nice, neat and humorous package. Although at one time both dramatic and comedic programs were written in half-hour time slots, the half-hour has now been almost entirely relegated to comedy programming, specifically the situation comedy.

Episodic drama—60 minutes long, consisting of four acts. (Or, in some cases, four acts and a teaser. In most cases, a montage of scenes from the particular episode is assembled into a teaser of sorts.) Dramas were assigned a 60-minute slot because 30 minutes wasn't believed to be enough time to develop a dramatic plot of any substance, while 90-minute dramas just began losing viewers—unless, of course, the subject matter was truly exceptional. As a rule, 90-minute episodic dramas have gone the way of the furry goldfish into extinction. With the exception of variety programs and special broadcasts, the 90-minute program has largely vanished, its remains being swallowed up by the 60-minute drama and the television movie.

Movies for television—120 minutes long, generally consisting of six acts of equal length. Television Movies of the Week (MOWs, in the vernacular of the Industry) have grown into far greater prominence in recent years as staple programming at each network. One reason for this rests with the often exorbitant prices paid by a network for a first-run theatrical release; in many cases it would almost cost a network less to produce its own movie than to purchase the television rights to a theatrical motion picture. Usual length 101-120 pages, film format.

Since most freelance television sales are made in episodic drama and comedy, we'll turn our attention first and foremost to this area.

Writing the Episodic Program

Probably the single most important step to take before you can begin writing a script for episodic television is to perform a market analysis of the program you intend to write for. Translation—watch the show. (Don't laugh; you'd be surprised at the number of scriptwriters who submit work based on little more than the synopses that appear in *TV Guide*, without having actually seen a single episode.)

It is absolutely *vital* to study the series you intend to submit your work to. You must develop a genuine feel for the characters, the situation, the location where the program takes place, and the types of shows that comprise the series. These elements are important because no matter *what* your script may be about, you have to deal with these preexistent factors—of which characterization is the most essential, particularly for the situation-comedy market. Because of the built-in limitations of a sitcom in terms of sets, locations, and personnel, you have to build your scripts almost entirely around the way the characters deal with their surroundings and with one another.

Keep a notepad beside you while you watch your target series. (Having a tape recorder handy is also of considerable help, since it allows you to play the episode over and over and study the way the characters speak. A videotape recorder (VTR) is even handier.) Write down everything you can about the show and its characters. Look at their appearance, their attitudes, habits, eccentricities, and listen for any colloquialisms they use, even any nicknames they refer to one another by. (A character who calls her father "Father" is considerably different from one who calls him "Daddy." From that fact alone, you can probably infer something about both characters' relationships.

A good example of how important a solid grasp of characterization is came during the production of one of my scripts. Upon returning from lunch, I spotted a cast member sitting off by himself, writing furiously. I asked him what he was doing. "Writing out my character's history," he said, holding up several sheets of fact-filled paper. "This is where I was born, where I went to school, who my parents were . . . the whole thing.

This way I have a better grasp of who my character is, and why he acts the way he does." Working from the inferences written into the script, he was able to backtrack and create an entire history. Every character you ever use, whether your own invention or someone else's, must have a personal history, even if you're the only person who will ever know all of it. Not only does that lead to better, more well-rounded characters, it also makes the writing itself easier, and this rule applies not only to television scripting, but to *any* writing.

It's like this: Think of your best friend for a moment. (If you don't have one, then fake it, or borrow someone else's.) Now, mentally visualizing your friend, place him or her in a darkened living room. Have your friend walk from one end of the room to the other, accidentally hitting his or her knee on the coffee table en route. Knowing your friend as you do, you know *exactly* what your friend will say when his or her knee contacts the coffee table. *The same principle applies for characters!* You must know them so well that you don't have to work at making them speak and move. You simply place them in a situation, and let your intimate familiarity and understanding of the characters create the dialogue for you.

Sounds simple, doesn't it? Actually, it is, but it takes a *lot* of practice before it becomes simple. Author Gene Fowler once made this observation about the profession: "Writing is easy; all you do is sit staring at a blank sheet of paper until the drops of blood form on your forehead."

Other points you should look for in doing a market analysis of a television series: How many acts make up an episode? Does the program use a tag or a teaser (since both are rarely used together)? How long is each act and/or tag? What sorts of stories are generally favored? Are social issues tackled, or is the subject matter too light for such endeavors? Is there just one primary plot, or are a number of sub-plots sprinkled through the show? Who is the show aimed at—what age range, social level, educational level, and sex? Are there any running themes present—to varying degrees—in each episode?

The question of running themes of similar plot lines is vital in developing an idea for an episode of that series. If the series demonstrates an active social conscience, then a script deficient in this area will probably be rejected out of hand. If the series presents programs that usually fall under one particular topic—the problems of a single girl in a big city, for instance—are there any angles that haven't been covered within that category? It is helpful to have a large backlog of synopses, either of your own or provided by *TV Guide*. Such synopses, as we mentioned earlier, can't tell you *everything* you need to know about a show in order to write it, but it *can* tell you what topics have been dealt with in previous shows.

No matter what kind of topic or brand of episodic television program you finally decide upon, there are certain requirements that have to be met. These commonalities not only are important to remember in terms of television writing, but are, in many cases, rules of good drama to be maintained in anything you write.

If you are writing for a situation comedy series, it is necessary that you limit the number of sets your script requires. Most sitcoms utilize just two sets, the primary set (such as the living room in *All In The Family*), and one ancillary set generally determined by the particular script (a welfare office, for example, or a meeting hall). Some situation comedies have a larger number of primary sets—sometimes called standing sets—that are used semiregularly. This is particularly true of ensemble programs, where it is often necessary to follow various characters as they go about their business. If the program you choose to write for has a number of these standing sets, feel free to use them *as they may be required by your plot*, not simply because they are available. You should still keep any new sets that will be used only in your script down to one. This may seem an arbitrary decision by the producers, but it's not. Each new set constructed to be used only once is a considerable drain on the production budget, and I've seen more than a few scripts rejected solely because they required too many additional sets.

(Actually, no matter *what* kind of show you choose to write for, it's always a good idea to keep one eye on the budget at all times. It's not at all uncommon for producers to go a little over-budget on an occasional show or two, thereby making a script that can be produced at or even *below* their regular budget a desirable commodity.

(There's an apocryphal story floating around Hollywood these days— at least, I *hope* it's apocryphal—that illustrates this point very nicely. A writer calls a producer to pitch an idea for an episode of his show. "All right," the producer says, "what's it about?" "Oh, about half your standard per-show budget," the writer says. "I'll take it," concludes the producer.)

Another basic requirement is that the episode be *about* something. It must, in other words, have a plot. Although it would seem that such a basic necessity of drama is taken for granted, that is not always the case, particularly with sitcoms. Many first-time television writers put together a comedy script believing that it is enough simply to string together a long series of jokes or sketches, tie them together loosely with a theme of one sort or another, and call it a script. They quickly find out that this just doesn't work, usually after deluging a producer with one plotless script after another—a process guaranteed to send any sane producer (assuming there is such a character) into an absolute dither. As Gary Goldberg, producer of such programs as *The Tony Randall Show* and *Lou Grant*, once remarked to me, "If there is no plot, there is no show. Period."

So . . . the show must be *about* something. The characters must strive to achieve something, to avoid something, or to do something to somebody else. There must also be a conflict, a process impeding that striving, whether the conflict be embodied in another character or as a social situation.

The rules for constructing a plot for a telescript are much the same as for writing a short story. The process for plot development in an episodic teleplay tends to run in this order:

1. Reintroduction of character(s). A week has gone by since the program's characters last paid a televised visit, so it is always wise to take a few moments at the beginning of a script to refamiliarize the audience with the characters. This is usually accomplished by a bit of dialogue or business between two or more main characters that reaffirms their personalities for the viewers. This brief segment usually has nothing to do with the plot, which emerges soon afterward. From a writer's perspective, this time gives you a chance to take a breath, play with the characters a little, develop a feeling for them, and show off any talent for interplay before plunging into the plot. It is often difficult for many writers to immediately bring the primary plot into focus at the beginning of a show. It is also impractical creatively, since the plot—particularly a complex one—may so involve the viewer's cerebral talents that he might not pay much attention to the characters, leading to the impression that the characters are listless and flat. Besides, jumping into a plot is an artificiality not even remotely echoed in real life. You don't generally wake up in the morning and *immediately* confront a new problem . . . unless, of course, you happen to be married to it. And it is only infrequently that a problem pops right into bed with you. (It is also immoral in several states, but that's another book.) Before dealing with any problems that arise, you usually get up, have breakfast, encounter all the necessary and potentially dangerous daily habits of shaving and cooking breakfast, and follow this by riding the bus or driving to work. Any of these events makes good grist for characterization.

Incidentally, these stretches of characterization tend to follow a teaser and are largely separate from it. In a dramatic-series teaser, the main character often is not involved; but it reflects the plot yet to come. For example: The teaser shows a trained assassin loading a high-powered rifle, a picture of a well-known political figure, marked with an X, on the table in front of him. The show proper begins with the hero—for our purposes a detective—complaining about the potentially lethal coffee served in the cafeteria one floor below. He is then given the assignment of protecting the politician (whose picture we saw before) while the statesman is visiting locally. This gets the plot off and running. It also provides a certain amount of dramatic tension; we the audience know an assassin is on the loose, but will the detective figure that out in time? (Usually he does.)

Bringing the main character immediately into the plot without sacrificing characterization or dramatic tension is easily accomplished: Simply change the picture in the teaser from the mugshot of the politician to a newspaper clipping embellished with a photograph of our fearless detective. This allows us to go ahead with our bit of characterization, with a new question added in the viewer's mind: When will the assassin strike, and how will the detective avoid getting killed, or at least having his hair creased in a different style?

2. Truth in characterization. Since we're already well into the topic of characterization, it seems wise to take a moment to consider the issue more thoroughly. Now, everyone—with the possible exception of certain political and sports figures—has some sort of character—good character, bad character, or good character brought into a bad situation through forces beyond his control. But no one is composed of just one single element of characterization, and to create a character without taking time to invest him with a wide range of emotions—the whole emotion-fraught heritage of our collective humanity—is to end up with a flat, lifeless character and an unsalable script.

Because you're dealing with characters created by someone else, it's important to follow through with the study of these characters. Nothing results in a faster rejection by a producer than an action that is absolutely outside a running character's normal pattern of behavior.

When introducing a character of your own, you can be somewhat freer in terms of creative control. Within certain limits, that is. If, for instance, the program deals honestly with the lives of simple, down-to-earth people, it would little profit you to write a script in which the main characters are kidnapped by Venusians and forced to listen to four hours of recorded bagpipe music. You must be certain, therefore, that your new characters—introduced to create or advance a plot—correspond to the general tone of the series under discussion.

Finally, when introducing new characters of your own design, it is absolutely imperative that you get the characters in and out cleanly. Translation: If you are introducing a character on a one-time-only basis, for the purposes of this single script, you do *not* have that character move in next door to your main character. New characters must be *program-specific*—you must not leave them lying around for other writers to deal with unless the producer asked you to create a new *running character* in the first place. Along these same lines, you should make any changes in the main character equally program-specific. Writing a script in which the main character loses both legs will probably be an excercise in futility, particularly if the show is the ongoing story of a high school physical education teacher. You can have that character break a leg, and thereby deal with the problems of limited mobility, but you'd darn well better have the character on his feet by the end of the program. The only exceptions are, again, any long-term changes specifically indicated.

How much latitude you have through a producer's decision to change a character depends in part on how sneaky you are. For example, a freelance writer contributing to one of the more popular soap operas was given a continuity breakdown on the series that at one point called for one of the primary characters to be hospitalized. (A continuity breakdown is an outline specifying in broad terms what will happen to the characters during the season. Its use is largely confined to soap operas and other programs whose episodes are directly connected to each other by one linear, running plot.) With this information in hand, the writer— who had a little medical knowledge of his own—proceeded to write a script in which the main character had an automobile accident and went into a coma. The producer was pleased by this, since the whole purpose of putting the character in a hospital in the beginning was to get her out of the way while other plotlines were being developed, and how much more out of the way can someone be than in a coma? Then an interesting situation occurred. The writer, armed with his medical knowledge, had called for a particular kind of injury to cause the coma and was the only one who knew what procedures were necessary to eventually bring the character out of it. He also knew, though, that his assignment would last only as long as she *remained* in a coma. So he just decided to keep the character comatose for as long as he could manage to placate the producer—which turned out to be twice as long as had originally been planned. The writer secured twice his expected fees, the actress earned her salary by just lying there, and the plotlines continued in their development, although the producer was just a bit miffed by the whole thing. One story circulating after this event is that some time following the completion of this assignment, the writer tried contacting the same producer about some more work. "I'm sorry," the secretary told him, "she's unavailable." "Well," the writer asked, "when *will* she be available?" "We don't know," the secretary replied dryly, "she's in a coma, and there's no telling *how* long it'll be before you can take your call."

3. Introduction to the plot. After you have reintroduced the series' running characters and one or more of the new characters, you move into the introduction of the plot. It is at this point that the problem is presented or the goal to be achieved is fully described.

Probably the single most essential key to solid plot development is basing all plotting on characterization—the reason why this section follows our discussion of characterization. Whenever you develop or introduce a plot, always remember this simple rule: No one does anything without a reason. That reason may not always be a valid one in terms of our own world-views, such as the psychotic killer who takes up a position as a sniper atop the World Trade Center, but there must always be a reason intelligible to the character involved. For instance, our sniper may imagine he is surrounded by invading armies. Whatever the individual case may be, never have a character do something just because it might be kinda nifty. Anything your character does must be within the parameters defined by his behavioral and psychological profile.

4. Pursuing the plot. The strivings of your characters toward their goals constitutes the bulk of your script. Once again, the issue of characterization is of primary importance here. Just as the person who introduces the problem does so for a reason, the way the main character responds to and deals with the problem is a direct consequence of his or her personality. A hardened detective—given the threat of the sniper previously described—would react one way; a priest, a reporter, a potential victim, and the sniper's mother would, because of their differing backgrounds, react in ways unique unto themselves.

This factor, alternately called *character response* or *reactive characterization*, is probably the most evident one in detective and police-oriented television series. The basic plots of these series don't vary much from one another, consisting as they do of the standard robberies, assaults, and murder mysteries. What *does* make each series different is the way the main characters respond to the crisis under consideration. Detective series are built almost entirely on the personality of the lead character—ranging from the lollipop-sucking Kojack to the befuddled Columbo and the fretful Rockford—and less on the actual event that gives rise to the plot.

5. Plot resolution. Whatever plot you eventually choose to develop, and however you might plan out your characters' reactions, it is necessary to resolve the plot by the end of the program. (The exception to this rule would be two-part episodes, which are, incidentally, falling into less and less favor with network executives because of the risk involved: If one episode of a series fails to attract reasonable ratings—presumably because of the particular story—that's something the networks can live with—however uncomfortable the living arrangements might be. But if the program is a two-parter, and the first part fares poorly on the overnight ratings, it's reasonable to assume the following week's installment will do even worse, since those who watched the first part—and didn't like it—don't watch the second part, and those who missed the first part won't want to come in in the middle of the plot.)

Because of the necessity of tying up all the loose threads of plot by the conclusion of an episode, many television scriptwriters tend to work backward, starting with the resolution and moving back to the beginning, dropping in plot complications and an occasional red herring wherever possible. This way, the scriptwriter always knows exactly where he wants to end up, and how he intends to get there.

In attempting to provide a nice, tidy resolution, many beginning script-writers make the same mistake—the kind of error that constantly per-turbs producers as they break in novitiates. *Your characters must work their own way out of their conflicts.* It is *they* who must provide the means of resolving your story. By this, I do not necessarily refer to avoid-ing the *deus ex machina* solution—some previously unseen character suddenly walking in from outside with the answer to everyone's prob-lems. What I *do* mean is that the means for resolving your plot must be generated from within your characters, calling upon their special skills, abilities, resourcefulness, and determination. The trouble-making char-acter's (the antagonist) suddenly dying of a heart attack, the episode-spe-cific character's saving the hero's neck, the main character's remaining solvent by receiving a gift from his parents or a secondary character—all these generally are bad moves. Avoid anything that might minimize the effectiveness of your main characters and don't make them too reliant on the whims of fate or the last-minute interventions of a secondary character.

6. Denouement. Like the short story, another brief, encapsulated form, the climax and resolution of a television episode is followed by a dénoue-ment, a period for tying up the remaining subplots, and/or providing an-other glimpse into the personality of your main character. (The former of these two is more common to detective or adventure series; the latter is endemic to the half-hour situation comedy.) The telescript dénouement, in the case of a one-hour program, usually occupies the last three or four minutes of the final act. Half-hour programs usually have two ways of dealing with a dénouement, depending on whether the series has a tag. If it does, the dénouement may be contained entirely therein. If not, the last act contains the dénouement, separated from the main body of the act by a transition indicating that we have moved forward in time. (Note: Some producers, probably in an attempt to confuse the hell out of new writers, sometimes combine the two approaches when a tag is present. They place the dénouement at the conclusion of the final act, and use the entire tag for a characterization piece, sometimes to the point where the tag has virtually nothing to do with the preceding program. The best example of this was *Welcome Back, Kotter*, where the tag was a lengthy excursion in-to joke-telling. A less extreme example of this kind of tag—what some headache-causing troublemakers have dubbed a "sub-dénouement"—would be the main character's watching a news broadcast and comment-ing on some particularly irritating facet of the presentation.)

So . . . to sum up the creative considerations that go into constructing an episodic telescript, we can organize each point into a brief checklist:

1. Select your preferred medium—60 minutes or 30 minutes.

2. Select an individual series out of that specific area.
3. Study that series in a comprehensive, critical fashion.
   A) Get a feeling for the characters.
   B) Make a note of the number of acts.
   C) Determine what topics, plots, and themes are targeted.
   D) Make a rough estimate of the show's intended audience.
   E) Determine the available number of sets.
   F) Note if the show seems to have a high or low budget.
4. Develop a plot in accordance with these factors.
5. Follow the process of plot development for that series.
   A) A reintroduction of characters.
   B) Be sure your interpretations are valid and that your additional characters are program-specific.
   C) Introduce the plot.
   D) Using your understanding of the characters, have them tackle the plot in ways natural to them.
   E) Resolve the plot neatly in one episode.
   F) Provide a dénouement that shows character or further resolves the plot.

The Craft of Telescripting

This subhead may look suspiciously familiar, but there is a subtle—though quite important—difference. The *art* of scriptwriting has to do with the creative and conceptual considerations underlying the genesis of a television script. The *craft* of scriptwriting deals with the most effective and systematic means of implementing those creative decisions—and doing so with the greatest possible professionalism. Failing to perceive that there is a difference between art and craft, and acting upon that lack of understanding, is pernicious. It produces creative scriptwriters who can't sell, and selling scriptwriters who are somewhat bereft of the creative impetus to do Great Things.

In a published interview, Garry Marshall—creator/producer of such series as *Happy Days* and *Laverne and Shirley*—once discussed the question of craftworthiness. "[Scriptwriting] is a craft, not so much an art form," he said. "It takes a certain kind of head. You sit at a table and you sit there until you're finished. It sounds like a joke, but when you'd look for comedy writers, you'd look for people who had a terrible social life . . . they had no other life, and they'd stay there, night after night. It's a tough job. There is no looking around, saying, 'I think I'll go for a walk and look at the sky, and maybe I'll get a brilliant idea.' "

So having an idea, and having the discipline to sit there and come up with one idea after another, is certainly a good thing. Without such creativity, the entertainment business would come to a screeching halt.

But as we discussed briefly at the start of this chapter, having an idea is not enough. Despite this, networks are continually besieged by telephone callers offering ideas; performers and directors receive massive amounts of mail from people who have ideas for television; and workshops are regularly crammed with people with nifty ideas—all looking for someone else to actually do the writing for them.

For the offical record, *nothing* is more representative of amateurism (at its worst) than someone trying to peddle his or her ideas, provided that someone else does the work.

The simple, blunt, painful truth is that writers and producers of programs for network television are just plain not interested in isolated ideas from freelancers. As we'll discuss in more detail later, for legal reasons they'll actually go out of their way to *avoid* these ideas. There is simply no market for programming ideas from new freelance writers. (The operative word, of course, is *new*. An established freelance telescripter with a reliable track record can scribble an idea on the back of a paper sack and sell it. This can be done by such professionals as Larry Gelbart (*M*A*S*H*), Garry Marshall, and such other literary luminaries as Ray Bradbury and Neil Simon, because people in the position to purchase ideas know they have the skill and ability to follow through on the ideas.) Nearly everyone in this business has heard stories about people who have walked right off the street into a producer's office and sold an idea for a new series or for an individual episode of a current series. Rest assured that with a few very, very rare exceptions, such stories either are blatantly false or minimize the actual contribution of the writer. (The exceptions usually involve the offspring, friends, or relatives of someone already employed in the Industry.)

If you have the ideas but not the wherewithal to carry them through to conclusion, you may as well put this book away now and write the whole thing off as a bad idea, 'cause it just ain't gonna work. Television doesn't work that way. About the only alternative you have is to find someone who *can* transform those ideas into reality, and form a writing team. That such partnerships exist is testified to by the multiple credits on many programs. Should you choose to find such a person, give *him* a copy of this book. Better still, let him buy his own copy. I won't mind.

For the moment, however, we will assume that you want to develop and market your own manuscripts, and are prepared to do everything to fulfill that desire. (As for the others, well, you can stay for the ride if you choose, but you'll *have* to stop riffling your papers and talking in the back rows.)

There, now. Having successfully alienated half the people likely to purchase this book, we can now go on to discuss one of the reasons *why* no one wants your ideas.

There are two primary reasons behind this disinclination. One has to do with the ever-present threat of a plagiarism lawsuit, which we will examine more closely in the section on placing your manuscript with a producer. The other reason has to do with a producer's rights of territoriality.

To explain . . .

A producer gets to be a producer because he or she is efficient at producing—and the major task of a producer is to maintain a constant flow of ideas. He develops the ideas himself; or they arise during story conferences with writers and are written down for future use; or offhand suggestions come from friends, staffers, and in casual conversation with other production-related intimates; or they are developed by the story editor, who is also responsible for maintaining the show's creative continuity. There is, therefore, no lack of ideas. Producers stay alive by swimming in a virtual sea of ideas—good, bad, and mediocre—and by culling the better ones out of the brine. The best ideas are those that clearly fall within the province of a producer's program and are different from any done before, or that take a different *approach* to an old topic. Your ideas must fall into those two categories; either that, or the ways in which you handle the show and its characters must be so appealing that it would be impossible for an intelligent producer (and there are a few) to turn you down.

But there's no way a producer can tell whether or not you can do that from three or four sentences on a sheet of paper.

What, then, *does* a producer need to have in order to determine whether or not your work is worth his time? And what do you, as a telescripter, have to do in order to develop and implement your ideas for his series?

Answer: You must know the steps underlying the craft of telescripting, follow those steps through to a finished script, and communicate to the producer both this familiarity and your utility with putting those steps into practice.

Here, then, are those stages of development.

The synopsis. This is a telescript in its most basic form. It consists of the essential nut of your idea, written in brief, narrative form. A synopsis can be as short as a paragraph (a la *TV Guide*), or as long as a page and a half to two pages. The optimum length preferred by most producers is one double-spaced page.

A synopsis is, therefore, simply a statement explaining what your projected episode is about. While a producer may be interested in seeing your synopses *after* he has become familiar with your work, the primary reason for a synopsis is scriptwriter-oriented. It helps you keep on track, and lets you stand back and take an objective look at the idea you've developed. Many times, an idea may seem valid when first conceived, but when you sit down behind the typewriter and attempt to sum it up and extend it out, it sorta falls apart. If that happens to you, don't worry about it—better you should find out the idea doesn't work at the synopsis stage than when halfway through a 40-plus page telescript.

(A number of new writers have a hard time boiling their ideas down. "It's too complex, too layered," goes the usual explanation. "If you're going to understand what my idea's about, it takes more than a page to do it in." That feeling is understandable. [I get the same reaction when I've labored over a lengthy piece that's taken me four weeks' arduous research, and then some fur-ball-brained twit fresh from a speed-reading course reads it in forty-five seconds.] However, the ability to summarize your idea is imperative. And it's not impossible. After all, most writers have little trouble explaining—in 25 words or less—the entire plot of a movie they've seen the previous night. In other words, you've got to be able to distance yourself enough from your work so you can concisely and accurately summarize it with minimal bias.)

A synopsis also is handy from an agent's perspective. Case in point . . . I know an agent who's with International Creative Management (ICM), one of the biggest agencies in the country, with offices in Paris, London, Rome, New York, Las Vegas, Hollywood, and, for all I know, on Mars. As a packager, ICM handles writers, actors, and directors. The fellow I'm referring to handles writers. He has an egg timer on top of his desk, which he puts to good use: When he receives a salable script that has arrived without a synopsis (or with one he doesn't like), he'll create his own. He'll sit there, egg timer in hand, and proceed verbally to boil down the essential script elements into as brief a form as possible. "If I can explain a script in three minutes or less," he once told me, "I can sell *anything*." Just for the record, his claim is far from braggadocio. I've seen him do it, although why he doesn't exchange his egg timer for a digital watch is something I've never understood. On a bet, I once asked him if he could synopsize *Moby Dick*. He thought about it for a moment. "It's all about this nut chasing a big fish, see . . . " You get the idea.

When you write your synopsis, keep it as simple and straightforward as possible, making sure that you've indicated which characters appear in the episode, how many sets will be used, what the program-specific characters should look like, and so forth.

To give you a better idea about what a synopsis looks, feels, and sounds like, we'll take this opportunity to develop a script together, just you and I. Depending on our needs as we go, we will follow the development from idea to actual portions of finished script.

For our purposes, we'll choose the episodic comedy series *M*A*S*H*, since it's both a popular *and* long-enduring series. Between prime time broadcasts and individual episodes currently in syndication, it's a fair bet most of the people likely to read this book have seen at least one episode of *M*A*S*H*. We will also assume that the preliminary steps of market analysis—studying the series and its characters—have already been carried out and begin with the actual process of creating and developing an idea.

Let's begin.

As a comedy series, M*A*S*H only loosely fits the description of a situation comedy. It is frequently allowed to go beyond the limitations of standing sets and onto limited location shooting. To maximize our chances of selling this script, however, we should restrict ourselves to the standing sets—the compound and its surrounding tents. (It will not, however, actually be marketed, since it was written exclusively for this book.)

Because the series is very much an ensemble show, with each character pulling his own artistic weight, we'll assume that there will have to be at least two running plots. Given M*A*S*H's mix of the serious and the comic, we'll make one plot humorous, and the other considerably less lighthearted. Since Hawkeye Pierce is the character most given to outrageous behavior, we'll assign the comic plot to him. So on whom do we lay the serious plot? Ideally, we should find someone who is often passed over, for two reasons: One, it allows you the freedom to explore a character about whom not as many behavioral ground rules have been established, thereby giving you a little more creative freedom. Two, it's a fair bet to assume that behind that character there's an actor who would relish the opportunity to take center stage and sink his teeth into a larger role. We will, therefore, construct our secondary plot around the camp chaplain, Father Mulcahy.

Having selected our subjects, the next logical step is to determine *what* the episode will be about. (This process also works in the opposite direction—starting with the storyline and then finding characters that fit. This is just the way *I* tend to work.) Hawkeye is anarchistic and uninhibited, with a flair for the dramatic; Mulcahy is reserved and soft-spoken—he's the one everybody comes to when they're trying to work something through. What we need to do, therefore, is to find some plot element that either emphasizes or conflicts with these aspects of their characters.

We'll start with Hawkeye, who is always on the lookout for something to divert himself and his comrades from the work that is so much a part of their lives, and combine that interest with his flair for showmanship. Our primary plot, then, will concern the arrival of a package for Hawkeye, containing a mail-order movie camera, which he will use to make his own movie.

As for Mulcahy, well . . . let's do a turn around. Whereas people always come to him for help in resolving a problem, let's give him a problem, one he has a hard time talking to anyone about. Whom does he have to turn to? Next comes the question of what that problem should be. In a place where death and pain is an everyday fact, what could be upsetting in comparison? Answer—the death of someone stateside; a friend, for instance. Since the men dying in Korea are doing so for a reason, we'll make the death in America senseless—an automobile accident.

And there we have our plots, which in a very brief synopsis, look like this:

> Upon receiving a home movie camera in the mail, Hawkeye Pierce wreaks havoc at the 4077th M*A*S*H unit by attempting to become South Korea's answer to Otto Preminger. Meanwhile, as the chaos ensues, Father Mulcahy attempts to deal quietly with another, less amusing piece of news that also arrives in the day's mail— the report of the senseless death of his childhood friend in an automobile accident stateside.

And there it is. Moreover, not only do we have the characters dealing with their own individual stories, but there is also room for some conflict as well. In his bereaved state of mind, how will Father Mulcahy deal with Hawkeye's latest antics? How will they relate during this time? Who will Mulcahy finally talk to about all this? The questions arise quickly, and each one leads to yet another facet of the story, another shading of characterization.

What we need to do at this point is broaden the idea, flesh it out a bit with the other characters in the series, and include the ongoing activities that are a constant part of life at a M*A*S*H unit. (Remember, no one's life revolves around only one incident. Life's not that simple.) Knowing what we now do about the general structure of an episodic program, let's expand our summary into the more accepted one-page (250 words) synopsis. We do this primarily by factoring in the interrelations of Hawkeye and Mulcahy with the series' other characters, and by examining the possible consequences of their individual behaviors. It is at this point— when you begin anticipating the actions of your characters—that the firm knowledge of your cast of characters becomes absolutely essential.

So . . . on to our revised, polished synopsis.

> On the morning of an otherwise slow day, punctuated only by a spirited argument with Charles Emerson Winchester about who secretly borrowed whose cologne, Hawkeye receives a long-awaited package in the day's mail, delivered to the Swamp by Corporal Klinger, who is smart enough to avoid the argument altogether. Upon opening the package, Hawkeye finds a home movie camera, which he had sent for long ago through a mail-order house. New toy in hand, Hawkeye proclaims himself the logical successor to Otto Preminger and waddles out to begin his show business career.
>
> Continuing his rounds, Klinger drops off a letter at the Chapel,

where Father Mulcahy is going through his suggestion box. Mulca- hy obviously finds the contents of the letter quite disturbing, but prefers not to discuss it at the moment.

As the day progresses, Hawkeye wreaks havoc on the camp, bringing his form of *cinema-verite* into the women's shower tent, the mess hall, and into direct confrontation with Charles' nerves. Along the way, he enlists the aid of B.J. (with little success) and Klinger (who not only consents, but assumes the pseudonym of "Francoise Klinger"). He also attempts to enlist Mulcahy's assist- ance, but finds the Father not only reluctant, but actually resentful of Hawkeye's rambunctious activities, something that has never happened before. That some problem is bothering the Father be- comes obvious even to Colonel Potter during an operation, and to Major Houlihan, who encounters the somewhat sullen Mulcahy in the mess tent during lunch. That the Father is going through some very personal problem is obvious, and they all agree to try to be ex- tra-nice to him—which he senses and *also* resents.

Finally, at a mess-tent showing of Hawkeye's film, which was de- veloped quickly but under less-than-honest circumstances, Father Mulcahy slips out. Colonel Potter follows, and at last is confided in by Mulcahy, who explains that he has just received news of the death of his childhood friend—a friend who had also gone through the seminary, but lost his faith and dropped out. Mulcahy finds his friend's death senseless, with nothing left to show for his life. Potter disagrees, pointing out that important memories have been left, and that as long as those memories persist, Mulcahy's friend will live on. Mulcahy reluctantly agrees, and asks if he can stop by Potter's tent later, to talk about his friend. Potter agrees.

In a later scene, Mulcahy has finally regained his sense of bal- ance, and further indicates his recovered sense of humor by slip- ping a whoopee cushion under Winchester.

There are several points worth noticing about our finalized synopsis. First, we have indicated how the two main characters dealt with their en- deavors, and how each resolved his task—Hawkeye finished his film, and Mulcahy learned how to deal with the death of his friend. A synopsis should never simply present the problem and indicate that a resolution can be found in a finished draft of the telescript. That is a red flag to many producers, signalling the possibility that maybe you really *don't* know how to get your characters out of the jam you've created.

Second, we have included other primary characters found in the se- ries, an important point, given the group effort and ensemble perform- ances associated with the series. Each character is given something to do that would be natural for that character.

Third, we indicated what sets would be used, and in what basic order. This way, both you and the producer know what you're going to be dealing with in terms of exterior or location shooting and budgetary considerations.

Finally, it is straightforward and objective. It does not begin with a line like, "In this marvelous, exciting episode . . . " or "In what is sure to become the dramatic highlight of the season . . . " If your concept is good, it doesn't need the hype. Let your ideas sell your product. As my friend at ICM is so fond of saying, "A good script glows in the dark."

There is, however, one important drawback. For an episode of a popular comedy/drama series, it really isn't very funny. At least, it doesn't *look* funny—and *that's* why synopses are of secondary importance to the actual script. In examining the brief synopsis, it's possible to see the points that could be handled in comic fashion. But the question in the producer's mind is, "Can the writer transform these possibilities into reality?" Some familiarity on his part with previous submissions—where you've proven your comic ability—help allay that concern, and make it easier for you to get an assignment based on a synopsis.

(Needless to say, this problem is virtually nonexistent in a dramatic series, where, if you've worked out the basic plot, you don't have to worry about being funny as well. It's only when you create a synopsis for a situation comedy—which, by nature of its brevity, must be very serious— that your creative capabilities come under the darkest shadow.)

With our synopsis in hand, we are now prepared to take the next step in the development of an episodic telescript, armed with a clearer idea of just where we're going and how we're going to get there.

The treatment. A treatment is a substantially longer version of your idea, usually running five to eight pages, and rarely longer than ten pages, written in narrative form very much like a short story. Whereas the synopsis indicated *that* a certain group of characters interacted, a treatment dwells more extensively on *how* they interact. It gives a more accurate feeling for the way your characters move, speak, and act.

Most importantly of all, a treatment allows you to include a reasonable amount of dialogue, demonstrating your ability to make the characters speak in ways that are natural and serve to advance the plot. For this reason alone, most producers—when given a choice between seeing a synopsis and a treatment—generally opt for the treatment. It is simply a more accurate indicator of your abilities as a scriptwriter. Although it requires terribly abusing an old cliché, it would probably be safe to say that one good treatment is worth a thousand synopses.

Incidentally . . . about the time you start working on your treatment, it's a good idea to have a working title in mind. It's always been my belief that a well-chosen title adds another dimension to the finished piece, and helps set the tone for all that follows. I say this even though something like 80 percent of all the titles for episodic television are never shown on screen. In this sense, a title is generally for your benefit and the producer's; but don't let that disclaimer result in deemphasizing the importance of a title, however. I've met many producers who feel that if a writer can't come up with an exciting title, it's a fair bet to assume the script will be equally listless. I know that sounds harsh, and even less than entirely rational, since I've *also* known writers who could produce great scripts but had a terrible time with titles. For good or ill, a title can be essential in getting a producer to look at your script.

Or, as Don Freeman—a nationally respected television columnist for the *San Diego Union*—once remarked to me, "A solid, audience-grabbing title may not be half the battle, but it never hurt Hemingway."

So for our purposes, we shall entitle our scriptwriting endeavor "A Finer Balance," since it deals in part with weighing one death stateside against so many in Korea, and because the fulcrum of our conflict is based on two emotional extremes, Hawkeye's rambunctiousness and Mulcahy's somber attitude, urging the two into a golden medium somewhere in between.

In actually writing a treatment, you should always include the basic elements a producer needs to evaluate the dramatic potential of your concept. These consist of dialogue, directions, indications of physical movement, the denotation of entrances and exits, narrative descriptions of any program-specific characters, and the assignment of individual act and scene numbers.

When writing a treatment, keep your style loose and comfortable. Avoid overwriting, but don't get *too* vague. There are few things that irritate a producer more than treatments that read, in part, "At this point, a crisis develops in (Name)'s family, but his quick action and resourcefulness take care of it nicely." The first thing a producer will assume upon seeing a line like that is that the writer hasn't the vaguest idea *what* will happen, or what the nature of the crisis might be. It's considered a sign of sloppy development.

Make sure the tone of your treatment reconciles with its topic. If you're writing a treatment for a comedy, the treatment should have a light, humorous flavor. If you're writing for an episodic drama, be serious without sliding into melodrama.

Overall, you should attempt to give your treatment the feel of a well-written short story. It might not be a bad idea, therefore, to read a reasonable number of short stories (assuming you haven't already) before writing your treatment. In addition, while I personally don't care much for them, you might want to pick up a couple of novelizations of television programs during your next excursion to a bookstore. Such books, while parasitical from a literary perspective, at least manage to convey how you can put the events in a script into narrative form.

One important distinction between a treatment and a synopsis is that a treatment, like a short story, is written according to very specific typographical guidelines. This uniformity in presentation makes life easier for the producer, who has to wade through an incredible number of treatments each season, and helps to establish from the very beginning that you know something about telescripting.

The typographical requirements for a treatment are as follows:

The left and right margins should be set 1 inch from either side of the page. (This amounts to 10 spaces on a pica typewriter, and 12 on an elite typewriter. Since pica typing is almost mandatory in scriptwriting, however, all horizontal spacing requirements will henceforth be given only in picas.)

The title of the series you are submitting to should be placed 8 spaces from the top of the page. The title of the series should be capitalized, underlined, and centered on the page.

The title of the episode should be centered 2 spaces below the series title. It is written in upper- and lower-case letters, and bracketed by quotation marks.

Centered 4 spaces below the episode title are the words *Written By*, typed in upper- and lower-case letters, followed 2 vertical spaces later by your name, which is also centered.

Act numbers should be capitalized and set flush with the left margin, while individual scene numbers should be typed in upper- and lower-case letters, underlined, indented 5 spaces and placed at the beginning of the paragraph that begins the scene.

All paragraphs should begin with a 5-space indentation.

The treatment begins with ACT ONE placed halfway down the first page. Each subsequent page begins 8 spaces from the top of the page.

The title of the episode should be placed 4 spaces from the top, in the left-hand corner of the second and all subsequent pages.

Each page number after the first page is placed 4 spaces from the top in the right-hand corner of the page at 75 picas.

Needless to say, you should always pick your strongest slices of dialogue for the treatment. In addition, you would include more dialogue in a comedy treatment than in a dramatic treatment simply because a comedy depends more upon sharp, witty lines.

Using all these rules, therefore, we'll now examine what the first few pages of our treatment for "A Finer Balance" should look like this. (See Fig. 1 and 2.)

The treatment continues in this fashion until finished. In this case, the total work amounted to 10 pages. (Although space requirements do not allow for the total printing here of finished treatments and scripts, each has been written in its entirety for my own reference.)

Because a treatment is broken up into acts that correspond to those used regularly in the series, it is necessary for you to end each act on a high note, more commonly known as a *hook*. A hook is precisely that—a

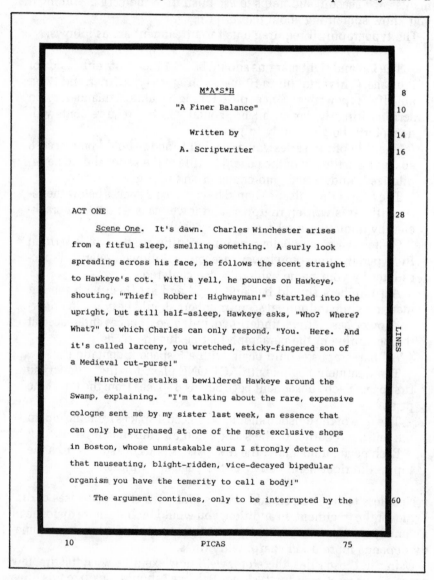

```
                        M*A*S*H                        8
                   "A Finer Balance"                   10

                      Written by                       14

                   A. Scriptwriter                     16


     ACT ONE                                           28

         Scene One.  It's dawn.  Charles Winchester arises
     from a fitful sleep, smelling something.  A surly look
     spreading across his face, he follows the scent straight
     to Hawkeye's cot.  With a yell, he pounces on Hawkeye,
     shouting, "Thief!  Robber!  Highwayman!"  Startled into the
     upright, but still half-asleep, Hawkeye asks, "Who?  Where?
     What?" to which Charles can only respond, "You.  Here.  And
     it's called larceny, you wretched, sticky-fingered son of
     a Medieval cut-purse!"
         Winchester stalks a bewildered Hawkeye around the
     Swamp, explaining.  "I'm talking about the rare, expensive
     cologne sent me by my sister last week, an essence that
     can only be purchased at one of the most exclusive shops
     in Boston, whose unmistakable aura I strongly detect on
     that nauseating, blight-ridden, vice-decayed bipedular
     organism you have the temerity to call a body!"
         The argument continues, only to be interrupted by the   60


              10              PICAS              75
```

Fig. 1

device for grabbing the audience and making sure they return for the following act. In a dramatic series, a hook is often action-oriented—a gunshot, the hero finding a bomb in an airplane, the heroine being seized from behind by an unseen assailant, or a main character clinging by his or her fingers from the roof of an 18-story skyscraper. In a comedy series, hooks are more often verbal, but they too help to advance the plot, trigger an action, and make the viewer wonder, *"Now* what's going to happen?"

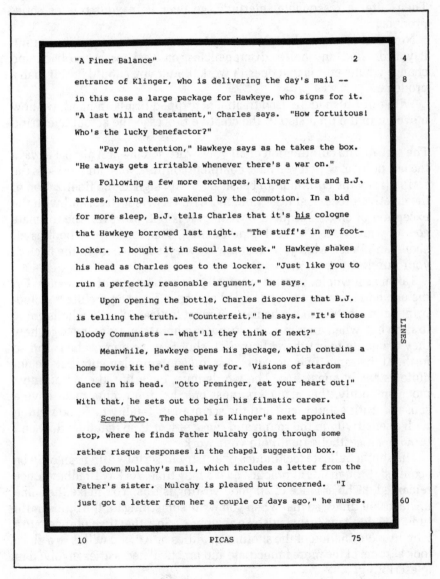

```
"A Finer Balance"                                    2       4

entrance of Klinger, who is delivering the day's mail --      8
in this case a large package for Hawkeye, who signs for it.
"A last will and testament," Charles says.  "How fortuitous!
Who's the lucky benefactor?"
     "Pay no attention," Hawkeye says as he takes the box.
"He always gets irritable whenever there's a war on."
     Following a few more exchanges, Klinger exits and B.J.
arises, having been awakened by the commotion.  In a bid
for more sleep, B.J. tells Charles that it's his cologne
that Hawkeye borrowed last night.  "The stuff's in my foot-
locker.  I bought it in Seoul last week."  Hawkeye shakes
his head as Charles goes to the locker.  "Just like you to
ruin a perfectly reasonable argument," he says.
     Upon opening the bottle, Charles discovers that B.J.
is telling the truth.  "Counterfeit," he says.  "It's those
bloody Communists -- what'll they think of next?"
     Meanwhile, Hawkeye opens his package, which contains a
home movie kit he'd sent away for.  Visions of stardom
dance in his head.  "Otto Preminger, eat your heart out!"
With that, he sets out to begin his filmatic career.
     Scene Two.  The chapel is Klinger's next appointed
stop, where he finds Father Mulcahy going through some
rather risque responses in the chapel suggestion box.  He
sets down Mulcahy's mail, which includes a letter from the
Father's sister.  Mulcahy is pleased but concerned.  "I
just got a letter from her a couple of days ago," he muses.   60

     10                  PICAS                   75
```

Fig. 2

It is in the finished treatment that your idea exists in its most comprehensive form short of an actual script. Once completed, however, it becomes incumbent upon you to do a little second-guessing. Switch roles for a moment from writer to producer, and try your damnedest to poke holes in your treatment. Look at your work as dispassionately as possible, and find any weaknesses that might injure the treatment and, later, the script itself. Put the treatment away somewhere for a couple of days. Then, after a reasonable interlude, go over it in your role as series producer.

Now that you have the opportunity to examine your concept as a unit, if you do find any holes, discrepancies, or weaknesses, go back and change whatever it is that doesn't work. Better you should find it than a producer.

With our finished, revised treatment gripped firmly in hand, we now move on to the final step in the creative process—the actual telescript.

The script. The culmination of all your work so far—and almost always the last point at which you have complete control over your work—is the script. (I say the *culmination* because a script signals the finalization of the creative process, at least from the writer's perspective, and with the exception of any subsequent rewriting. It is not, however, the ultimate *goal* of your work. The goal is production. That's what this book is all about, and that's what you must always keep somewhere in the back of your mind as you write.)

Taken as a whole, a script is actually a combination of opposites. On the one hand, a script is as detailed and specific as an architect's blueprint or an electrician's schematic. It must indicate clearly who is going to say what, when they are going to move, where they are going to go, how they are going to get there, how each shot is to be approached, and so forth. At the same time, however, a script contains elements that are not quite as easily quantified. The words must have life, the action must move smoothly, the characters must breathe, the events must have a sense of truth about them, and the script in its totality must be written with a sensitivity to the sound and sense of words so that they flow and provide an aesthetic quality to your work.

The subtle delicate techniques of artistry in scriptwriting can only be acquired through lots of practice over a long time. As Ray Bradbury once remarked, "The essence of all good writing is this: You make the same mistake 999 times, so that when you write something for the thousandth time, you don't make that mistake anymore." So rather than plunge into a lengthy examination of the sublime qualities of Art, we will take a close look at some of the more immediate and practical necessities involved in telescripting.

Little things . . . like how to do it.

A good telescript is always spare. It contains only those elements necessary to its production. Here are some of the things you will not find in a script, because they are not necessary to its production: longwinded speeches that run two or more pages long; frequent asides to the director or the cast; explanations or clarifications of the plot (if you have to explain it to the director, how do you expect the viewer to figure it out?); action which is gratuitous or downright irrelevant; lines of dialogue tossed in to fill up time; hand-drawn lines that indicate where bits of dialogue or scenes were supposed to go, but that were placed out of sequence; numerous and—most importantly—inexcusable typos; as well as a general feeling of sloppiness and disorganization.

Here are some of the things you will always find in a production-quality telescript: short, precise directions that make their point and let the action continue; dialogue that is succinct and to the point; acts and scenes that are clearly marked and laid out in a comprehensible, sequential form; neatness in presentation; a sense for what works visually; and an adherence to the typographical format associated with the target series.

Overall, there are probably two elements of telescripting that trip up new writers the most—dealing with camera angles, and blocking. Let's take these one at a time.

The novice scriptwriter frequently feels it's necessary to spell out every single camera angle in order for the full meaning of his script to be understood. I have seen scripts that have more lines of incredibly detailed camera directions than they have lines of dialogue. For writers who, in their quest for clarity, wander and become trapped in the tarpit of visual excess, I have one word of advice: *Relax.*It's not written anywhere that you have to figure out how every shot is to be set up. That's what directors are for. You gave yourself an ulcer bringing your script to life and that's enough. Now it's *his* turn.

So . . . to what degree *should* you worry about including camera angles in your script? As before, the answer rests in sparsity: You should only interject those directions crucial to the development of your story. If it is necessary that your audience see a character sneaking a pistol into his jacket, and if that action is crucial to what is going to happen shortly, then naturally you want to make sure the action takes prominence in the mind of the viewer. This is accomplished by signalling for an insert—in this case, a closeup of the character's hand surreptitiously picking up the gun and placing it into a jacket pocket. After that, you return to the scene by simply writing BACK TO SCENE. (A glossary of camera terminology and the way in which it is used can be found at the back of this book.)

As a rule, you will tend to find more explicit camera directions in dramatic scripts than in comedy scripts. This is particularly true for situation comedies that utilize three cameras and a live audience. Because we are generally dealing with a very finite visual universe—usually just one or two sets—there aren't a whole lot of camera angles you can really call for. Because all the editing is done electronically during production by switching from one camera to another, most of the emphasis will be on reactive shots—angles that display a character's reactions to an event or another character to the best possible effect—and these are virtually impossible to set up until a technical rehearsal can be held.

What, I hear you ask, is a technical rehearsal? That's when the cast and crew assemble on the set for the first time, usually following standard rehearsals elsewhere. At this point, the director sits down behind the three monitors that display what each camera sees and begins roughly sketching out what cameras he wants to use, in what order, and from what angle, depending upon where the actors are at any given moment. This process is then refined even further until a precise, second-by-second outline has been created. Once this has been done, the live taping may proceed.

(Just as a distantly-related-but-actually-rather-interesting aside, you might be intrigued to know that nearly every situation comedy produced in front of a live audience is actually taped *twice*. There are several good reasons for this. No two audiences are ever the same, and a line that gets a small laugh during the first taping might get absolute howls during the second. In the final mixing, the portions that were best received during either taping are edited together to form a cohesive whole. In addition, it is not uncommon that only after an initial audience reaction do the director and producer realize that something just isn't working. When this happens, the writer can usually be found just offstage, shaking his head and muttering, "I *told* you it wouldn't work." I say he *can* be found because an all-out effort to find him is made whenever part of the show turns out to be a stinker. That section is then reworked and rewritten until the final kinks are ironed out, and a second taping is undertaken. While sitting in on the taping of one show, I saw the cast and writer rewrite an entire *act* in the hour and a half between the first and second tapings. If that doesn't tell you something about television writing and the reason it pays so well, nothing will.)

Our conclusion, therefore, is that you should keep camera directions to a minimum in dramatic scripts, and virtually eliminate them in comedy scripts. In terms of blocking, however, the emphasis should be about the same between the two. (Blocking is a stage term for how the characters move and what they do while the cameras are on them.) While no one ever speaks while remaining totally motionless, and while there is nothing more boring to the eye than a script devoid of character directions, you must strive to keep such directions only to those called for by your story.

A facility with character direction is essential for a telescripter in either comedy or drama. A single move can heighten the sense of humor or tension in a script. A classic example of this cropped up in an episode of the situation comedy series *Too Close for Comfort*, wherein the lead character is deciding whether or not to have an affair. The action takes place in a hotel lobby. His potential partner is five floors up. In his indecision, he paces the lobby; enters the elevator; exits the elevator; enters the elevator, goes up three floors, then comes down again; walks upstairs; walks downstairs; walks upstairs and takes the elevator downstairs— and all without a single word of dialogue, and with the camera shooting straight ahead from one angle. It was a brilliant piece of blocking, and it was received with unbounded enthusiasm by the audience.

Probably one of the best ways to gain a working knowledge of scriptwriting and how to balance camera angles, dialogue and blocking (short of this book, of course) is simply to read as many produced television scripts as you can, comparing what you see on the page with what appears onscreen. Surprisingly, it's not difficult at all to secure such scripts, either in original or bound form. Here are some examples of where to go to find produced television scripts:

Libraries. Public libraries frequently stock books that contain scripts from the Golden Age of Television; college or university libraries often have more recent material. One of the best collections of telescripts is *Great Television Plays*, published in two volumes by Dell Press (paperback $1.25). It contains such classics as Gerald DiPego's *I Heard the Owl Call My Name* and Rod Serling's *A Storm in Summer*, among others.

Magazines. Publications about the television industry can be gold mines of information on how to find television scripts. Foremost among these is *American Film*, the magazine of the American Film Institute. From time to time, magazines sometimes reprint scripts: *Twilight Zone Magazine* has carried a number of early *Twilight Zone* scripts by Rod Serling, Richard Matheson and others.

Bookstores. Browse around the television and film sections of your local bookstore, and the odds are fair that you'll find at least a few printed and bound television scripts, many of which include photographs from the productions. Somewhere on these dusty shelves, you can find bound versions of *The Phantom of the Open Hearth*, Jean Shepherd's award-winning television movie produced by the Public Broadcasting System, and available in book form from Doubleday Dolphin (paperback, $4.95). As a double bonus, Harlan Ellison's collection of short fiction *From the Land of Fear* (Belmont Tower, paperback, $1.25) not only contains his telescript "Soldier," produced for the television series *Outer Limits*, but a second version of the story in narrative fiction form. Two other television works by Ellison can be found in books—an episode of *The Young Lawyers* appears in his collection of television columns *The Other Glass Teat*

(Pyramid, paperback, $1.50), and his telescript for "The City on the Edge of Forever," an episode of *Star Trek* that won the Most Outstanding Teleplay award from the Writers Guild of America, appears in *Six Science Fiction Plays*, edited by Roger Elwood (Pocket Books, paperback, $1.95). (I cannot commend the works of Harlan Ellison to you too strongly. His teleplays are generally outstanding, his media criticism—originally published in the *Los Angeles Free Press*—are so to-the-point that they are often used as textbooks, and his fiction can stand up to that produced by anyone else—and beat it to a pulp. His encounters with network television executives are legendary, and his ongoing struggle for literary integrity has inspired not a few novice writers.)

Depending upon where you live, it is sometimes possible to find a bookstore that carries television scripts in their original form. If you don't happen to live near a large city, you might want to start by trying (visiting or writing) the Hollywood Book and Poster Company at 1706 North Las Palmas Avenue in Los Angeles. They have one of the widest and most up-to-date selections of telescripts available. Also, for the diehard *Star Trek* fans among us, all the scripts for this series and every other Gene Roddenberry production are available from Lincoln Enterprises, 1614 Wilcox Avenue in Los Angeles.

And finally . . .

Studios. When in doubt, go straight to the source. Although the networks do not make it a point to publicize the fact, scripts for television series are frequently available directly from the original production company. I cannot stress enough, however, that this route should *only* be used as a last resort. When I say "last resort," I mean cases when you really have your heart set on writing for a particular series, you've turned up empty-handed on all other sources, and you feel you cannot possibly do a reasonable job on the script unless you examine a produced script. This is not, by the way, an altogether unreasonable point of view. Having an actual production script in your hands can be of considerable help in getting the rhythms and patterns of speech correct for each of the different characters.

So if you find yourself in this desperate position, your first step should be to locate the production company responsible for the series. (A sizable list can be found at the end of this book. Beyond that, you're on your own.) Tell them, in a query letter, that you're interested in submitting a script on a speculative basis, and that in order to make your submission as close to their standards as possible, you'd like the opportunity to examine one of their scripts. As a further incentive, you may want to include proper postage, which can be figured simply by working out the script's approximate number of pages, adding another half-ounce for the manuscript cover and fasteners, and using the current postal rates to arrive at a precise amount. You can probably expect to receive a script in the mail in eight out of every ten attempts.

Be certain, however, that you take this step only when you can see no other way around it, because if the studios are deluged with too many requests they'll probably put an end to the practice altogether.

Those are the steps necessary to securing copies of produced telescripts. But you need not go through any of them simply to get an idea of what a telescript looks like. To do that, you need merely read on . . .

Formats. There are probably a dozen or more ways a beginning telescripter trips himself up when it comes time to make a submission. But one of the most immediate and damning errors is not adhering to standard script formats *as they apply to the series in question.* You see, there are a variety of formats for television scripts, and knowing when to use the right one is like knowing the password into a speakeasy—it tells the people in charge that you know what you're getting yourself into, and that you are somewhat more familiar with the medium than some other writer whose improperly formatted script arrived the same day.

With a couple of exceptions too infrequently used to warrant mention here, there are four distinct television script formats currently in use. Which of these is to be used at any given time depends entirely upon the nature of the program. There is a specific script format for programs that are shot on film, situation comedies videotaped before a live audience, live variety shows or videotaped variety shows, and a dual-purpose two-column script that, though still in use, is (happily) declining in popularity.

In examining each of these formats, we shall take the following approach: First, we'll look at the format itself, its typographical requirements, and general approach, after discussing them briefly in a paragraph or two. After the explanation and the visual format, we'll put the format to use by taking a scene from our *M*A*S*H* script and dropping one each into two of the four available formats. This will provide a better means of contrasting the different typographical forms.

Format #1: Film. Nearly every one-hour dramatic series is shot on film. This is because they frequently require a lot of on-location filming, and exterior shots look better on film than they do on tape. There is also more editing to be done on such programs, and film can be edited much more precisely. Film also has greater depth of field, does not flatten its images nearly so much as videotape does, and just plain looks nicer.

There are, however, some programs that qualify as comedies that are shot on film. These include the serio-comic *Lou Grant* series, *The Love Boat,* and *M*A*S*H.* (Therefore, this is the correct format for the script we've been writing throughout this chapter.) If you're unsure, you can always tell a filmed program from one videotaped by looking for the qualities mentioned—a lot of intercutting and editing, a richness of depth of field, and so on.

Here are the typographical dimensions of a telescript intended for production on film. Each film-format page equals about one minute. Set your tabs and margins accordingly.

Act numbers are centered on the page, and are placed 7 spaces from the top of the page. Make another scene denotation at 75 picas.

Page numbers are located in the upper right-hand corner of the page at 79 picas and 4 lines from the top.

Scene numbers are at 15 picas. Each scene should be individually numbered, and preceded by some transition. If a scene is carried across two pages, the word CONTINUED, printed in all caps, should follow the scene number on each subsequent page. Make another scene denotation at 75 picas.

Dialogue is placed in the center of the page between 30 and 60 picas, and single-spaced.

Dialogue directions are indented 5 spaces further in—35 picas— and set in parentheses without use of upper-case letters, except for characters' names.

Names of characters are placed at 40 picas and are always capitalized.

Camera, scene and blocking directions are placed between 20 and 70 picas. Within this section, the names of characters are CAPITALIZED when first introduced, and written in upper- and lower-case letters each time thereafter. Always single-space.

Scene indications are also placed between 20 and 70 picas and single-spaced. The difference between a scene indication and a direction is that indications of scenes are always capitalized, and begin with the denotation INT. or EXT., thereby establishing that the scene in question takes place in an Interior or Exterior location.

Transitional and *continuational* notations are typed at 68 picas.

The first page begins with the words FADE IN in all caps set flush against the left margin (20 picas), 12 lines from the top. The first scene is typed 2 spaces below that, and all subsequent scenes, descriptions, and individual blocks of dialogue are double-spaced from one another.

Subsequent pages begin with the scene continuation 6 spaces from the top, and the action itself begins 2 spaces below that. Each new act begins with the format used for the first page, with the end of each act clearly indicated in all caps, centered on the page, approximately 6 lines below the last line of dialogue or description. FADE OUT is only used once, at the very end of the telescript.

Having now established, in specific typographical terms, what format must be adhered to, we'll take a look at a visual representation of that script, followed by a couple of pages of our M*A*S*H script that utilize that format. (For a longer example of a film format, see the chapter on motion pictures.) (See Fig. 3 through 5.)

Format #2: Situation comedies/videotape. While it may prove impracti-

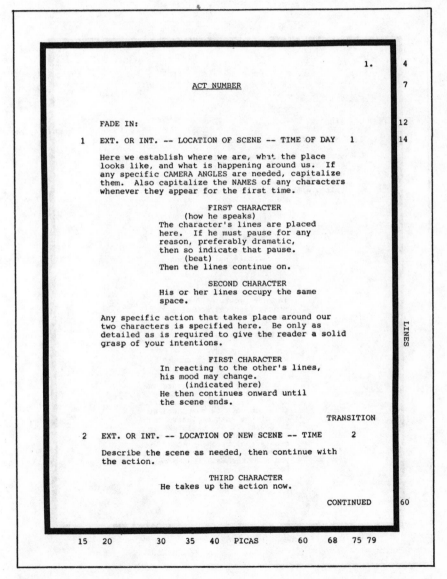

Fig. 3

cal to use videotape in location shots—if only because the crew must truck along a massive amount of additional equipment, monitor the taping, and edit during production—videotaping is perfectly suited to production on an enclosed set. Nothing needs to be shipped out, all three cameras are on hand, you don't have to stop shooting whenever a plane passes overhead, and there's a fully equipped control room that puts the director in complete command of everything happening on the studio

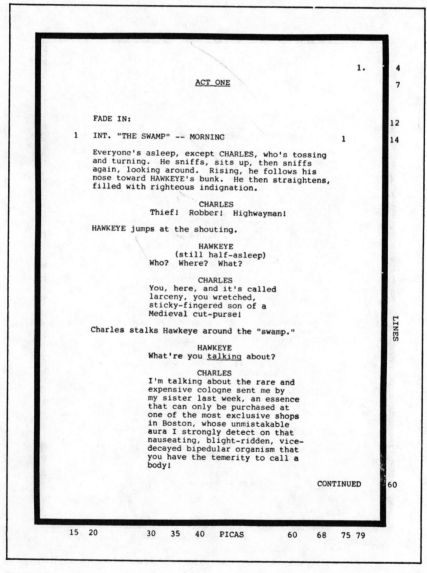

```
                                                          1.      4

                         ACT ONE                                  7


        FADE IN:                                                  12

    1   INT. "THE SWAMP" -- MORNING              1               14

        Everyone's asleep, except CHARLES, who's tossing
        and turning.  He sniffs, sits up, then sniffs
        again, looking around.  Rising, he follows his
        nose toward HAWKEYE's bunk.  He then straightens,
        filled with righteous indignation.

                         CHARLES
                Thief!  Robber!  Highwayman!

        HAWKEYE jumps at the shouting.

                         HAWKEYE
                     (still half-asleep)
                Who?  Where?  What?

                         CHARLES
                You, here, and it's called
                larceny, you wretched,
                sticky-fingered son of a
                Medieval cut-purse!

        Charles stalks Hawkeye around the "swamp."

                         HAWKEYE
                What're you talking about?

                         CHARLES
                I'm talking about the rare and
                expensive cologne sent me by
                my sister last week, an essence
                that can only be purchased at
                one of the most exclusive shops
                in Boston, whose unmistakable
                aura I strongly detect on that
                nauseating, blight-ridden, vice-
                decayed bipedular organism that
                you have the temerity to call a
                body!

                                        CONTINUED     60


        15   20      30   35   40   PICAS     60   68   75 79
```

Fig. 4

floor. As a result, nearly every half-hour situation comedy is produced on videotape, usually in front of a live audience.

Because of the unique requirements of television production on tape, a script format that deals with these needs with minimal fuss has emerged. The most vital aspect of videotape production facilitated by this kind of script is the constant need for last-minute revision. As you may have noted on the film script format, the single-spaced approach doesn't leave

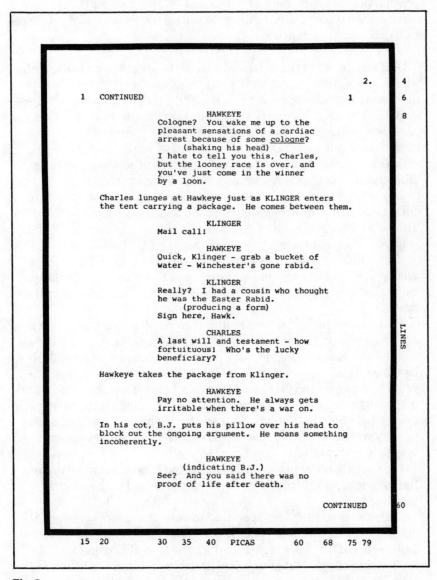

Fig. 5

much room for changes: That's because there is usually sufficient time between shootings for the production assistants to retype pages that need changing. Situation comedies simply don't provide that luxury; the production must be wrapped up quickly, and any twelfth-hour changes must be pencilled in on the original script. This, plus the fact that camera and blocking directions are usually written along the margins of the script, translates into the need for a lot of blank space on the finished telescript. As such, each page equals about 30 to 40 seconds.

Here are the typographical dimensions for a television situation comedy script to be videotaped:

Act numbers are centered and placed 12 spaces from the top of the page. Centered directly above the act number are the series title (8 spaces from the top) and the episode title (10 spaces from the top). The series title and act number are always capitalized and underlined, while the episode title is written in upper- and lower-case letters, bracketed with quotation marks, and underlined. (The two titles are, of course, omitted on the first pages of acts two and three, although the act number remains 12 spaces from the top.)

In addition, *each page*—inclusive of the first page—must feature an act and scene number notation in the upper right-hand corner of the page. This is placed at 65 picas, 3 spaces from the top of the page, capitalized and underlined. (Example, *ACT I, SC. 1,* and *ACT II, SC. 3.*) This helps locate a particular scene in the episode more easily during rehearsal and production. (There are, incidentally, only about three scenes per act in any given situation comedy script.)

Cast names for the actors required to participate in any given scene are placed directly (one line) below the act and scene notation in the right-hand corner, and single-spaced between 60 and 75 picas. Cast names are written in upper- and lower-case letters, separated by commas and bracketed by parentheses. They are used only at the beginning of a given scene, with the page number appearing 2 spaces below (about 7 lines from the top). They are omitted from subsequent pages of the same scene, with the page number rising to 5 spaces from the top.

Page numbers are placed at 75 picas, and spaced from the top of the page according to the specifications spelled out in the preceding paragraph.

Dialogue is written in upper- and lower-case letters between 20 and 50 picas, and double-spaced. You should refrain wherever possible from continuing a section of dialogue from first page to another. Because of the double-spacing, however, this can be difficult at times. So if a continuation becomes necessary, write the word

"MORE" directly below the last line of dialogue on the one page, and put the abbreviation (CONT'D) directly beside the character's name on the following page, with the dialogue picking up where it left off 2 spaces below, in the usual manner.

Names of characters are capitalized at 30 picas, and placed 2 spaces above the first line of dialogue.

Dialogue, scene, camera and *blocking directions* are all placed between 15 and 50 picas, capitalized, single-spaced and bracketed by parentheses.

Scene indications are capitalized, set within the same margins, and are not accompanied by numbers directly beside them. The scene numbers at the top of the page are sufficient. All that are required are the indications of INT. or EXT., the location, and whether the action takes place at night or during the day.

Transitions and *continuations* are also handled simply. Each act begins with *FADE IN:* and ends with *FADE OUT* in capitals and underlined, and placed at the far left margin (15 picas). Transitions are usually confined to simple blackouts, freeze-frames, and dissolves. They are placed at 65 picas and capitalized.

Each scene following a transition begins on a new page, with the scene indication beginning at 10 spaces from the top of the page.

Actually, all this sounds a lot more complicated than it really is. The result is simply a television script that has a lot of "air" and is set largely on the left of the page, with constant little reminders about where we are on a scene-by-scene basis. A pure example of this kind of script appears on the following page. After that, we have an example of what another part of our M*A*S*H script would look like if it were being videotaped as a situation comedy in front of a live studio audience. (See Fig. 6, 7, 8.)

Format #3: Live, comedy/variety programs on videotape. Just as situation comedy telescripts must be fashioned in a way that leaves them open for last-minute revision, so too must a television sketch or other live-broadcast material be open to changes. More so, in fact, because of the frenetic requirements of such programs.

The most immediately noticeable difference between the two formats is that the body of a television situation comedy script is placed to the left of the page, while live or variety programs have the bulk of their material on the far right side of the page. This may seem rather arbitrary, but in the case of the live or variety telescript, there is actually a good reason for the distinction. You see, it's not at all uncommon for these scripts to be changed, revised, polished, pulled and put into a program at the last minute to fill up time when the program runs short. This occurs to the understandable consternation of the cast members, who may find it difficult to memorize all the new lines without sufficient lead time. Sometimes the studio uses a teleprompter—a device that scans a sheet of paper and electronically displays the written copy on a screen directly above the television camera. And it just happens that teleprompters are built so that they scan the right side of the page.

So it's not really quite as arbitrary as it seems, is it? (Of course, you might well ask why the situation comedy producers don't switch over to

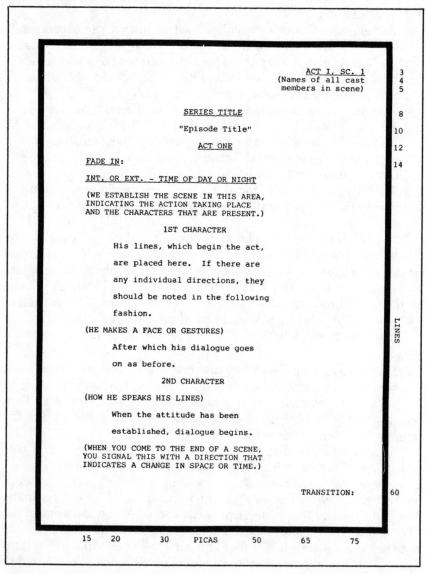

Fig. 6

this format and thereby create a little consistency in comedy scriptwriting. It's an obvious question. In fact, I asked it of several producers myself, and in each case got about the same response—a quizzical look, a shrug, and "because we've *always* done it this way, and always will" for a response. Go try and figure the world.)

Another important distinction of this format is that it is not divided into acts. Instead, each individual segment of the show (inclusive of come-

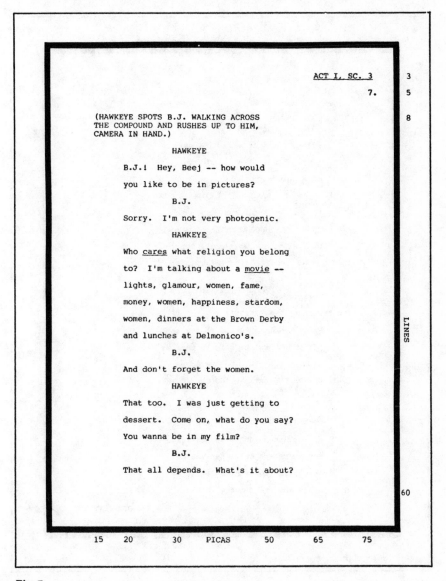

Fig. 7

dy sketches, films, and musical appearances by guest groups) is called an
item. Further, each item is given its own number, according to its sequence in the show, and is typed separately from the surrounding items.
This way, should a producer decide at the last minute to replace one
comedy sketch with another, he can do so without having to rewrite or retype the surrounding pages.

   Finally, there's no need to designate interior or exterior scenes. Every-

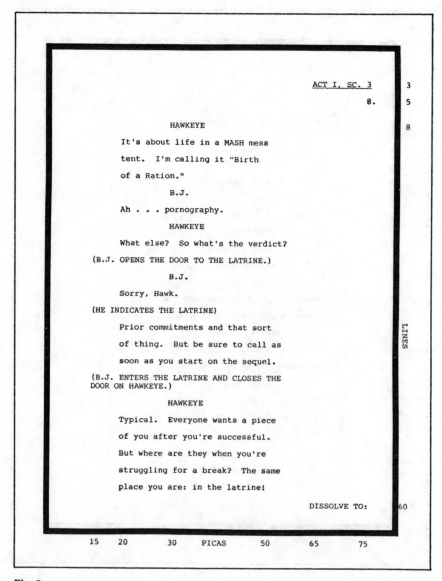

Fig. 8

thing is shot inside the studio. But you are required to specify what kind of set is required, usually beginning with the words UP ON, which indicates that the camera dissolves to that set after taping the previous segment. (For example, UP ON: A UNIVERSITY AUDITORIUM tells the director that the sketch takes place on a set built to resemble the interior of a large auditorium, with desks, a chalkboard, and so on.)

From time to time, however, you will notice programs featuring segments videotaped on location, usually with a minicam accompanied by a skeleton crew. (I'm referring to programs like NBC's *Saturday Night Live*, ABC's *Fridays* and the independently produced *Second City Television.*) In order to differentiate between the two, items written for production in-studio during live taping are accompanied by the notation (LIVE), while those that require exterior taping are indicated with the abbreviation (VTR). This means that the item is to be taped before the show, edited, and cued up by the director during the studio taping. The videotape recording—VTR—is then shown on studio monitors for the audience. In addition, the microphones recording audience response are left open, so that any applause and laughter can be broadcast along with the visual tape.

It should be noted here that while the format for writing a sketch that is pre-taped and shown during production is the same as a live sketch, the typewritten sketch is not included in the script used during live production. Because the pre-taped sketch has already been completed, there's no need to include all the dialogue in the production script. That merely brings up the cost of typing and duplicating. Instead, a single page is inserted into the production script, containing the title of the sketch, the length in minutes and seconds, the opening shot that begins the sketch (which tells the director whether or not the tape has been cued up to the right point), and the outcue—the last word, sentence or scene that finishes the sketch—that tells the director the scene is concluding and to segue into the next item.

In order to facilitate the transition from one item to another, and to make sure that nothing gets out of sequence, the last line on the last page of each item gives the cue for the following item. For instance, on the bottom of the last page of an item immediately preceding a sketch about pirates would be the line (INTO: PIRATE SPOT).

Once again, this all sounds a lot more complicated than it really is. In reality, sketch writing is probably the easiest and simplest form of telescripting there is. You don't have to worry about dividing the action into separate acts, or maintaining an involved plot over a full thirty minutes. The sole task of a sketch writer is to get in quickly, get the laughs, then run like hell so the next sketch can start.

Here, then, are the typographical standards for comedy/variety show sketches, applicable both to live and videotaped items.

Page numbers are placed 3 spaces from the top of the page at 75 picas.

Item numbers are set at 33 picas, 5 lines from the top of the page, capitalized and underlined. On the first page of the individual item, the full number is spelled out. (For example, *ITEM #4.*) On subsequent pages, however, only the actual number is used, bracketed by quotes—in this case, (4).

Sketch titles also appear at the fifth vertical line from the top of each page at 53 picas. Titles are capitalized and underlined, and should be as brief as possible a version of the full title. (Example: *PIRATE ATTACK ON THE U.S.S. HERMITAGE* would be written simply as *PIRATE ATTACK.*)

Live or videotaped notations appear directly after the title of the sketch, written in all caps and bracketed by parentheses. Hence, the above would read, in full, *PIRATE ATTACK (LIVE)* or *PIRATE ATTACK (VTR)*.

Cast names for those actors required in the sketch are, as in the situation comedy format, written directly beneath the sketch title in upper- and lower-case letters, bracketed by parentheses.

Scene indications appear 12 lines from the top of the page, starting at 33 picas and ending at approximately 63 picas. As mentioned, scene indications always begin with the words UP ON, followed by the designation of the required set. They are written in capital letters and bracketed by parentheses, and are always single-spaced.

Scene descriptions and blocking directions are written in the same fashion as scene indications, occupying the same pica space on the page and using the same rules of capitalization.

Dialogue is double-spaced between 38 and 75 picas, written in upper- and lower-case letters.

Names of characters are typed in all caps at 53 picas. Double-space between the name of a character and his or her first line of dialogue. (Note: When a sketch is first turned in by a writer, it may or may not use the actual cast names in place of characters. If a sketch is written specifically for one of the cast members, this is so stated. As a rule, however, producers prefer to get a sketch using only the characters' names, allowing them to determine who will play any given role.)

Transitional Flags signalling the upcoming sketch are written on the last line of the sketch, centered, written in caps and bracketed by parentheses.

If you have written a sketch to be videotaped for later showing during the live production, you should also include the one-page substitution sheet that will be used in the final production sheet, the one that gives the director his cuing information.

Here are the specifications for that accompanying page:

The typographical rules concerning *item numbers, page numbers, sketch titles,* and *indications for the following sketch* are followed in precisely the manner outlined before.

Videotape recording notations are made directly after the title using the following: (VTR).

A *VTR data box* is made by putting a line of dashes from 33 picas to 75 picas at a point 12 spaces from the top of the page, and 2 spaces from the bottom of the last line of your outcue.

All the following are written in capitals, underlined, followed by a colon, double-spaced from one another, and typed at 33 picas.

VTR: This space, to be left blank on your page, is for the code number of the videotape upon which your sketch has been recorded. This lets the director place the tapes in the order in which they will be cued up.

TIME: This contains the approximate running time of your sketch in minutes and seconds.

OPENING SHOT: In as few words as possible, this describes what the director should be seeing on his monitor if the tape has been cued up properly to the beginning of the sketch.

OUTCUE: The signal for the director to prepare for the next scene—the last sentence or visual cue ending the sketch.

Once again, in order to get a better understanding of this script format, we'll illustrate the point with a few samples of the sketch and accompanying page formats. Because the requirements of this kind of script are so radically different from either one discussed previously, we'll have to diverge momentarily from our excursions into the world of *M*A*S*H* and replace it with an actual sketch—once again written exclusively for this book. (See Fig. 9 through 14.)

Format #4: Two-column scripts. This particular format—the last we will examine in this chapter—was originally developed as an all-purpose kind of format. In recent years, however, the rise of format specialization we discussed earlier has steadily eroded that overall utility. As of this writing, two-column scripts have almost entirely been relegated to television commercials.

This format can be distinguished from all the others considered so far by the fact that the script is neatly divided down the center, the visual directions on one side, dialogue on the other. There is a reason for this: Most television commercials, if you really study them, consist mainly of narrations dubbed over a series of images of the product being hawked. It becomes tiring after a while, however, to keep writing (VOICE-OVER) on every slice of dialogue on each page. In addition, dividing the two parts makes it easier to signal images in a montage without interrupting the flow of dialogue on the typewritten page.

It is important to note, however, that networks do not produce commercials, their own or anybody else's. (The exceptions are commercials

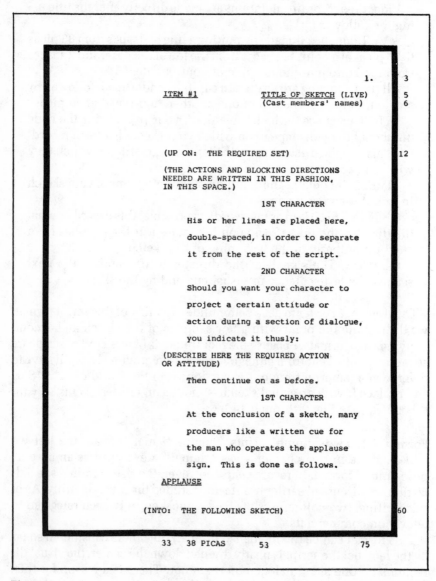

Fig. 9

consisting exclusively of a segment from an upcoming program, plugged by a voice-over giving the date and time of the scheduled broadcast.) Virtually all television commercials are produced by advertising agencies. The format is being included here because it is a simple fact of life that many of today's television writers got their start by writing commercials. (This is *not*, though, a path I recommend to anyone.) Some writers find it a satisfactory means of learning about television production in a "hands-

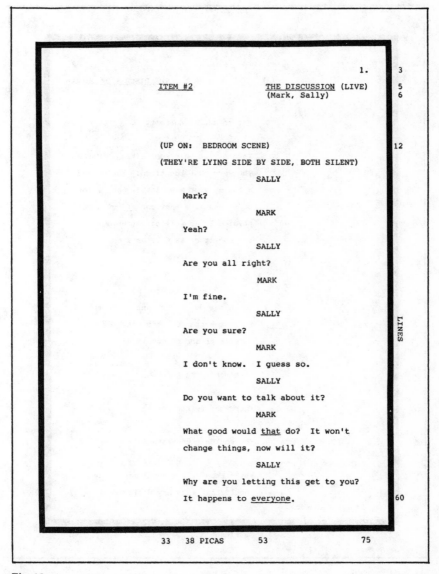

Fig. 10

on" situation, where they can get first-hand experience with tape editing, mixing, camera work and so forth.

So if you're the kind of person interested in writing television commercials, I recommend the following attack:

1. Write anywhere from three to five one-minute spots using the following format. Pick large, well-known sponsors.

2. Go through your telephone book and locate those advertising agen-

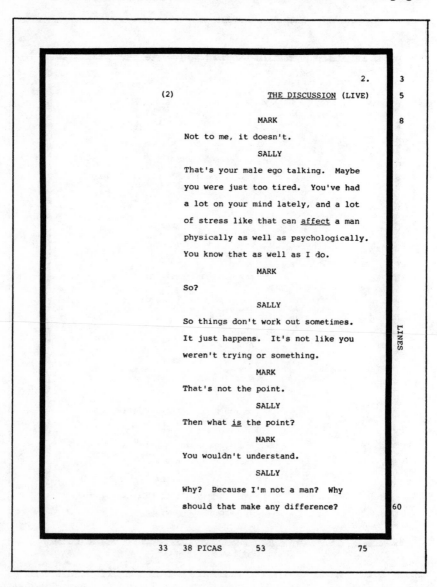

Fig. 11

cies in your community that produce commercials.

3. Write a letter of inquiry to the agency, stating your interest in writing television commercials for them on a freelance basis. Tell them that you'd like to send along a few samples of your work to give them a better idea of your skills.

4. Assuming a positive response to your inquiry, send off your packet of commercials and follow up with a request for an interview after they

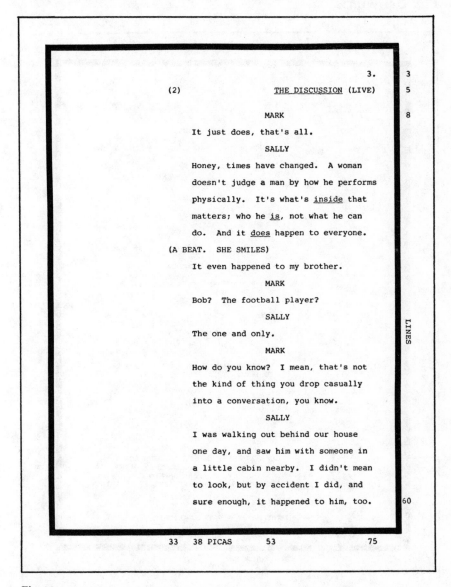

Fig. 12

have finished examining your material. If your scripts are good, there is a strong possibility they will give you one or two assignments on speculation to see how you handle their clients. Should those turn out satisfactorily, the number of assignments will increase with time.

It's usually better to approach a small agency first; because of their less extensive staff, it is more likely that they would be receptive to freelance material than a large agency that is fully staffed with a fair number of full-time copywriters.

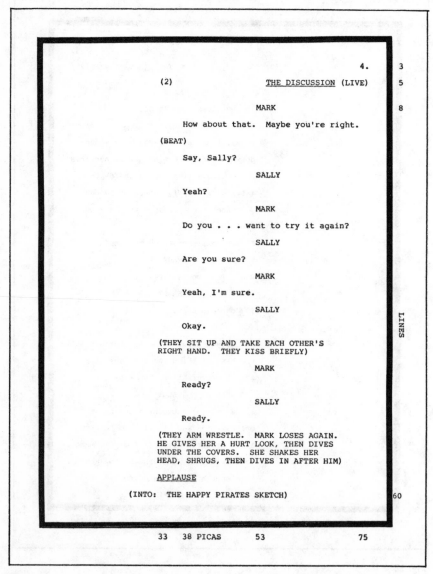

```
                                          4.        3

     (2)                    THE DISCUSSION (LIVE)    5

                          MARK                       8

            How about that.  Maybe you're right.
     (BEAT)
            Say, Sally?

                          SALLY

            Yeah?

                          MARK

            Do you . . . want to try it again?

                          SALLY

            Are you sure?

                          MARK

            Yeah, I'm sure.

                          SALLY                          L
                                                         I
            Okay.                                        N
                                                         E
     (THEY SIT UP AND TAKE EACH OTHER'S                  S
     RIGHT HAND.  THEY KISS BRIEFLY)

                          MARK

            Ready?

                          SALLY

            Ready.

     (THEY ARM WRESTLE.  MARK LOSES AGAIN.
     HE GIVES HER A HURT LOOK, THEN DIVES
     UNDER THE COVERS.  SHE SHAKES HER
     HEAD, SHRUGS, THEN DIVES IN AFTER HIM)

     APPLAUSE

     (INTO:  THE HAPPY PIRATES SKETCH)             60


       33    38 PICAS        53            75
```

Fig. 13

Here, then, are the typographical dimensions for a television commercial script.

The *name and address* of the advertising agency appears at a point 8 spaces from the top of the page, and 8 picas from the left-hand edge of the page. (Note: If you are operating as an independent, your name and address appear in this space.)

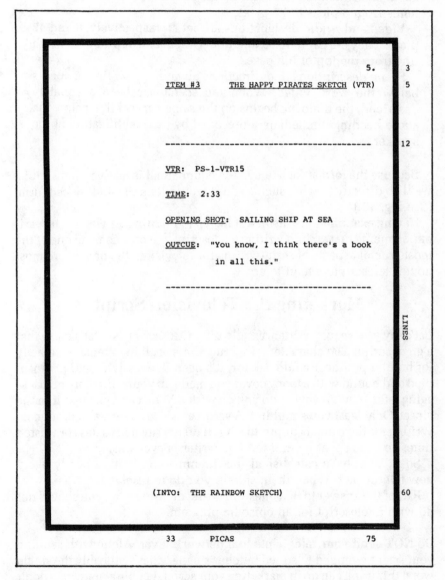

```
                                        5.          3

        ITEM #3        THE HAPPY PIRATES SKETCH (VTR)    5


        -------------------------------------------     12


        VTR:  PS-1-VTR15

        TIME:  2:33

        OPENING SHOT:  SAILING SHIP AT SEA

        OUTCUE:  "You know, I think there's a book
                  in all this."

        -------------------------------------------
```

LINES

```
        (INTO:   THE RAINBOW SKETCH)                     60

              33      PICAS              75
```

Fig. 14

Client information appears at 42 picas, 8 spaces from the top of the page. One line apiece (flush left) goes to the name of the client, the product, the title of the commercial, the length of the spot, and the production number (left blank until a number has been assigned by the advertising agency).

A *line* appears 14 lines from the top, separating the information about the commercial from the actual body of the spot. The line extends from 8 picas to 75 picas.

Video and *Audio* designations are set at, respectively, 8 and 42 picas. They are capitalized and underlined, and appear at the 16th line from the top of the page.

Scene descriptions and directions always appear first, 2 spaces below the word *video*. When the scene has been adequately described, the dialogue begins on the same vertical line below the audio heading, immediately preceded by the identification of the speaker.

Because the format for a television commercial is really rather simple, we'll go directly to what such a script would look like in finished form. (See Fig. 15.)

Having examined the history of television writing, as well as the various elements that go into writing a telescript, we now come to one of the most crucial aspects of scriptwriting for television, the one where most novice telescripters tend to err.

Marketing the Television Script

Let's say you've just written a really nifty little script. No, let's make that a *great* script. The characters ring true, there is all the drama or comedy (or both) a producer could ask for, it's been flawlessly typed, photocopied and bound with a fancy cover you made up yourself. (More on packaging later.) But *now* what do you do with it? You can't just toss it in the closet. Or at least you shouldn't. A script exists to be seen and produced. Writing for the trunk is unproductive. (I do *not* say it is useless or wasted time; no time spent behind the typewriter is *ever* wasted.)

So . . . we have established the dilemma confronting nearly every new telescripter. What, then, should you do to resolve it?

Part of the answer to that question is first defining what you should *not* do with a telescript for an episodic program.

Do NOT send your telescripts to a network. Ever. Along with sending your script wrapped in soiled butcher's paper, that's probably the single worst thing you can do in marketing your script. People at networks don't want to see scripts, don't want to hear about how you spent the last five years putting one together, and would generally prefer that you ceased bothering them and dropped into a convenient chuckhole somewhere. Why, I hear you ask, does this attitude prevail? It's simple.

Networks, you see, do not produce programs in the first place! Networks *underwrite* programming. There's a very important and subtle distinction between the two, and understanding that difference is vital to selling your scripts.

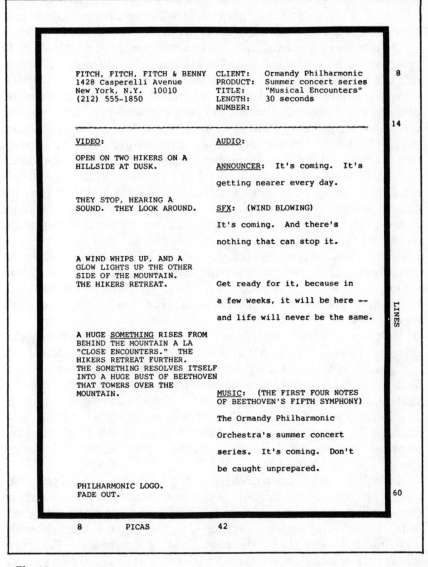

Fig. 15

The process works something like this; An established producer of television programs—someone the networks trust and know to be capable of delivering what he promises—approaches a network with an idea for a television series. Depending upon how reputable the producer is, he may have to present several scripts and a cast with his idea, or just the idea. (Norman Lear is reported to have sold several series with just a one-paragraph synopsis and an improvised scene from the pilot episode.) He also provides a written estimate of what the shows will cost, individually and in groups of six, twelve and eighteen. Should the network find the concept interesting, they have the option of financing the series.

At one time, each network financed a new series for an entire season. In recent years, however, as ratings have become steadily more important, that period of support has decreased severely. The networks now underwrite the production of six episodes, and the scripting of six more. Should the series bomb, the network ceases its underwriting, writes the additional scripts off as a loss, and the series dies. If, on the other hand, the ratings indicate a potential hit, the networks will approve the production of six or twelve more shows, depending upon how late in the season the series debuts, and how confident they are of its eventual success. (It is at this point that we see why the networks commission six full episodes and six scripts to begin with. The okay for additional episodes often comes at the last possible minute, and without scripts on hand, it would be impossible to keep production on schedule.)

Thus is a television series born. As the seasons pass, it will be financed by the networks for as long as it pulls in the ratings . . . which leads to yet *another* interesting situation. It is actually possible for a producer to lose money with a successful series, and make money on a series that's been cancelled.

Don't look at me like that. I *know* how it sounds. It sounds screwy. But it makes a lot of sense. Since the networks only underwrite the actual cost of production, the production company responsible for the series isn't making a profit. Their expenses are being covered, and everyone's getting a salary, but the non-production-related expenses incurred by any organization grow with time, steadily whittling away at the company's finances. (The networks make a profit by charging extraordinary amounts of money for commercial airtime during a given series—an amount which is determined by ratings.)

The only circumstances under which a producer and his company make a profit are in syndication. In the past, reruns on independent stations and network affiliates started only after the series was cancelled. But that has been changing lately; one of the first shows to break the mold was *The Mary Tyler Moore Show*, which (according to one MTM representative) was losing money even though it was a top-rated program. As a consequence, the producers demanded—and received—permission to syndicate the series even though it was still being aired in prime time. The networks initially were unhappy with the idea, afraid (naturally!) that such syndication might hurt the new shows. As it happened, however, the syndication not only didn't *hurt* the evening ratings, in many instances it seemed to *help*. As a consequence, it is now much easier for other series to receive similar permission, with the resultant money going into the development of new series.

In summation, it is to the producer of a series that you must submit your scripts. At this point, we will look at the step-by-step procedure of getting your script into the hands of a television producer. (This is a "do-it-yourself" procedure; we'll examine the role of agents, and how they make nearly everything much simpler, in the appendix entitled *Agents*.)

Selling the Episodic Script

Step one: Locate the producer. There are several ways of going about this, depending upon how much time and money you want to invest, and the kind of information you want.

To start, if you carefully watch the credits as they roll by at the conclusion of the program you want to write for, you will spot the name of the production company. You can find the name of the producer either in the opening or closing credits—occasionally in both. Next, you dial Directory Assistance for the metropolitan area in which the show is produced (usually either New York or Los Angeles), and ask for the phone number and, if the operator will provide it, the address of the production company. Although this frequently results in the mailing information you need, it does not *always* work; a given production company may be only an informal arm of another, larger company, and therefore may not have a separate listing. Besides, this method doesn't supply you with the supplementary information you need to approach a producer.

(Incidentally—the most comprehensive listing of production company phone numbers and mailing addresses for television and film appears in the *Pacific Coast Studio Directory*, 6331 Hollywood Boulevard, Hollywood, California. It's published quarterly, and also features a list of unions, agents, artist's representatives, publicity organizations and television stations. Included in its coverage are such other states as Arizona, Colorado, Hawaii, Canadian British Columbia and Utah, among others. Once again, though, you have to know the name of the company before you can use the directory.)

The two publications that consistently provide the most important information to aspiring television writers are the *Scriptwriters' Marketplace*, published quarterly by the *Hollywood Reporter*, 6715 Sunset Boulevard, Hollywood, California, and the *Writers Guild of America, West, Newsletter*, published by the WGAw, 8955 Beverly Boulevard, Los Angeles, California.

The *Scriptwriters' Marketplace* provides the phone number and address of the production company, indexed by both the name of the show and the name of the company itself; the person in charge of scriptwriting assignments; and tells you whether they are open to outside submissions. It does not, however, tell you what programs are in development, or are staff-written, or have all the scripts they need, and because it is published quarterly, the names of production company representatives may not always be accurate. (Television has an incredibly high turnover.)

The *Writers Guild Newsletter* does supply you with this information, and because it is published monthly, its listings are more extensive and up to date. Unfortunately, while it provides the production companies' phone numbers, addresses aren't given, so you may end up either buying one of the other publications anyway, or calling the company and asking for their mailing address. (Any way you look at it, you're probably going to end up spending some money.) Other advantages of the *Newsletter* are that each edition can be purchased separately and far more cheaply than the *Scriptwriters' Marketplace*, and it also contains nifty articles about the business of writing written exclusively by, and for, television writers.

(Another source of television production company listings is *Daily Variety*, 1400 North Cahuenga Boulevard, Los Angeles, although few of these listings are skewed toward writers.)

Step two: Contact. Once you have the name and address of the person responsible for scriptwriting assignments, you draft a letter of inquiry. In this letter, you should state:

1. Your familiarity with the show and its characters, and the great enthusiasm you have for it.

2. The fact that you have studied the show in detail to get a feeling for what it is trying to accomplish, and the kinds of plots it tends to present.

3. That after studying the program, you have developed several ideas that seem consistent with the program's format, characters, plots and point of view.

4. That you have followed one of these ideas through its process of development, from concept to synopsis to treatment to script.

5. That you would like to submit either the completed telescript or the treatment for his/her examination on a purely speculative basis.

6. That you will be enclosing a standard release form with your script or treatment, unless there is a specific release used by their company, which you would appreciate receiving.

7. List your previous writing credentials and/or the points that

help qualify you to write for the show. (For instance, being a doctor is a big advantage when you submit a script to a television series about a physician.) If your credentials are minimal or nonexistent, it's better to say nothing at all. An interpersonal oddity is that if a producer receives a well-written, thoughtful query letter without a list of credentials, he will often assume that you have more background than you really do. I have yet to figure out why this is so.

8. Close by reaffirming your familiarity with the series, your conviction that the idea you have developed is suitable for the series, and add that you hope to hear from him on this matter in the near future.

If you'll look back at points 3 and 4, you'll notice a certain careful phrasing. You must tell the producer *that* you have developed a certain idea, but not *what* the idea is. There's a reason for this. You should never, *ever* send anything to a producer unannounced or unsolicited. If you send in a script, it will be returned in a larger envelope, unopened (although there will often be a tiny tear in one of the corners of the original envelope, made by a secretary to verify that it contained a script). If you send a one-page synopsis in a regular number ten envelope, it will be returned, opened (since they had no way of knowing what it was), with a curt note asking that you not bother them any more.

Unsolicited manuscripts are the constant nightmare of every producer. It's like this: Let's say that, based upon your market analysis of a series, you have developed an idea and a script that you believe is just perfect for the show, and send it off to the unsuspecting producer. Upon its arrival, let's assume that one of the secretaries accidentally opens the envelope containing your script. Within seconds, she starts repackaging your script and sends it back with a note explaining that they don't accept unsolicited manuscripts. You finally receive the returned script, assume because it was removed from its original envelope that they at least *looked* at it, and accept the rejection quietly.

But now things start to get tricky, because if your market analysis was accurate, there's a substantial chance that the series will eventually feature an episode along the lines of your script. It may even be that they have a similar one already in development. When that episode finally airs, you could very well accuse the producer of plagiarism and take him to court. You could also very possibly win the case, since any plagiarism suit hinges on the question of access, and when the secretary opened the envelope containing your script, the company gained access to your idea. It then becomes incumbent upon them to prove beyond a reasonable doubt that they did not take advantage of this accessibility, which is hard indeed.

A considerate, well-written query letter and a release form are the only protection a producer has against plagiarism suits. (A model standard release form is included in the appendices.) By showing these small concerns, you have a fair to good chance that the producer will agree to look at your manuscript. In fact, I daresay that this tack works in nine out of every ten instances. Remember, producers are always on the lookout for new material and new writers. The only criteria here is that they are writers who seem to know what they're doing, and who follow all the correct procedures.

Step three: Follow-up. Assuming that you do, indeed, receive a positive response from the producer, your next step is to prepare your manuscript for immediate mailing. You should make a photocopy of the script or treatment that is clean and clear, on crisp paper. You should also make up a cover sheet for your manuscript, as well as one sheet for your casting and set requirements. These two pages will look like this: (See Fig. 16 and 17.)

It would also profit you to copy your cover onto heavy (40 lb. or so), colored stock, and provide a backing sheet of the same stock. This keeps the script from bending too much in mailing, and makes for a neater presentation. Don't choose too flashy a color—just primary colors and subtle shades, like dark green, deep blue, rust or gray.

Finally, punch three holes along the left side of your script and bind it with brass paper fasteners. This should look really nifty, and further convince the producer that you know what you're doing.

Then prepare your accompanying letter, confirming your receipt of the producer's go-ahead to submit the script (just in case a secretary might mistake it for an unsolicited manuscript), your enthusiasm for the series, your conviction that the script may prove suitable for the series, and then close on the usual amenities. Slip the letter, a self-addressed, stamped return envelope, and your signed release form into your mailing envelope. Somewhere on the exterior of the mailing envelope should be written, in large, friendly letters, the following: RELEASE FORM ENCLOSED. If you don't, it will just get bounced right back to you again, since these three words are the only clue a secretary has that you've cleared this submission with the producer—a possibility that she will verify by checking the cover letter and asking the producer.

After preparing your manuscript and dropping it into the corner mailbox comes the hardest part of all—waiting and silently wondering *What are they doing with my child?*

Step four: Dealing with the response. Reaction from the producer, which generally takes anywhere from two to four weeks, will come in one of three forms: rejection of the script, acceptance of the script, or rejection of the script but not of you as its writer.

Let's take these one at a time, starting with the worst possible scenario.

Flat-out rejection. The note accompanying your returned script thanks you for giving them the opportunity to examine your manuscript, but it does not meet their current needs, etc. Your immediate reaction to this news is entirely up to you. If it makes you feel better to punch a wall, do it. Jump up and down on the letter, cast aspersions on the producer's sexual proclivities, malign his lineage, make faces, yell at the cat, stick pins

Fig. 16

into a little clay doll labeled *Producer* . . . do whatever you want, for five minutes. Then go back to your typewriter. If you really feel that you can write for the series, then dash off another note to the producer. Confirm your receipt of the script and his letter, thank him for examining the work, and ask if you could submit another script for his examination that incorporates the suggestions or observations mentioned in his letter. (Note: There will almost always be some explanation of why your script

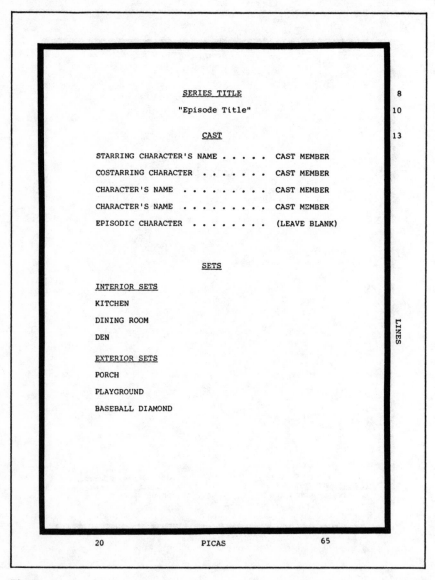

```
                        SERIES TITLE                         8

                       "Episode Title"                      10


                           CAST                             13

        STARRING CHARACTER'S NAME . . . . .   CAST MEMBER

        COSTARRING CHARACTER  . . . . . . .   CAST MEMBER

        CHARACTER'S NAME  . . . . . . . . .   CAST MEMBER

        CHARACTER'S NAME  . . . . . . . . .   CAST MEMBER

        EPISODIC CHARACTER  . . . . . . . .   (LEAVE BLANK)




                           SETS

        INTERIOR SETS

        KITCHEN

        DINING ROOM

        DEN

        EXTERIOR SETS

        PORCH

        PLAYGROUND

        BASEBALL DIAMOND
```

LINES

20   PICAS   65

Fig. 17

was rejected.) Remember, persistence is as necessary to telescripting as talent. Then mail it off. The worst they can do is say *No*, in which case you simply move on to another series. But the odds are about even that, if your script was even fairly written, you'll be given one more opportunity to submit your work. If the producer acknowledges that an additional submission is okay, then write another script and go for it.

Semi-rejection. In many cases, the producer may like the way you handled the characters, but not the plot you developed—or the other way around. In this event, the producer has two options. First, he can tell you why the script was rejected, what you could do to improve your handling of the series, and encourage you to develop another script that incorporates these points. A second option, should the producer be exceptionally impressed with your work, is to farm out an idea that he's been tossing around for a while, and see what you can do with it on a speculative basis. In either event, the producer has left a door open for you, and it is now up to you to go the rest of the way.

Acceptance. Just as there are two levels of rejection, acceptance is not always a cut-and-dried sort of thing. He may be only accepting you, and not the plot. (This is, by the way, exceptionally common.) Should this occur, the producer will either farm out an idea of his own, or ask you to develop another one for him—often asking that you submit a treatment on the idea before you follow it through to script form. The difference between this, and semi-rejection, is that the work will be done on assignment, not speculation. This means that no matter what happens, you will get paid for your work.

The final option a producer can exercise is actually to buy the script you originally submitted. Far from being the end of your obligations, however, this point is only the beginning. A number of things happen to your script, and you, after your first sale.

Right off the top, you will be required to join the Writers Guild of America, East or West, depending upon which side of the Mississippi River you live on. Among other things, all of which are discussed in greater detail in the chapters that follow and are carefully delineated in the appendix concerning the Guild, the WGA establishes certain set minimums for television writing. These fees break down as follows:

	3/1/81 to 6/30/82	7/1/82 to 6/30/83	7/1/83 to 6/30/84	7/1/84 to 6/30/85
TELEPLAY ONLY				
15-Minute Telescript	$3,173	$3,553	$3,944	$4,299
30-Minute Telescript	$5,153	$5,771	$6,406	$6,982
45-Minute Telescript	$5,449	$6,102	$6,774	$7,383
60-Minute Telescript	$6,952	$7,786	$8,642	$9,420

	3/1/81 to 6/30/82	7/1/82 to 6/30/83	7/1/83 to 6/30/84	7/1/84 to 6/30/85
90-Minute Telescript	$9,661	$10,820	$12,101	$13,571
120-Minute Telescript	$12,396	$13,883	$15,410	$17,414

STORY AND TELE-PLAY

15-Minute Telescript	$3,925	$4,396	$4,879	$5,318
30-Minute Telescript	$7,186	$8,048	$8,933	$9,737
45-Minute Telescript	$8,281	$9,274	$10,294	$11,221
60-Minute Telescript	$10,566	$11,833	$13,135	$14,317
90-Minute Telescript	$14,339	$16,059	$17,826	$20,143
120-Minute Telescript	$18,868	$21,132	$23,456	$26,506

To make sure all television purchases are handled properly, the Guild also has provided a basic contract form for use by television producers and telescripters. This contract, which you will receive upon the agreement to puchase your material, will be identical to the one that follows:

STANDARD FREELANCE TELEVISION WRITER'S EMPLOYMENT CONTRACT

Agreement entered into at _____, this _____ day of _____, 19____, between _____, hereinafter called "Company" and _____, hereinafter called "Writer."

WITNESSETH:

1. Company hereby employs the Writer to render services in the writing, composition, preparation and revision of the literary material described in Paragraph 2 hereof, hereinafter for convenience referred to as "work." The Writer accepts such employment and agrees to render his services hereunder and devote his best talents, efforts and abilities in accordance with the instructions, control and directions of the Company.

2. DESCRIPTION OF WORK
    (a) IDENTIFICATION
        Series Title:_____
        Program Title:_____
        Based on:_____
    (b) FORM
        ( ) Story
        ( ) Teleplay
        ( ) Rewrite
        ( ) Sketch
        ( ) Format
        ( ) Non Commercial Openings and Closings
        ( ) Plot Outline—Narrative Synopsis of Story
        ( ) Option for Teleplay

( ) Pilot
( ) Polish
( ) Narration
(c) TYPE OF PROGRAM
( ) Episodic Series   ( ) Unit Series   ( )Single Unit
(d) PROGRAM LENGTH: _____ Minutes
(e) METHODS OF PRODUCTION & DISTRIBUTION
( ) Film   ( ) Syndication
( ) Network   ( ) Live
( ) Videotape

3. (a) The Writer represents that (s)he is a member in good standing of the Writers Guild of America (West or East) Inc., and warrants that he will maintain such membership in good standing during the term of his employment.

(b) The Company warrants it is a party to the Writers Guild of America 1981 Basic Agreement (which agreement is herein designated MBA).

(c) Should any of the terms hereof be less advantageous to the Writer than the minimums provided in said MBA, then the terms of the MBA shall supersede such terms hereof; and in the event this Agreement shall fail to provide benefits for the Writer which are provided by the MBA, then such benefits for the Writer provided by the terms of the MBA are deemed incorporated herein. Without limiting the generality of the foregoing, it is agreed that screen credits for authorship shall be determined pursuant to the provisions of Schedule A and the MBA in accordance with its terms at the time of such determination.

4. DELIVERY

If the Writer has agreed to complete and deliver the work, and/or any changes and revisions, within a certain period or periods of time, then such agreement will be expressed in this paragraph as follows:

5. COMPENSATION

As full compensation for all services to be rendered hereunder, the rights granted to the Company with respect to the Work, and the undertakings and agreements assumed by the Writer, and upon condition that the Writer shall fully perform such undertakings and agreements, Company will pay the Writer the following amounts:

(a) Compensation for services $_____
(b) Advance for television reruns $_____
(c) Advance for theatrical use $_____

6. RIGHT TO OFFSET:

With respect to Writer's warranties and indemnification agreement, the Company and the Writer agree that upon the presentation of any claim or the institution of any action involving a breach of warranty, the party receiving notice thereof will promptly notify the other party in regard thereto. Company agrees that the pendency of any such claim or action shall not relieve the Company of its obligation to pay the Writer any monies until it has sustained a loss or suffered an adverse judgment or decree by reason of such claim or action.

IN WITNESS WHEREOF, the parties hereto have duly executed this agreement on the day and year first above written.

_____   _____
        (Writer)   (Company)

With this contract, and the initial payment, you will be required to pay your WGA dues. That you can make the sale at all as a non-Guild member—since producers can *only* purchase scripts from Guild members—is through the intervention of the Taft-Hartley Act, which stipulates that any nonunion worker can perform a union activity, at full payment, once—after that he must join the union having jurisdiction in that area.

Next comes your first meeting with the producer, assuming you live close enough to the production company for this to be practical. (And even if you don't, you may want to consider investing in some travel, if only because personal contact, a definite plus, is the main reason most telescripters live near the areas of production.)

Several things will be happening during this meeting. The producer will be attempting to estimate how easy you are to work with (and therefore if you should be on the set during production), how well you respond to criticism, how succinctly you can discuss your idea and—most importantly—what concepts you have for future episodes of the series. Because most producers do not as a general rule like to work with one-time-only writers—preferring instead to develop a long-term creative relationship—you can be certain that the producer will ask you what additional ideas you have. Instead of writing them out, however, you will be asked to verbalize them—a practice known as *pitching an idea*. Most television scriptwriters, after breaking the ice with a producer, receive the assignment to develop a script after pitching it to the producer in his office. This is one reason we placed so much emphasis on developing a solid synopsis earlier in this chapter. A well-crafted synopsis should contain all the elements of plot, characterization, and action required to pitch an idea successfully.

In order to protect their ideas, many writers make it a practice to sketch out a few typewritten lines about each plot idea on a single sheet of paper. Then, after the ideas are pitched, the sheet is handed to the producer, who initials it. This proves that he heard your ideas and serves as a legal record should there be any question of plagiarism. Without this record, since the ideas were expressed verbally, the courts would have only your word against his.

One brief word about plagiarism: It happens. Not as often as some would have you believe, but it happens. Often it's unintentional—a producer will generate what he thinks is an idea of his own to a staff writer, forgetting it was pitched to him several months ago. It is wiser to go in prepared to protect your ideas in a thoughtful and careful way than to fight it out in court later—an act that will not help convince other producers to examine your work.

Following the sale of your script (all rights to which have been purchased as a work-for-hire) and your meeting with the producer, comes the process known as *story conferencing*.

Here is the recipe for a story conference: Begin with a harried producer, a nervous writer, a story editor (whose task it is to keep the series' continuity going from episode to episode), several staff writers (who have their own ideas about your script, and how it might be improved), one or two associate producers, and occasional hangers-on. Stuff them all into the same smoke-filled room, add several pots of coffee and some Chinese food from around the corner. Start the cooking process by debating the propriety of each line of the script, baste liberally with some nicely developed egos, and lock the door. The goal and the eternal hope of story conferencing is that the resultant explosion will produce a solid production script.

Story conferencing is one of the hardest things for a new telescripter to handle. It's the first definite indication you have that your words are not sacrosanct. There's a terrible feeling that arises from the pit of your stomach when the producer or the story editor says, "I think act two, scene three is a little too slow—let's just drop it," and there's sufficient agreement for the scene to be dropped. It doesn't particularly matter if you spent nearly three weeks on act two, scene three, or that it's your favorite scene of the whole script.

Whenever you find yourself in this position, try to follow this rule of thumb: Only fight for something if you feel it is vital to your story. Don't fight every single line change simply because you want it to stay as you originally wrote it, but don't crumble either. Let your creative integrity be your guide.

The creation of a production script is not, however, the last time your script can be revised. The next step is a group reading by the series' full cast, at which point a performer is free to suggest a line change if he or she feels the character wouldn't deliver the line in quite the same manner indicated in the script. Further changes can be made right up until the moment of actual production.

After production is completed, the only changes that can be made take place in the editing room. Should the producer discover, for instance, that the length of a scene was misjudged, thereby causing the episode to run overtime, something will have to be cut. If the show can be put back on track simply by editing out a few seconds of panning or tracking shots—points where no dialogue is being spoken and no action necessary to the plot is taking place—the cuts will normally be made there. But if several minutes must be edited out, some superfluous lines will have to be eliminated. (I've always found it amusing that a producer can go into a taping confident there isn't a single line of unnecessary dialogue in the script, only to discover—when he's in the editing room with an overtimed show and his neck is on the line—that there are suddenly entire blocks of dialogue that can be deleted without hurting the episode.)

Following the production of your first honest-to-god, no-kidding television script come the two best things about being a television writer: First, starting work on your next script; and second, throwing a big party the day your program is aired.

Be sure to invite all those people who said you'd never make it as a writer. Have a good time—you've earned it.

After you've been scriptwriting professionally for a while, you'll discover that you've developed a track record—a reputation. Producers come to know what they can expect from you in terms of style, plot, and your ability to adhere to deadlines. When this happens, you'll find that producers start coming to you with their ideas. Remember, producing is a costly and erratic business, and reliability is nearly as important as creativity. Producers feel most comfortable when they're dealing with a known quantity. That's why some writers make it a point to develop specific reputations. Some are good rewriters (*body and fender men*, to use a common, though sexist term); some are good at plotting, while others find their forte is scripting dialogue (with the two often working together, which is why you so often see two names on a scriptwriting credit); others specialize by genre.

My own track record highlights two aspects of my work. First, I can switch from one medium to another quickly and—from a production viewpoint—effectively. Second, I am fast. Whether or not my work possesses any rudimentary quality is something I will leave to those better able to judge than I. But I am nothing if not fast.

Which leads me to an anecdote that I think may illustrate some of the insane things that happen to television scriptwriters. A few years ago, I was approached by a producer who was putting together a pilot situation comedy. He had already commissioned a script from another writer, but the finished product was—to address the matter as charitably as possible—deficient. So he contacted me, having seen some of my work in other areas, and arranged a meeting. We met at 6:30 p.m. on a Saturday evening at a restaurant. (You'd be surprised how much business takes place over a club sandwich and coffee.) He outlined the concept of the series, explained the characters, and gave me an idea of the program's point of view. He then told me that he needed an entirely new script, replete with a new plot, characterizations to be shaded differently, a couple of new supporting sub-plots, a certain kind of banter between the characters—the whole thing. After about an hour of discussion and negotiation, at which point I felt I had a fair grasp of what he wanted, I finally agreed to take the assignment. "When do you have to have the script?" I asked, already sensing that he had probably waited until the last minute to dump the previous script and contact me—hoping that he wouldn't have to eat the money he had paid for the original script.

I wasn't prepared for his answer, however. "We go into rehearsal tomorrow morning at ten."

I remember having stared at him for what seemed like five minutes before I finally managed to say, "You'll have it." (I think my response surprised him as much as it did me.)

To make an already long story short, I arrived home by 8:00 p.m., put on a huge pot of coffee, turned on the stereo, warmed up my trusty Smith Corona, and went to work. I had finished the script, and even had time to go back and fine-tune a few pages here and there, by a little after nine o'clock the next morning, just ten minutes before he picked it up.

Surprisingly, this was one of my few scripts to undergo only a handful of changes between the time it left my typewriter and the day it went in front of a camera.

I have made it a point, however, never to agree to do another overnighter (unless, of course, I am paid one hell of a bonus), even though word of that assignment prompted a film producer to put me under contract a few months later for my first motion picture screenplay.

But that's another story, and another chapter.

A word about series pilots and television movies. Whenever I teach scriptwriting, either at the university level or at workshops, I constantly hear comments like this: "I've got a really great idea for a new television series—how do I sell somebody the idea?"

Although, as we discussed at the beginning of this chapter, the networks are not interested in the direct acquisition of literary materials or ideas from freelance writers, whenever we start discussing pilot television series we are dealing with a different bird altogether. Networks can only charge advertisers in accordance with the program ratings—and these programs can *only* pull in the ratings by providing content that is timely and in tune with society as a whole. Network programming must change as the surrounding culture changes or face the video equivalent of extinction.

As a consequence, each network has created a division whose sole task is to develop new concepts for original programming. They are headed by vice presidents in charge of dramatic programming, or vice presidents for comedy development, and so on—each balanced on the edge of a knife. If they give the go-ahead to a series that turns out to be a genuine stinker, they very probably face termination. But the reverse also holds true. As one agent told me concerning a prominent writer/producer, "If he goes to a network with an idea, having had so many successes in the past, they're usually afraid *not* to give him the go-ahead, because if he then takes it to another network, and it succeeds, the person at the network who canned his idea will usually be either demoted or fired."

The development of original pilot series can be a highly paranoid affair for a network. So it was in an effort to minimize ulcers that two primary means of developing new programming concepts came about.

First, the heads of development at each network make it a point to watch what the *other* two are doing, and keep an eye on the box office receipts of newly released motion pictures. If they spot an idea that works, they'll contact a producer with an idea for a spinoff. (Thus did *Saturday Night Live* give birth to *Fridays* on another network. This same phenomenon led to a rash of television series about fraternity life after the success of National Lampoon's feature film debut, *Animal House*.)

Second, many of the larger producers have their *own* divisions for program development. They work with the staff writers they already employ, and regularly turn out batches of programming concepts. They then bring these concepts to the networks, and hope for a go-ahead to proceed with script development.

Actually, most new series are sold in treatment form, rather than with a finished script. Networks are sometimes even *leery* of scripts, because if it's gotten that far in the first place it was—in their estimation—probably commissioned, then turned down by another network.

Do your family, friends, and loved ones a favor—don't *ever* become a network programming executive. You could go *nuts* from such a business.

Perry Lafferty, the man who gave us such programs as *Rawhide*, *The Twilight Zone*, *All in the Family*, *Maude*, and *The Mary Tyler Moore Show* as a prime time programming executive at CBS, succinctly described the plight of the networks—and the television writer—as it relates to original programs: "Each network gets in the vicinity of three thousand bona fide submissions a year. Most of them are quickly discarded because they're bad. It usually comes down to ordering up about one hundred scripts out of those three thousand ideas, and out of those hundred scripts, you make about twenty-five pilots, and out of those twenty-five pilots, you may get about four on the air. And out of the four, maybe one will last and continue into a second season. These are the worst odds I've ever heard, but everybody in town is trying to sell the networks programs."

As a footnote to the preceding, the remaining twenty-one pilots are almost always aired sooner or later, though not necessarily in prime time. The networks can't afford *not* to try to recoup their losses somehow— usually by broadcasting the programs late at night, when they hope no one important is watching, with just enough charged to the advertisers to balance out the cost of production.

So if you're a freelance writer trying to sell an idea for a new series, your chances are pretty slim if you're going it alone. Having an agent helps, or a producer who's willing to back you up (and who the networks know can come in and bail them out if your show runs into trouble), but it's still a rough road. There have been instances of writers managing to badger their way into a programming executive's office and finally sell him on an idea, but this is the exception rather than the rule.

Which is not to say that there aren't other, sneakier ways of getting your ideas into the hands of network executives. The solution rests in one of the two purposes of the television movie.

Movies made exclusively for television have recently grown in prominence and quantity, because (as mentioned earlier) it now costs almost as much to rent a theatrical film for a first-run television showing as it does to actually produce an entire television movie. In addition, the audience for first-run motion picture showings on television has decreased, largely because of the pay cable industry. Why should a viewer watch a sanitized version of a popular motion picture on commercial television when he can—and probably may—watch an unedited version of the movie on pay cable, without commercial interruption?

That, friends, is why you can see a nifty motion picture in a theater one week, and then, several weeks later, find a movie-for-television that deals with a similar topic, the point of view slanted enough to make it different. The philosophy here is that the appetite of a massive potential audience has been whetted by the film, thereby almost guaranteeing a hefty rating for a television movie along similar lines.

Television movies are, therefore, usually extremely topical, often dealing with the latest news headlines before the newsprint has had the chance to dry. Whenever a spectacular court case takes place, network executives and producers are generally on hand, trying to purchase the principal's rights to the story, racing to be the first network to air a TV movie based on the case.

However, there are other kinds of television movies—movies that are simply good drama. The television movie has the potential—should it be well-received—of being turned into a regular prime time series. This is known in the business as "getting a back-door series."

This means exactly what it sounds like—you've circumvented the usual development route and have created a potential pilot television series.

Writing a television movie—particularly one you wish to later adapt into a series—requires three steps. First, write a full treatment for the two-hour movie. Second, based upon this treatment, write the script, using the film format examined in this chapter. (Also, see the chapter on motion pictures.) Third, write another treatment, briefer than the first, that examines how the movie could be translated into a weekly series. This treatment should provide extensive information about the characters, how they relate over time, what makes the show different from others currently on the air (or what makes it similar to a successful series on another network), and what kinds of stories could be presented in such a series. Whatever your idea might be, it must always have the potential for new plots to develop spontaneously. If no new characters can be added without forcing the issue, the series will stagnate and run out of ideas.

In order to sell such a program, it is almost mandatory to have some kind of representation, usually an agent. But if you've got a dynamite television movie script on your hands, you probably won't have much trouble getting an agent to represent it, and you. Also, if the concept is that good, the odds are fair you'll at least get the networks to look at it.

After that, it's entirely up to your craft as a scriptwriter.

A Look at the Future

One nice thing about this book is the fact that my contract with Writer's Digest Books requires that future editions be revised periodically to keep up with any changes in the areas it covers. This comes in particularly handy in this chapter, because in the decade following the publication of this book, television will undergo a remarkable evolution.

We will take a brief look at a few of these coming changes, and what they will mean to the telescripting business.

For nearly all of television's history, the three networks had a singular and seemingly unbreakable grip on programming. Viewers had to take whatever was offered because, with the exception of syndicated reruns and movies on independent local stations, there simply wasn't much else to look at. Then came cable television, pay cable, videocassette recorders, videodiscs and direct broadcast satellite operations—and the impact made by these breakthroughs in technology already is significant. Network and independent studies have shown that in the brief two-year span between November 1978 and November 1980, competing program sources such as these eroded the networks' share of the total national viewing audience from 93.3 percent to 88.5 percent.

While this may be less than reassuring news for the networks, the rise of competing program sources signals a boom of immense proportions for television writers. We'll examine how each of these programmers/producers provides an outlet for telescripters.

Basic cable. The cable industry started simply as a means of routing television signals to locations too distant or obscured by natural obstacles to receive signals clearly. But because the cable companies were capable of carrying an immense number of signals, new local stations cropped up—independent programmers who couldn't afford to open a broadcast station, but could handle the less exorbitant costs of cablecasting. This has led to a vast increase in locally and minority-oriented programs. Where none existed before, there are Spanish- and Japanese-language television stations, religious stations, public service and information stations—all requiring written material. Stations such as these have proven an excellent educational tool for local television writers without the experience to approach the networks. It is expected that independent cablecasting will continue to grow at a rapid rate, providing an ever-increasing stream of opportunities for fledgling telescripters.

Along with the independent cablecasters, whole cable networks have appeared, starting with Ted Turner's Cable News Networks (CNN and CNN2) and the Entertainment and Sports Programming Network (ESPN), each carried without additional charge by the subscribing cable company, and each supplemented by advertising revenues. Even CBS Television, sensing the changing tides, eventually unveiled a "cultural network" carrying symphony, ballet, and other classical offerings, as well as stage plays.

Each of these cable networks has provided surges of work for telescripters, and as the networks' capability to produce original dramatic programming increases with their revenues—which are growing at a phenomenal rate—these opportunities will expand even further.

Pay cable. Along with the rise of basic cable, for which viewers pay a monthly service fee, soon came the idea of pay cable, which also was warmly received. For an additional monthly fee, or in some cases a per-program fee, the viewer is given a wide selection of movies and variety specials piped in along the same cable. (A decoder box is also required to unscramble the signal,thereby avoiding piracy.) By 1981, there were already three major pay cable programmers: Home Box Office (HBO), owned by Time, Inc.; Showtime, owned by Teleprompter and Viacom; and The Movie Channel, owned by Warner Communications and American Express. By that same year, each of these programmers was earning, respectively, $432 million, $96 million, and $48 million in yearly revenues. With more on the way, it is estimated that the total revenues for pay cable in 1985 will be $5.8 billion.

At first, it seemed as if the only impact this new service would have on scriptwriters would be a modest increase in revenues earned through residuals on produced motion pictures. But that has not turned out to be the case. The pay cable programmers discovered that their systems had a high rate of disconnects. Although the movies shown on their systems were cablecast before the networks were able to do so, it seemed that customers just weren't content to wait through three days of rerunning features to see something new. It soon became abundantly clear that they would need to expand to include original programming.

As a consequence, the pay cable industries have implemented the steps necessary to begin producing their own soap operas, serials, weekly series, mini-series, documentary specials, and biographical specials keyed to recent news events. When you consider those production outlets in the light of the rapidly growing number of pay cable programmers, the result is overwhelming. Where there were once only three primary avenues of television production, there will soon be dozens, each calling on the skills of producers and writers across the nation.

Amusingly enough, many of the pay cable programming executives are already saying it will be virtually impossible to avoid reruns to one degree or another because, in their estimation, there simply aren't enough writers in the entire nation to keep up with the demand that pay cable and the other programming sources will be making.

Subscription television. Similar in most of its essential elements to pay cable, subscription television (STV) differs in that its programs are broadcast over the air instead of through a land-based cable. (A decoder box is still required to unscramble the signal.) STV is already being heralded as the logical, legitimate successor to pay cable, primarily because there is less cost and risk to the programmer. In 1981 it cost over $100,000 to string cables in a large city, an expense not incurred by STV. But the reception quality is not as high as that of pay cable, so it may be premature to nominate STV as heir apparent. Conservative estimates place the 1985 revenues for STV services around the nation at $1.2 billion, supplied by about 5 million viewers, all of whom will be demanding the original programming pay cable has been required to provide.

Direct broadcast satellites. Six full channels of full-time programming— the equivalent of six networks—will begin national broadcasting through Comsat, a federally chartered corporation charged with operating the United States satellite communications network. Each channel will be devoted exclusively to news, sports, drama, entertainment, and other programming. Comsat will supply individual viewers with the three- or five-foot earth stations needed to pick up each of the channels.

Videocassettes and videodiscs. By 1981, the combined video software business was earning $3.6 billion annually, and growing fast. Videocassette recorders (VCRs) were the first to hit the market, and their impact was felt immediately. VCRs wreaked hell with the ratings system, because even though the television might be turned to one station, the VCR could very well be tuned to another network altogether, recording the program for later viewing.

It is interesting to note that the networks are themselves largely responsible for the increasing popularity of VCRs. It all started with the counterprogramming technique. If, for instance, ABC runs a blockbuster program at 9:00 p.m., CBS and NBC counter by running equally monumental programs at the same time. As a result, *everyone* loses. The viewers have to choose between three equally attractive options, and the networks only receive half or a third the possible ratings they might have secured if they ran their programs without such stiff competition. VCRs negate that dilemma.

But whatever the initial reason behind the rise of VCRs, the fact remains that the role of VCRs has expanded beyond merely recording counter-programmed television broadcasts. Movies are recorded and marketed shortly after being released in theaters, giving the consumer the opportunity to transform his home into a movie house.

Feature films on videocassette have two inherent problems, however. First, for our purposes, they provide little new material or opportunity for telescripters (although there are signs that, as in pay cable, this will change). Second, these prerecorded videocassettes cost quite a bit.

It was in order to provide a nice middle ground that videodiscs were developed. The conssiderably cheaper price of videodiscs—usually one-third or one-fourth that of a prerecorded videocassette—not only makes owning a feature film less intimidating, but also makes the possibility of original programming on videodisc a more realistic proposition. It is estimated by many that videodiscs will prove to be a watershed for independent producers and scriptwriters, who will need only to produce a finished videotape, then sell it to a videodisc distributor for a one-time purchase price plus residuals from each individual sale. In this sense, the videodisc market will soon resemble the book publishing or music industry, thereby lifting the restraints imposed whenever one completes a script as a work for hire that must meet a network's editorial standards, and instead increasing the emphasis on individual creativity.

Networks. Despite predictions from these new programmers—whose total combined revenue will, it is estimated, top $100 billion by 1991—the networks are not dead yet. (Neither should any signs of illness be anticipated.) Their lock on television programming will be loosened, yes; but networks have a way of springing back when knocked down by adversity. By 1985 they will still be earning a healthy $9.8 billion per year, and putting that money back into production.

Certain changes are, however, inevitable. The networks are already trying to merge with the coming cable technology, and are looking at new avenues for their work. In recent years, the number of television features released theatrically on the overseas market have dramatically increased; it is reasonable to assume that the line between television production and the creation of a motion picture for theatrical release will grow steadily less clear.

Every sign indicates that the networks will also continue their production of weekly drama and comedy programs. They've been doing it for a lot of years, and it's doubtful they will be overshadowed professionally for many more.

Conclusion. Although no one can accurately predict what these new opportunities will mean for writers, and how the new technologies will affect these opportunities, one thing is certain: They *are* coming. They are, in fact, already here.

It is also certain that as the entertainment options open to televiewers increase, their degree of selectivity will also grow. There is every probability that the coming years will see a preponderance of specialty stations and programmers—outlets that, like specialty magazines (which killed off the general-interest magazines), will cater to precisely defined viewing tastes. There will be channels devoted exclusively to cultural programming, sports, drama, concerts (particularly feasible with the better sound systems some television sets are now equipped with), community activities, and so forth.

With increasing viewer discretion, it is highly doubtful that audiences will settle for the same old diet of questionable- and low-quality programs. Television used to be like the weather—everyone liked to complain about it, but nobody did anything about it. Now something *is* being done, and consumers have a choice. It is up to television scriptwriters to create material of sufficient quality to survive in the day of the hundred-channel television set.

Whether this can be done or not remains to be seen.

But we're sure going to try.

It is not enough to pay attention to words only when you face the task of writing—that is like playing the violin only on the night of the concert. You must attend the words when you read, when you speak, when others speak. Words must become ever present in your waking life, an incessant concern, like color and design if the graphic arts matter to you, or pitch and rhythm if it is music, or speed and form if it is athletics. Words, in short, must be *there*, not unseen and unheard, as they probably are and have been up to now. It is proper for the ordinary reader to absorb the meaning of a story or description as if the words were a transparent sheet of glass. But he can do so only because the writer has taken pains to choose and adjust them with care. They were not glass to him, but mere lumps of potential meaning. He had to weigh them and fuse them before his purposed meaning could shine through.

—Jacques Barzun

2.
CRADIO

As of January, 1981, four-year programs in broadcasting were being offered at more than 228 colleges and universities throughout the United States. Nearly 80 percent of these also offered higher degrees in broadcasting, and more than sixty junior colleges nationwide offered two-year programs in broadcasting studies. Over a quarter of a *million* students graduate annually from broadcast-related programs in these schools.

From a distance, those figures are impressive. To the aspiring scriptwriter, they may be more than a little intimidating. But that need not be the case—particularly when it comes to scriptwriting for radio.

In nearly *every instance*, colleges offering programs in broadcasting are heavily oriented toward telecommunications and film. The reason behind this is easily apparent. Television is, as we mentioned in the first chapter, a significant force in American culture. Today's crop of students have grown up with television. They find it glamorous, exciting, dynamic—and want to become a part of it. It is precisely this demand that has led to the proliferation of broadcasting programs. As Jimmy Durante used to remark, "Everybody wants ta get inta the act!" This is particularly true of broadcasting students. They want to get into the act as performers, directors, technicians, stage managers, camerapersons . . . and writers. At times, it's almost funny. People who can't write a solid short story and wouldn't want to *try* a novel, who would never think of aspiring to be brain surgeons or computer programmers feel that they can sit down and, with precious little effort, turn out a television script. And why not? After all, they are children of television. All they have to do is regurgitate what they've been visually ingesting all their lives. (Which explains a lot about why modern television is the way it is.)

None of this is meant to detract from the importance of college-level broadcasting programs. They play a vital educational role, because if we do not bend our energies toward preparing each generation to deal with the ever-increasing power of the communications media, particularly television, then we will have lost a battle essential to our survival in a media-oriented world. Neither should these students be dismissed as a class (no pun intended), since many of our finest contemporary filmmakers have come out of broadcasting schools.

So . . . here we are with hundreds of educational institutions turning out students skilled in television and film, nearly all of whom have had some training in scriptwriting for these two media.

But what about radio? What about the medium that started it all? Don't any of these institutions prepare students for a career in radio? The answer to that is a resounding *yes*. But there is a subtle difference in the kinds of programs being offered, and understanding that difference is critical, because it leaves an easy opening for prospective scriptwriters.

With a very few exceptions—usually in the form of extension courses—most of these institutions offer little in the way of scriptwriting for radio. The programs that *do* exist are directed largely toward on-air activities—announcing, news reporting, and disc-jockey training—and are frequently spread out among different departments. News reporting and writing is usually taught by the journalism department, announcing is taught in cooperation with the dramatic arts department, and many colleges offer hands-on experience in tape editing and audio production through a low-power campus radio station. In some instances, radio copywriting is also taught through the journalism department.

What is the upshot of all this? It means that in a decade when radio—specifically radiodrama—is coming back stronger than ever before (as we will soon see), providing enormous opportunity for people who know how to write radio scripts, our educational institutions have not responded quickly enough to take up the slack. Although the demand for radio scripts is not as extensive as the need for television scripts, it is substantially easier for a scriptwriter with little or no experience to sell his scripts because there simply aren't enough writers around who would even *recognize* a radiodrama script.

In this chapter, therefore, we will take a look at writing for radio, concentrating primarily upon radiodrama scripting as well as on the ways to sell, syndicate, and even produce your scripts.

An Audio Retrospective

To better get a feeling of your potential future in radio scriptwriting, however, let's look at the historical development of radio, and the forces that have led to a renaissance of radio scriptwriting.

Radio has its earliest roots in the work of Scottish physicist James Clark Maxwell, who in 1864 theorized the existence of certain frequency waves, whose modulation could be controlled and varied for communication purposes. Although many of the leading scientists of his day patently dismissed his work as too far-fetched to merit serious consideration, some dedicated themselves to vindicating Maxwell's theory. In 1864, Guglielmo Marconi succeeded in transmitting the first radio signals capable of being received at a separate location without the use of an interceding wire or cable.

The first practical application of Marconi's discovery was in ship-to-ship communication, thereby solving a predicament that had previously baffled the navies of the world. It was, in fact, the United States Navy that first coined the word *radio* in May of 1912 as a replacement for the overused *wireless*, and later coined the term *broadcast*.

After having proven itself as a device with practical applications, radio was quick to find a home on land as well as at sea. Although no precise date is available, it's generally conceded that KDKA, operating on an experimental basis out of Pittsburgh, was the first American-based radio station. Not long afterward, the first license to operate a regular radio broadcasting station was awarded to WBZ in Springfield, Massachusetts, on September 15, 1921.

The Popularity of Radio

During the following thirty years, radio underwent a staggering growth cycle. The prospect of instananeous communication took America by storm, and by 1924 there were nearly 1,500 independent radio stations nationwide. These stations were almost entirely community-oriented, with occasional experiments in joint broadcasting (usually sporting events and presidential speeches).

On November 15, 1926, experimentation in networking took a giant leap into reality with the formation of the National Broadcasting Company (NBC), led by David Sarnoff. By 1928, NBC had acquired so many affiliates that it decided to divide its member stations into two divisions, called the Red and Blue Networks. In 1927 The Columbia Broadcasting system (CBS) opened its doors as a radio network.

The 1930s and '40s have come to be known as the Golden Age of Radio. Around the nation, as families had once crowded about the hearth, they now huddled around the box, listening to the adventures of the Shadow, the antics of Benny and Costello and Fields, and the weekly suspense series, *I Love A Mystery* and *Inner Sanctum*. These exciting days of radio are probably best described in the following excerpt from *Network at 50*, written by Norman Corwin, a man who shares with such giants as Arch Oboler and Orson Welles the distinction of being one of the greatest dramatists of radio's Golden Age.

Years of the electric ear!
The heavens crackling with report: far-flung, nearby, idle, consequential,
The worst of bad news and the best of good,
Seizures and frenzies of opinion
The massive respiration of government and commerce,
Sofa-sitters taken by kilocycle to the ball park, the concert hall, the scene of the crime;
Dramas that let us dress the sets ourselves;
Preachments and prizefights
The time at the tone, the weather will be, and now for a word,
The coming of wars and freeways,
Outcroppings of fragmented peace,
Singing commercials, and the Messiah.*

Just as in television, whose spectre was already looming ominously on the media horizon, there was always a certain adrenaline-filled frenzy to live radio. You could never be entirely sure that the program was going to go smoothly, as planned. In fact, about the only thing you *could* be sure of was that somehow, somewhere, *something* would go wrong. This probability was heightened by the fact that network programs were done live twice a day—once for the East Coast, and then again, three hours later, for the West Coast. It was also not uncommon for some of a show's cast and crew to go out for a few drinks between broadcasts, a situation that much increased the producer's anxiety.

There were also technical difficulties that had not yet been ironed out. Harry Saz, a renowned sound effects specialist of the period, once told me a story that illustrates the situation. "We were doing T-Men in Action, which always wound up with a lot of shooting—a problem since we were in a very small studio. In those days, mind you, the radio transmitting tubes were very sensitive. They didn't have automatic limiters on them to crunch the sound like they do now. So on one show, I was off with my gun as far off in a corner as I could get. But what I didn't know, and what the engineer didn't know, was that in that corner was a live microphone. So the cue came for the gunshots, and I fired. Over in the control booth, I could see the engineer gesturing because the needle registering the sound went way over. But we kept on going. You couldn't stop on a live show. I must have fired a dozen shots. Afterward, I could see the engineer on the phone. Then he came out and said, 'You know, you just knocked one of our affiliates off the air eight times in the last fifteen minutes.' "

When television made its inevitable appearance, many predicted it would mean the end of radio. As it happened, television did indeed man-

---

*From *Network at 50*, by Norman Corwin, broadcast on April 1, 1978. Used by permission of Norman Corwin.

age to steal away many of radio's greatest stars (Bob Hope, Jack Benny, George Burns and Gracie Allen, Amos 'n' Andy, Red Skelton, Ozzie and Harriet, and Kay Kaiser, to name but a few. Fred Allen was one of the few wholly unable to make the transition to television, which he called a medium "because it is neither rare nor well done."), and not a few people at the radio networks began wearing buttons that read "Help Stamp Out TV." But it was too late. As audiences turned more regularly to television for entertainment, the number of dramatic presentations on radio decreased. By the 1960s and early 1970s, radio had returned to its original community-oriented status. There were all-news stations, all-rock stations and all-country or classical stations, but drama was difficult, if not impossible, to find.

While radio networks continue to exist—CBS, NBC, the Mutual Radio Network and the like—their relationship to their member stations has changed considerably. The stations are largely independent of network control (except network-owned-and-operated stations); the role of the parent network has largely become that of providing hourly news reports. It is now also possible for a single station to be affiliated with more than one network. (During my tenure as theater and film critic for KSDO Newsradio, San Diego, the station was owned by the Gannett Corporation, and affiliated with the Mutual Radio Network and the CBS Radio Network.)

One very important change during this time has to do with what are known as "programming cycles." In the early years of radio, stations operated in half-hour and one-hour cycles (or blocks, as they were sometimes called). Modern television works in this fashion, programming shows in increments of thirty minutes. But bereft of their dramatic programs, the programming cycles of radio stations decreased in length and now run anywhere from eight to twenty minutes, depending on the station's format. (A good way of understanding the cycle concept is to listen to an all-news station, which repeats key stories at regular intervals.)

In the middle and late seventies, however, something peculiar started happening: Audiences began showing a revived interest in old radiodrama. A few new programs found large audiences suddenly. Some attribute this development to the fact that television's novelty had finally worn off, that audiences were tired of seeing the same ideas recycled season after season and wanted something more—something they could participate in on a creative level, which is impossible in television since everything is *right there* in front of you, and the imagination begins to stultify.

Unfortunately, radio stations around the nation resisted the idea of resurrecting radiodrama, primarily because it meant disrupting their established formats and programming cycles. (It should be noted here that this attitude was held almost exclusively by commercial radio stations. Noncommercial or public radio stations, which generally programmed in longer blocks of time, were far more receptive to a renewal of radiodrama. National Public Radio has, in fact, had a longstanding commitment to the preservation of radiodrama.)

Some stations responded to this new demand by rerunning Golden Age broadcasts with proven audience response, while others decided to take a chance on new programs. In either event, however, the stations almost invariably ran the programs late at night, when their formats would be least disrupted.

By the late seventies and early eighties, radiodrama went into what many have described as the beginning of a Silver Age. Radiodrama productions were being undertaken on both a national and local basis. These national programs included *CBS Mystery Theater, Earplay, NBCs National Radio Theater, Masterpiece Radio Theater* and *Enchantment Radio Theater.* Locally oriented excursions into radiodrama led to the creation of the *National Radio Theater of Chicago,* KPFK-Los Angeles' series *Los Angeles Theater of the Ear* (LATE), and a variety of others.

This revival of radiodrama has been caused in part by the development of new technology that allows far greater accuracy in sound effects, and which gives producers greater latitude in the kinds of shows they can do, particularly in the realm of science fiction. In addition, radiodrama is immensely less expensive to produce than television. (I once produced/wrote/directed a 45-minute live comedy with an eye toward experimentation: How little could it be done for? Using the resources of a college radio station and local actors [both groups volunteered their services for the experience] and a minimum of expenditures for props and photocopying, the total costs of production came to $25.)

Or, as my producer from *Alien Worlds,* Lee Hansen, once said in what can best be termed a slight exercise in hyperbole, "Hell, we could've done *Star Wars* for a buck ninety-five."

So it can safely be stated that radiodrama began undergoing an audio renaissance for the following reasons: Audiences wanted something different, individual radio stations began to relax their formats, and producers found that they could put together dramatic presentations for radio that were cheap and relatively authentic in sound and complexity.

But what about the scriptwriter? What benefits exist for the select few who sit behind their typewriters and struggle to paint pictures on the canvas of the mind's eye?

What about those people, anyway?

The Benefits of Radio Scripting

Working from a scriptwriter's perspective, there are a whole lot of really terrific little things about radiodrama writing. For one thing, as we mentioned earlier, it is a very accessible field for relatively inexperienced freelancers. Whereas selling a telescript may depend to some degree on your track record as a scripter, this is not necessarily true for radio scripting. If you know the medium and know what mechanics are involved in putting a reasonable-sounding script together, then it really doesn't *matter* what you've done in the past. The fact that you can do it at *all* is the only truly important issue at hand, and the only one that counts to a producer desperate for material.

To move away from the purely pragmatic for a moment, another, largely intangible benefit awaits radio scripters. From a creative point of view, radiodrama is probably the area most dependent on the writer's craft: Radio is a writer's perfect medium. In every other field of scriptwriting, there are creative loopholes. You can write a scene that you know is a bit weak, and rely on the actor's visual presence to hold attention. If you're writing a comedy, you can rely on sight gags instead of the harder-to-accomplish verbal humor. You can sit back and allow the background business, the director's camera angles, the performer's tricks, the lighting technician's maneuvers, and the costumer's creations to carry your story at times.

But not in radiodrama.

In radio, you gotta *work* to keep the attention of your audience.

And yet, at the same time, that's the best thing about it. If your program is a winner, it's because of your ability as a writer. Certainly, the cast members, the director, and the engineers have a hand in the quality of a produced program—and more than a few really good scripts have been crippled by faulty production values—but it is the writer's words that create the world the characters live in, create the characters themselves, and allow the audience to see everything that happens as clearly as if they were there.

Television, stage, motion pictures . . . in each of these areas there is a certain amount of forced collaboration, points of overlap between the different creative disciplines. But in radio, there's only a plurality of voices (whose inflections and pauses have been indicated in the script), the carefully assembled lines of dialogue and description (courtesy of the writer's imagination), the sound effects that help form a picture in the listener's mind (selected and inserted by the scriptwriter at crucial moments) and the music (whose tone and tenor have been indicated by You-Know-Who).

Because of this tremendous reliance on the scriptwriter, you as the creative force have more control over the script than would necessarily be the case in another medium. You hear the voices, you see the room where the murder takes place, you hear the music and you know the story and the characters better than anyone else, and as a consequence there isn't much that happens to your script after it leaves your typewriter that you don't know about, or have some input into. Whenever I've sold a radio-drama script, I have always been consulted about cast selection, potential script changes, the nature of the characters, and so forth.

I use the word *consulted* because most producers will actively solicit your suggestions. (And, as an afterthought, I use the word *most* here because, as dictated by the simple law of averages, there's always an occasional twit who thinks he can get by without any input from the writer, usually to the detriment of the finished product.) In some cases, when you are working with a major producer for the first time, you will be flown to the studio so you can get a look at the facilities, meet the cast, and be on hand for any last-minute script changes. And let me tell you . . . there's no feeling in the whole world like the one you get when you're sitting in the studio control room, watching a group of actors—separated from you by a huge sheet of glass and thousands of dollars worth of audio equipment—giving life to the words you've labored over in solitude.

For those who shun a highly technical field, radio is a wonderful medium for artistic expression. You don't have to worry about camera angles, transitions, what's possible to do on a modest budget . . . any of that. The vocabulary of radio is rather simple, the process far from frightening in its complexity, and budgets generally the least of your concerns. All you have to worry about is your story and your characterizations.

There is another, almost hidden, benefit in writing for radio, particularly if you place your script with an established national series: The sale enables you to join the Writers Guild of America. Once you've done that, it suddenly becomes much easier to sell your scripts to other media, specifically film and television. In fact, I've known several writers who in a rather roundabout way have used this situation to best advantage.

It's like this: You want to increase the chance of a television sale by convincing the producer that you know what the hell you're doing. What do you do? Well, you find a nice little radiodrama series, preferably one that's a Writers Guild signatory. (This means that they've signed an agreement with the guild promising to pay a certain minimum fee.) You write a script, submit it, and, because of the great demands of radiodrama, sell it. You are now qualified to join the Guild, and do so. Then you contact the producer, telling him that you're a Guild member, and that you'd like to submit a television script for his examination. The beauty of all this is that when most TV producers hear someone say he's a Guild member, they automatically assume that the writer in question has sold a script or two to television. This makes them even more open to looking at your material.

Now, mind you, I'm not saying you should go out of your way—should you take this route—to make a television producer think you've sold to television. But neither am I saying you should actively discourage that misapprehension. Just state the facts, and let the producer draw the conclusions. You should never, *ever* lie to a producer. If you do, you'll get blacklisted permanently. But I don't think there's any particular danger in drawing a teensey, weensey, ittsy, bittsy mustache on the truth through a careful omission. Just be sure, if you're asked point-blank about the matter, that you're forthright. It's a tough world, kiddies.

The final benefit of scriptwriting for radio is that it pays well, particularly if you get involved with a networked or syndicated series. Smaller programs can pay far less, of course, and some pay only in the experience you get as a budding scripter. As such, the rate of payment for a radiodrama script, depending on the length of the script and the nature of the series, can range from $75 or so right on up to one or two thousand dollars.

So having established *why* radio scripting can be a desirable and lucrative endeavor for writers to pursue, we'll now go on to consider the steps involved in *how* a radio script is put together.

The Art of Radiodrama Scripting

To begin writing radiodramas, one of the first things that you as a creative entity have to do is engage in a little self-reeducation. This is because radiodrama is a medium with requirements and eccentricities unique unto itself. While there are things you can do in radio that you simply couldn't do in television or film, there are also some things that can't be done in radio. You must, in essence, learn an entirely new set of dramatic cues and signals that serve to make the script comprehensible to someone who doesn't have your personal insight into the story.

To illustrate what's meant by this idea of reeducation, we'll look at a simple dramatic scene, as it might be done for film or television, and see what changes would have to be made to transfer the scene to the realm of radiodrama.

1.   EXT. HOUSE—FRONT PORCH—NIGHT   1.

GEORGE, a scholarly looking man in his late fifties, steps onto the porch, fumbles with his keys, then opens the front door and steps inside.

2.   INT. HOUSE—LIVING ROOM—NIGHT   2.

George shuts the door, flicks on the light, and hangs his coat on a rack on the door. He turns, then stops. Sitting in a chair across the room, and facing him, is FRANK, a grim-looking, shabbily-dressed hoodlum in his early thirties, a man who looks like he knows the streets. He is holding a .38 caliber pistol, pointing it carelessly at George.

> FRANK
> Well, well. What's up, doc?

> GEORGE
> (seeing the gun)
> What do you want?

> FRANK
> I think you know the answer to that.
> How's Sally these days?

> GEORGE
> Now see here! Either you stay away from
> my daughter, or—

He stands, advances, sputtering in rage.

> FRANK
> You'll what?

> GEORGE
> —or I'll kill you, I swear it!

> FRANK
> (laughing)
> Right. You're gonna hurt me. What are
> you going to do, doc? You figure on turn-
> ing into a man overnight?

George's face flushes; he is angry beyond words. He takes a step for-ward.

> GEORGE
> Why, you—

Before he can take another step, Frank pulls the trigger. George grasps his chest, then falls to the floor, dead. Frank rises, checks for a pulse, then—a look of realization crossing his features—he races out of the room and into the night outside the house.

FADE OUT.

Well, now . . . that certainly seems a simple enough scene. Nothing confusing about it at all. It's straightforward in what it tells us about the action and the characters, and it certainly gets the story moving. You've probably seen something similar to this a dozen times or more on television and film screens.

But if you were to produce this scene, as written, for radio, you would leave your listeners confused about who the characters are, what they're like, where the action is taking place, and even mislead them about who shot whom!

Let's take it point by point.

Setting

Question: Where are we? Answer: George's house, of course. But is it really that obvious when you take away the pictures? What information is there that tells an audience listening to their radio where all the action is taking place? Simply put, there ain't none. The scene could be taking place in an office, a large passenger cruiser, or a log cabin, for all the listener knows.

Your very first obligation, then, is to let your audience know *where* they are. There are three basic ways of accomplishing this.

First, you can incorporate a *narrator* into your script. The purpose of a narrator is to establish location and setting with a minimum of confusion; to provide a sense of continuity; to reveal things that may or may not be known to the characters involved (a device generally frowned upon); and to assist in the transition from one scene to another. But you have to remember that a narrator is not always necessary. There are, in fact, many instances where you want to avoid a narrator altogether, since an omniscient commentator might give away too much, thereby putting a crimp into your script, particularly if it's a mystery.

There are, therefore, two conditions under which it is desirable to use a narrator: when the program being written is part of a continuing series linked together by the presence of a narrator/host, or if your script has certain complex set requirements that demand the presence of a narrator. The latter condition exists most often in science-fiction radiodrama, where it would be virtually impossible for the audience to visualize a setting on a planet they've never even heard of before.

In any event, whenever you *do* use narration to set your scene, the scripted narration should be brief, brisk, vivid, and very sharp. You should get in, set the stage, and get out again as fast as possible. If you let your narrator sit back and pontificate on the characters, the plot, the ethical structure of the universe, or suchlike, you run the risk of letting your narrator become a character, which detracts from the story's characters. (Unless that's your intention. It's not uncommon in radio comedies to let the narrator assume a *persona* who sets the tone for the entire show.)

Given this situation, would it be desirable to use a narrator to facilitate the scene we witnessed earlier? Since it has not been established that the scene is part of a script for a continuing, narrated series, that rationale is out. So would the script benefit from the presence of a narrator? Probably not. The setting is hardly extraordinary in nature, and can you imagine what would happen to the suspense of the scene if the narrator were to simply *tell* you that George was about to find someone holding a gun in his living room, instead of letting you, the listener, discover that along with George?

No, that doesn't wash either. Which leaves one last resort, the basic tools of the radio scriptwriter: sound effects and dialogue. And yet, here we hit yet another complication. How can we realistically use these tools to establish the scene without getting corny? Now, were this scene taking place on a nuclear submarine, we'd have no problem at all. The sound effects would do all the work for us. If the scene were taking place in a hospital, the sound of a nurse's voice on the public address system could tell the listener where he or she is. If the characters were about to scale a mountain, you not only could use the sound effects of wind and snow-shoes crunching on ice, you could also allow the characters to discuss the mountain, marveling at the grandeur and the terror of those high peaks.

In this instance, however, we simply have a man returning home at night. This complicates the matter considerably, since there is no one sound associated with a house, and it would be rather silly for George to mutter to himself as he unlocked the front door, "Well, here I am, home at last."

In a word . . . yuck.

What's required from the scriptwriter, then, is subtlety and an attention to detail. Think of the task as painting a picture with sound. What kinds of sounds would one encounter coming home late at night?

Crickets. Crickets are the most beloved bugs in the history of radio. The chirruping of a cricket tells a listener that the scene under way is taking place outdoors, and that it's evening. The next step requires putting in a detail omitted from the film script, because it was a given: How did George get home? As viewers, we can assume that he drove home. But here we can use the device to help set the scene.

So:

We start with the sound of crickets. Then, we hear the sound of a car moving across a gravel road. The engine dies. The car door opens, then shuts. We hear a single set of footsteps move across the gravel, up a couple of wooden steps, and stop. We hear the rattling of keys, a key being inserted in a door, and the door opening and closing.

This, then, has established most of the needed information about the setting. Only one thing remains: to establish that this is George's *home.* Since *home* is a concept, it needs to be verbalized somehow, but without being obtrusive. So one of the two characters needs to drop that tiny slice of information, but without breaking character to do it. George is out of the question, for the reasons discussed before. That leaves us with Frank. Somehow, he has to establish that this is George's home, and do it in a brash, not-entirely-complimentary fashion. Given Frank's streetwise character, there's only one way he could pull this off, and that's with a line such as, "Welcome home, doc," possibly followed with, "Nice place you've got here."

And there we are. The flats have been painted, the scenery constructed, the stage set. It is important to remember, though, that you can't simply set the stage once, at the beginning of your script, and leave it at that. Throughout your script, you must continue to paint what are known in the radiodrama industry as *word pictures*. How often, and to what extent you do this, is directly related to the number of different locations you intend to use in your script, and how out of the ordinary they might be. To create word pictures, you can turn once again to the devices of narration or character exposition in combination with sound effects. Just be sure that your characters are not describing an everyday setting, since nobody—at least nobody I know—sits in his or her living room, during a casual conversation, and describes the room to a visitor . . . unless there is something special about the room. Be equally sure that your sound effects can reasonably be achieved during production. I once saw a rejected script that had the following sound effect cue to set the scene for all that followed: "Snow falling in a forest of elm trees."

To close out the discussion of setting, there are occasional circumstances where ambiguity actually adds a new dimension to your script. A good example of this would be a spy drama in which a person has been kidnapped at the opening of the script and is being held—blindfolded, of course—at the kidnappers' headquarters. Later, after the prisoner escapes (they *always* escape) while being moved to a new location, it becomes necessary to go back and find the headquarters for some reason or another. In this kind of script, you don't want the kidnappers to give more than a few tantalizing hints about where they are keeping the prisoner, and having a narrator establish the location destroys the suspense. So the only route left is to include a few of those inadvertent clues, balanced with a lot of sound effects. In this way, the whole thing becomes a game of sorts, played equally by the escaped prisoner and the listener. While captive, he or she hears such sounds as a train crossing, chickens squawking, a noon whistle at a factory, and so forth. The character then tries to track down the spot where all those sounds came together. In this way, your script has two basic plots: the kidnapping, and the search for a hidden base, using only sounds as clues. It takes skill to pull off a script like this, however, so it's wise to wait until you have a solid understanding of more common techniques before attempting a tricky one.

As an exercise in setting, you might want to try to pick out the sound effects that would signal any given location. Picture yourself on a small boat, in a prison, in an electrical generating plant, at a street rally, and imagine what sounds you would hear while you were there. After a while, you'll notice there are generally one or two primary sounds that more than anything else give the listener an immediate idea about where he or she is. *These* are the effects to include in your scripts.

Plot and Action

Like any other form of dramatic scriptwriting, a radiodrama must be about something. It must have a beginning, a middle, and an end. There is a slight difference, however, in the types of stories required for radio. As a general rule, because of the nonvisual nature of radio, you'll find a minimum of heavy action-oriented material: There are few car chases, slug-outs, and so forth. Such material may be appropriate for a purely visual medium, where you can see the hero clinging to the edge of a window ten floors up, but it often doesn't play well on radio. Which is one big reason why mysteries, suspense, comedy, and science fiction programs have probably been the favorite genres for radiodrama writers and producers.

Radiodrama tends to be a cerebral medium. It highlights the interplay between characters, carefully constructs a delicate framework of suspense and tension, and attempts to portray that which could not, or would not, be portrayed on network television or in film.

Which is one of the truly nifty things about radiodrama—you can do virtually anything the imagination conceives. For verification, I need only refer you to the great programs of the past. It has not been uncommon for radiodrama protagonists to travel to the planet Mars; to literally turn themselves inside-out (an effect accomplished by slowly removing a surgeon's rubber glove right next to the microphone); to deal with an entire planet populated by super-intelligent rats; to become invisible and walk among the streets clouding men's minds; or to travel back and forth through time.

(A further illustration: During one of his radio specials, Stan Freberg emptied Lake Michigan, filled it with hot chocolate, then shoved a 500-foot mountain of whipped cream into it; at that point the Royal Canadian Air Force appeared, towing a 10-ton maraschino cherry, which was dropped into the center of the whipped cream to the frenzied cheering of 20,000 extras. He topped the exercise with the challenge, "Let's see you do *that* on television!")

The fact that you can toss the laws of probability, and in the foregoing example, common sense, to the winds does not mean, however, that the radiodrama writer has a free hand to do *anything*. You may have an idea for the most incredible effect ever done in radio, but if it's not essential . . . forget it. Story, not effects, must always be the linchpin of your script.

Whatever your plot concerns itself with, one simple rule stands inviolate: Any action that takes place in your script must be capable of being visualized by the listener as accurately as possible. Sure, you may know what that sound effect signals, but if the listener shakes his or her head and says, "What happened? Did I miss something?" you're artistically dead in the water.

Let's take as an example of this the scripted scene we examined earlier. Question: Who shot whom? Answer . . . it depends. If you saw the scene on television, the answer would be obvious—Frank shot George.

But if the event took place on radio *exactly as written*, then the answer would again be obvious to the audience: George shot Frank!

Lest you conclude that the author is nuts, let's go back to the original scene and take a closer look at it. To start with, does any verbal exchange between the two characters indicate that one is holding a gun? No. Does a narrator announce its presence? Again no. The first and only indication the audience has that a gun is present is the actual gunshot. And when does that happen? Right after Frank has made a snippy remark, and George, his anger showing, shouts "Why, you . . . " The result: To the listener who hasn't seen the script, it appears that George, irritated by Frank's remark and angry at his presence, has pulled out a gun and shot him. This impression is further enhanced because no one speaks for the remainder of the scene. The listener would only become aware of the truth later, when Frank makes another appearance in another scene. The problem, though, is that the listener would probably undergo that one moment of confusion, that feeling of "But I thought he was dead!" that leaves the audience certain the writer has put together a sloppy script.

How can we resolve this little problem? Just as before, the solution depends on giving the audience subtle clues, without making the listener *conscious* that this is going on.

Very well, then. Our first task is to establish that Frank is armed. Probably one of the oldest (and silliest) ways of doing this is to have the offended character say something to the effect of, "Frank! Where did you get that gun?" If you listen to any of the older radiodramas, you'll hear that line a lot. The problem with a line like that is that it doesn't fit naturally into a conversation. The only purpose of the line is to establish that the other person is armed, after which the conversation continues toward its main point. After all, what else could the scripter have his character say after a question like that? "Oh, this? Why, I picked it up at J.C. Penney's last Thursday after work. It has a nice recoil action. Would you like to hold it and see for yourself?"

I mean . . . come on!

So that route is definitely out. What's left? Well, as is the case with any form of drama, when in doubt, go straight for your character. The answer will invariably be found there.

Frank is your basic street-punk type. His courage comes out of the business end of a gun, and even then only when it's pointed at an unarmed victim. So he wouldn't utter the line, in response to George's threatening tone, "You'll what?" without something to back up the statement. Since this is an implied threat, it gives us an opening where we can wedge in the information about Frank's gun. This can be done with a sound effect and a bit of dialogue that actually helps to expand the plot a little.

The effect would consist of the sound of a pistol hammer being cocked, a move consistent with Frank's character. It underlines the threat.

Which brings us to the next step, a simple rule of dramatics that's true for every medium, but especially helpful in radiodrama: For every character action, there is an equal reaction from the other character(s). It's just physics transposed a bit, a little rudimentary logic. After all, if you were speaking to someone, and that person pointed a gun at you and cocked the trigger, wouldn't it cause you to react in some way, if only with a pause? I should imagine so. It's very difficult to carry on business as usual when you're looking down the barrel of a .38 caliber interruption.

So George is bound to say something in reaction to the sight of Frank's gun. (It is also *necessary* that he do so, since the sound of a gun being cocked is not quite sufficient in and of itself. It's altogether possible that the listener who has never been around guns may mistake the sound for a key turning in a door, or an old metal cigarette lighter being clicked.) For our purposes, George—a not altogether unaggressive character himself— will respond, "Put that gun away."

Since that line interrupts the structure we established in the film scene, we must now alter Frank's lines to make everything fit together: He will respond, "No way, doc. Not until I have just a little more fun with Sally."

A final response from George, along the lines of "You lay your stinking hands on my daughter one more time, and I'll kill you, I swear it!" puts us right back on track again.

And there we have it. With a few added lines and a simple sound effect, we've not only established that Frank is armed, which makes it clearer later that it was he who did the shooting, but at the same time we've also managed to convey a little more about Frank's character, or lack thereof.

Speaking of which . . . this is a good time to move on to

Characterization

Establishing characterization in radiodrama can be a tricky business. If you write a country hick role for television, the producer simply puts out a call for character actors who look the part. The written lines get ranked second in primacy to the effect created by the performer's appearance and style of delivery. A good character actor can read the telephone book and make it sound convincingly countrified.

Naturally, that technique doesn't hold in radiodrama—at least not entirely. Admittedly, if you write a role for a country hick, a radiodrama producer will go out and find an actor skilled at backwoods accents. But there's more to the creation of such a character than an accent. A whole different way of speaking and thinking is involved, and while it's imperative at all times to trust your actors, you can't rely on them to bring out all the subtleties just through their delivery.

Case in point: While teaching creative writing at a large university, I encountered a student who could do *very* convincing accents. One day, I brought in a monologue from one of my plays and without telling the class where it was from or who the original character was, had the student read it aloud using a Southern accent. Afterward, I asked the class for their reaction to the reading. They agreed unanimously that the monologue had been effectively delivered, but . . . something about it wasn't quite right. It didn't ring true. The rhythms seemed strange, the syntax subtly out of sync. They couldn't quite place what the problem was, but they knew *something* was wrong.

And they were right, because the monologue was culled from a dialogue between two characters reared in London during the early 1900s.

I didn't tell the class that. They went into the reading as if it were just a simple exercise. But *instinctively*, they *knew* that some part of the exercise was screwy. It just didn't sound right, didn't ring true.

The point here is that while it's important to make your dialogue sound authentic in any field of dramatics, particularly when dealing with regionalisms, this importance increases substantially when the only point of reference your audience has is the spoken word.

The beginning radio scripter must develop an ear for the way people speak and know what that manner of speech says about the person doing the talking. A speech pattern is like a fingerprint—no two are ever alike. A professor of literature, a car mechanic, an accountant, a professional model . . . each has his or her own particular method of speaking, which often gives the person's profession away. But more than an occupation can be deduced from the way someone talks: The cadences, the pauses, the inflections, the choice of words, the inclusion or omission of certain phrases, all these tell us something about the speaker. Even if no overt attempt at identification is made during a radio program, the listener should be able to tell which of the characters is the street punk, which is the California surfer, and which is the widow from the Midwest.

(There is, of course, the danger of going too far, and having your characters turn into stereotypes or, worse yet, unintentional caricatures. That's what I referred to earlier as the "tricky" part. It's a fine line to walk, and I'm afraid that you won't find any shortcuts in this book. Learning to walk that line is a skill that comes simply with trial and error, experience, and the development of a good ear for dialogue.)

So you should always listen carefully to people, even when they have nothing in particular to say (especially then, since the ability to speak while saying virtually nothing is a talent that can be acquired and applied to writing plays like *Waiting for Godot*, or to a solid political career).

In the case of our little scene before with Frank and George, both characters have a certain amount of contextual characterization built into their dialogue, more than enough for a visual medium. While it might also be sufficient for a radio script, it never hurts to expedite the exposition a bit. In this instance, Frank's lines could do with some more shading, something to point them a bit more toward the streets. We can, for example, take the line developed earlier—"Not until I have just a little more fun with Sally"—and flavor it a bit. After all, the structure of his statement would probably be a little more informal, less grammatical. A good alternative would be, "First, me and Sally, we're gonna have us a little fun, just like old times, y'know?"

This subtle change—and others that can be plugged into the script—heightens the menace of Frank's character, tells the audience more about his lack of education, and generally helps round him out. While it can be argued that this is only a trivial detail, it should also be pointed out that a good radiodrama, like a painting, is composed of small, individually selected and deliberately placed brush strokes which, when perceived together, form a whole picture.

And making pictures out of words is *precisely* what the art of radiodrama is all about.

The Craft of Radiodrama Scripting

As was the case with television writing, radiodrama scripting can also be divided into considerations of *art* and *craft*, with the latter largely concerned with the technical details encountered whenever you write for any of the electronic media.

As is *also* the case with every other endeavor of consequence, craft is something you can learn in a few hours. Craft is learning which end of the nail is supposed to be struck. Art, however, is something not learnable in the usual sense. Art is the application of experience, perception, and imagination—and each of these grows and changes with the passage of a year, a day, a minute. Your art is viewed as complete only after your demise. No living person has ever learned all there is to know about art, and no one ever will.

But a knowledge of craft is necessary, since it's only through the rudimentary tools of one's profession that art is able to be born.

In brief, craft is a Good Thing. It is imperative not to let the appearance of the tools scare you off. Once you figure out which end of the nail to hit, you'll be surprised at how many things you can make. In the pages that follow, therefore, we'll take a look at the nuts-and-bolts techniques that underlie the construction of a radiodrama script. In the process, we'll also see how some of the creative decisions we made in the preceding section on how best to adapt a visual script to a radiodrama format actually translate into something on the typewritten page.

But first, we must begin at the beginning.

Birth of a Notion

In addition to a couple of other esoteric items, one thing this book *ain't* gonna do is teach you how to come up with ideas for scripts. Ideas come out of your personal experience, angled just *so*, in such a way that it becomes drama. You don't look for ideas in someone else's *Weltanschauung*, or in your local public library. (I've heard of budding writers who have inquired at bookstores and libraries for *The Book of Ideas*, a nonexistent tome that supposedly contains every possible idea for a fictional plot, and needs only to be adapted to the individual's needs.) The only real consideration that must be given to the basis for your idea is whether it's entirely original in its format and characters, or if it has been written specifically as an episode for a continuing radio series—a topic we'll discuss in greater detail when we get to the section on marketing.

So: In the beginning, there is an idea. Since it's not necessary, as we did in the chapter on telescripting, to choose a program that has wide audience familiarity—it is, in fact, almost impossible, since there are few radiodrama series that can claim their characters are widely known—we'll take as our example a produced radiodrama script written by your humble author. The script is entitled "Encounter at Twilight," and it was written on direct commission from the Mutual Radio Network, acting through Great Dane Enterprises, a California-based radio production company.

What the network was looking for was a fast-paced radiodrama that fell into the action/adventure genre. A certain amount of science fiction or fantasy would also be acceptable. There were no continuing characters to worry about. My only requirements were that the material be realistic, the characters strong yet sympathetic; it had to move quickly, and take the listener somewhere he or she had never been before.

"With or without mustard?" I asked my producer.

He didn't laugh. Some people have *no* sense of humor.

I must've put together more than a dozen different concepts during the following three or four days, and none seemed quite right. Spies, escapes from East Berlin, war stories, safaris that turned out to be more than the hunter bargained for . . . I went through the entire routine and turned up empty-handed. Finally, I decided to put the whole thing on a back burner and not *try* to come up with something, since that's when most really exciting ideas are born. So I read, I watched television, I browsed through bookstores, and looked through my almanacs.

Then I stumbled onto something. While glancing through one of the almanacs that fill my reference shelf, I discovered that there have been several submarines lost at sea, a find which, in itself, was not particularly noteworthy. But then I noticed that a clear majority of them vanished in spring, although their disappearances were years apart. It seemed curious to me that they would follow such an unusual pattern, particularly since many vanished in calm seas. What, I wondered, could have happened to them? And why did it all happen in the spring?

Although logically I knew that it was all simply coincidence, the little fantasy-spinner that lives in the back of my head went to work with a barrage of "What ifs?" *What if* they all encountered a similar fate? *What if* they were destroyed trying to accomplish some specific task? I began to tie it all in with the legends of the Bermuda Triangle, the *Flying Dutchman,* and so forth.

Working on a hunch, I looked back through an index of naval disasters to see if I could find anything significant enough that it might have some bearing on this situation.

Sure enough, I hit the jackpot. According to my index, the passenger ship *Lusitania* had been torpedoed and sunk by a German U-Boat on May 7, 1915. A little more digging brought out the fact that there had been considerable speculation at the time as to whether or not the *Lusitania* had secretly been carrying arms for use against Germany during the First World War. And *that's* when it all came together with a final what if: *What if* those lost subs had encountered some force that attempted to draw them back in time to save the more than one thousand civilian passengers on the *Lusitania?*

An idea was born. I immediately slipped a sheet of fresh bond into the typewriter and began setting down the concept, which follows exactly as it was written:

> An American nuclear submarine, the pride of the fleet, encounters a strange force while on test maneuvers in the Atlantic. The force propels them back in time to the year 1915, where they attempt to prevent the *Lusitania* from being sunk by a German U-Boat.

With that concept worked out as fully as I could at the moment, I called my producer and read it to him. He liked it, and gave me the go-ahead to begin work.

The next step in the creation of a radiodrama script is similar to the process of writing a telescript: the creation of a treatment. In this case, the next step involved not only further plot development, but a fair amount of research as well. Since more of the plot would—I felt—probably come out of the research, I did my homework first. I tracked down where the *Lusitania* had been sunk (five miles off the coast of Ireland), the longitude and latitude of its last reported position, the type of U-Boat it encountered, how many passengers were aboard the liner, and so on. It was also necessary to find out all I could about the inner workings of a modern nuclear submarine, since once again a feel of authenticity is absolutely vital if you are to create a valid auditory setting. In this instance, that required calling up the Department of the Navy and finding out all I could on the average speed, cruising depth, and arms capabilities of your basic nuclear sub. As you might expect, I was referred up from one officer to another—right up to a lieutenant commander—all of whom wanted to know why I *really* wanted the information. In time, I managed to convince them that I *was* a writer, honest-to-god-truly, and that I wasn't trying to get my hands on any classified information. Then they were more than willing to cooperate, and proved very helpful.

With that done, I returned to my plot. Naturally, I couldn't have the sub's captain actually save the *Lusitania*, since everyone knows that it did, indeed, sink. Changing history may be nice from a dramatic perspective, but it shatters your credibility with an audience. So the *Lusitania* had to be sunk. And that made for bad drama, since nothing's unexpected there. This led to what I viewed as a crucial element of the story: The *Lusitania* would be sunk, yes—but there would have to be some question about *which* ship actually did it, the U-Boat or, through some accident, the nuclear sub itself!

But if history can't be changed, then why bring the ship back in the first place? Why not vengeance? A little more digging showed that the U-Boat that sank the *Lusitania* never returned to its home port, and was reported lost at sea. (As a research footnote, I have to admit that some other sources indicated that the sub *had* returned home. This was one of those cases where the author decided to close one eye and squint a little at the facts. Dramatic license and all that—you understand.)

This finally led to the creation of a full-scale synopsis and a treatment, which was essentially a longer, more complex version of the synopsis in narrative fiction form. Rather than print the entire treatment here, we'll just take a look at the expanded synopsis. (For further information on how to write a treatment, see the appropriate section in the chapter on telescripting, if you haven't read it already—and if not, how come?)

On May 7, 1980, a United States nuclear submarine, the *Trident*, is engaged in test maneuvers five miles off the coast of Ireland. Life goes on as usual until suddenly they encounter a strange disturbance—a long, black wall of mist or storm that runs clear across the horizon. Rather than risk the possibility of running headlong into a storm of some sort, the captain orders that the sub dive to a safe depth.

Once below the surface, however, the disturbance rushes over their position. The ship is tossed back and forth, and all its navigational instruments fail. When they go to visual tracking, they discover that they can see nothing outside. Although they do not yet know it, they have been transported back in time exactly sixty-five years, to a point not far from where a German U-Boat is about to torpedo the passenger ship *Lusitania*.

While the captain and crew of the *Trident* attempt to figure out what's happened, life goes on as usual on the liner, and the crew of the U-Boat prepare for the attack. Finally, just as the *Trident's* instruments return to normal, shortly after sighting the *Lusitania* through their periscope, the U-Boat fires off a torpedo at the passenger ship.

The first one misses. The captain of the *Trident*, even though he is at a loss to explain how he and the rest have traveled back in time, realizes that they are nonetheless in a state of war, and must fight to protect the *Lusitania*.

Just then, the U-Boat fires off a second torpedo. The *Trident*, in turn, fires off one of its own to intercept the German torpedo. The radar operator counts down the narrowing chase. Just then, there is an explosion! The *Lusitania* has been hit amidships. The *Trident* prepares to surface and aid the survivors. Suddenly, however, the U-Boat, which has become aware of the sub, fires off an attack on the *Trident*. They manage to avoid the first assault, then give chase.

The *Trident* chases the U-Boat through the murky waters, closing in steadily. It fires off a torpedo. The radar operator counts down the interception. Suddenly, both the U-Boat and the torpedo vanish. Rather than waste further time looking for them, the captain turns the sub around to look for survivors from the *Lusitania*. Just then, however, they encounter the strange force once again.

At a later scene in Command Headquarters, a Navy official explains to the captain that after receiving his report, a search team was sent to the location of the strange event. All the divers were able to find were the ruins of a German U-Boat that had been lying on the bottom of the sea for at least sixty years. He tells the captain that the whole event will probably go on the record as unexplainable.

The captain, as he leaves, wishes that one thing *was* explainable: Was it his torpedo, or the one from the U-Boat that actually hit and sunk the *Lusitania*?

They will never know.

And there it was. It was a good little story, and I knew it would work. As a matter of fact, it was such a terrific storyline that, about a year later, a movie titled *Final Countdown* opened with a very similar plot: A nuclear aircraft carrier, the *Nimitz*, travels back in time and attempts to prevent Pearl Harbor from being attacked by the Japanese. It was just one more instance of two people coming up with a similar idea at about the same time. Another person might have screamed plagiarism, but I knew this wasn't the case, since pre-production on the film would have started at roughly the same time I was putting my story together. So it didn't bother me. So *what* if, had I just come up with the idea a little sooner, *I* could have written a movie that starred Kirk Douglas and went on to make a fair amount of money at the box office. It doesn't upset me. Really, it doesn't.

(Now, if you'll excuse me, I have to go take my ulcer medicine.)

Back to business.

With the storyline firmly worked out, the next step was to present the story in standard radiodrama structure, first by breaking down the story into its component parts and plugging it into the progression of acts and scenes, and finally by actually writing the script itself.

Structure

The best way to learn the basics of script structure is to read every script you can lay your hands on. When it comes to radiodrama, however, we run into a slight problem. Because the field slumped during the late fifties, sixties, and early seventies, books about and collections of radiodramas were published infrequently, if at all. Consequently, there aren't a whole lot of books available on the subject. (Except this one, naturally.) A close scrutiny of your corner bookstore will probably prove useless in your search unless it carries a large number of used books, in which case you may stumble upon one or two.

Public and university libraries will probably be your best bet in finding written, published scripts for radio. Some of the very best of these are the collections written by Norman Corwin which, though often available in university libraries, are harder than hell to track down on the open market. These publications include *Thirteen by Corwin*, *More by Corwin*, and *On a Note of Triumph*, which contains the entire script for the famous nationwide broadcast aired on V-E Day. Other noteworthy resources include *Radio Sketches*, a book first published in 1936 and, although out of date, still a handy reference from a historical perspective, and the more recently published paperback *The Panic Broadcast* by Howard Koch, a fascinating look at the events surrounding Orson Welles' infamous recreation of *The War of the Worlds*, including the entire script from that hysteria-provoking program.

Happily, it is not at *all* difficult to acquire actual recordings of classic radiodramas. Just about any reasonably sized record store carries a full complement of old-time radio broadcasts, including episodes of *The Shadow, The Green Hornet, Inner Sanctum, I Love a Mystery, Buck Rogers* and many others, including such special, one-time programs as the aforementioned *On a Note of Triumph.* Recordings such as these give you an idea of the types of shows that have been done, how certain effects were accomplished, and the process by which the story was developed.

(One brief caveat: Radiodrama has matured considerably in recent years—in spite of certain of its practitioners—and you should be careful not to inadvertently recreate the 1930s all over again.)

Finally, you should attempt to locate stations in your community that either carry current radiodrama series or broadcast old radiodramas. Once you locate them, tape each broadcast and study it at your leisure.

During research, you're bound to discover that not all radiodramas are created equal. Depending upon the writer, the nature of the program, and the size of the budget, the construction of the programs will vary considerably from one another. This is particularly true of the early broadcasts. In recent years, radiodrama structure has been standardized a little, at least the programs carried by commercial stations. We'll deal with noncommercial, or public, radio a little later. For the moment, we'll look at the individual components that make up a radiodrama, armed with the realization that while some series may omit one facet or another, *all* of them, to varying degrees, use the basic elements of script construction as presented below.

Prologue. This is the opening sequence of your script, wherein the characters and situations to follow are first introduced. In this sense, it is roughly equivalent to a teaser in television scripting. A prologue usually consists of a narrative introduction to the characters and the series itself, followed by a brief scene featuring those characters. A prologue, using this format, can accomplish a number of things, depending upon your requirements. It can be used to show the day-to-day, mundane activities of your characters and thereby let the audience get a feeling for what the characters are like in circumstances other than the extraordinary ones that will follow. On the other hand, it can be used to introduce the situation itself very vividly, along the lines of "Mount Everest has several thousand small ridges and individual cliffs, each suspended hundreds or thousands of feet above the snow-coated ground. Hanging from one of these is Jeremy Fastworth, who at this moment is wondering how many seconds of life he can reasonably expect to enjoy." You then cut to Jeremy himself.

A prologue should get the listener's attention immediately. In this case, it should make the listener wonder who Jeremy Fastworth is, why he's on Mount Everest, how he got into his present predicament, and how on earth he's ever going to get down again, short of a nasty run-in with gravity. Like any good exercise in scriptwriting, it should make the audience *want* to stick around and find out what happens next.

Generally, depending upon the individual series, a prologue can run anywhere from one to three minutes and is usually organized in the following sequence: narrative introduction to the characters; brief, scripted scene featuring the characters and/or their predicament; narrative recap and invitation to stick around; series theme music; commercial break. (Note: An exception to this rule is the series which chooses to put its theme music at the top of the prologue instead of the bottom. Again, this is one of those cases where it's essential to really know the series you're submitting to.)

Acts. These are lengthier dramatic units that make up the body of your script. A half-hour program generally consists of three acts, with the first act around 5 minutes long, the second act approximately 10 minutes, and the last act rounding out at anywhere from 7 to 9 minutes. You may have a minute or two of leeway, depending upon how long your prologue is. When produced dry (without commercials added in), a half-hour radiodrama actually runs about 24 minutes.

One-hour programs can be a little tricky, depending upon the series and whether or not it's being carried by a radio network. As a rule, there are four complete acts in an hour-long program, with each act running about 9 to 12 minutes. If this seems like a wide margin of error, there's good reason for it. Let's take, for example, the series *CBS Mystery Theater*, which has been very popular for a number of years. Ostensibly, that series consists of daily programs one hour in length. But actually, they're not. First, virtually any network breaks into the individual stations at the top of the hour for 10 minutes of news. So this already cuts 10 minutes out of the program. Second, for an hour-long program to show a profit, it has to include at least 10 minutes' worth of commercial advertisements, which decreases the total running time of your 60-minute program to a grand total of 40 minutes.

Surrounding an act are a narrative recap and/or a tie-back (discussed in more detail shortly); a series of dramatic scenes that are related in some fashion, preferably through the use of a plot; and a narrative comment at the end of the act.

Scenes. These dramatic sub-units have caused more dissension among radiodrama producers than just about anything else. The controversy centers around the optimum length of any individual scene. Some producers see no reason why a single scene cannot last the entire act. Others shrink back in horror at that thought, some actually insisting that *no* single scene should ever run more than 2 minutes.

It's my personal feeling—one that, I might add, seems to be borne out by production figures—that the *best* radiodrama is one that combines both long and short scenes. A long scene of, say, 3 or 4 minutes allows the audience to spend a little more time setting the stage, and gives the scriptwriter more freedom in establishing solid characterizations. Interspersing these with short scenes of a minute or so helps keep the program moving, and makes it seem to go by faster than it really does. This combination approach makes the most sense from a dramatic point of view, because setting a mandatory—and rather arbitrary—length simply means that the writer will end up either padding some scenes (thereby making the action drag considerably) or cutting others (and thereby reducing the amount of possible characterization in that scene).

One final aside on the subject of scene length: Many of the proponents of a multitude of brief scenes insist that this is the only way to hold the interest of an audience whose attention span has been systematically reduced through the influence of television. Should you come across someone with this attitude, simply remind him that by tuning in to a *radio*drama, the listener has made a direct statment, to wit: that he or she is looking for something *different*, something that's *not* television. Why, therefore, should a producer just throw more of the same thing at an audience that is looking for some variety? Huh? Answer *that* one if you can!

Anyway . . . one of the most common errors made by novice radioscripters is the tendency to stick with the same location for each scene, with only the time element varying from scene to scene. In the technical jargon of radiodrama, this is known as a Bad Thing. Unless your script specifically calls for just one character—something that's very difficult to pull off—you will generally have a variety of characters and locations to play around with. Use that variety to your best advantage. If your script centers around the last will and testament of a dying man, then spend some time with the soon-to-be-deceased, some with his attorney, and some with those who stand to inherit a substantial sum from his passage. This opens up a wealth of dramatic possibilities. You can show the dying man telling his attorney what he *really* thinks of his family; and how those family members act among themselves—backbiting and jockeying for position—and in the presence of the patriarch, to whom they are uncommonly sweet. Not only does this pick up the action and increase the drama, it also saves you, the writer, a lot of cumbersome exposition. The dying man needn't give long, detailed descriptions of his relatives' true natures; it can be *shown* instead. (In "Encounter at Twilight," I bounced from the *Trident* to the German sub and the *Lusitania*, giving each character a chance to have his or her own say. It also increased the dramatic effect to have the German sub captain counting down the time until the first torpedo was launched, while the passengers on the ocean liner went blissfully about their business.)

In assembling the scenes, many writers—myself included—tend to favor what's informally known as the "circular and segmented" approach. In other words, as far as locations are concerned, you start with location A, then cut to B, then C, then back to B and finally again to A. You end up back where you started. In addition, you balance out each scene by making some short and others long. (Example: The second act of "Encounter at Twilight" begins with the Trident crew trying to figure out if that really is the Lusitania they see through the periscope; the next scene is a brief one as the U-Boat readies for the attack; the third scene takes place on the sundeck of the Lusitania, as a married couple gathers their children to go to supper; the fourth scene is back on the U-Boat, with one of the crew swearing he saw another periscope in the water, although when the captain takes a look it's vanished; and the last scene is back on the Trident as the power comes back to their instruments, and the radar operator spots the first torpedo being launched at the Lusitania.)

Tie-backs. In those cases where a narrative recap is not expected to carry all the weight, a tie-back is used following a commercial to reintroduce the audience to the story. A tie-back takes place at the top of the second and subsequent acts, and consists of the following: a brief, narrative summation of the previous act, right up to a highly dramatic moment; the actual recreation of that moment in scripted form; and a narrative introduction to the action about to take place.

A tie-back or some kind of narrative recap is often considered necessary because a commercial is an intrusive device, and it can break the continuity of your story. Devices such as these help bring the audience right back into your story, and refresh their memory of the last dramatic scene. A tie-back takes about 1 minute, or at most 90 seconds.

Hooks. Each act should end in such a fashion that, like a prologue, it makes the listener *want* to come back after the commercial break to find out what happens next. In addition, a hook works well from the standpoint of the producer. It forms a dramatic high point, the moment where the threat is issued, the music reaches a thundering crescendo, and the narrator invokes the prospect of death, destruction, imminent marriage or other un-nicenesses.

Transitions. Any movement in time (past to present and back) or space (from one location to another) that serves to advance the plot is called a transition. There are a number of ways to accomplish this. One is simply to throw a musical transition between two scenes. (The catch with this technique is that in order to avoid having your audience wonder where you've taken them, the first few lines of dialogue following the musical transition should somehow indicate where we are, and who's doing the talking, sometimes along the line of, "But George, do you really think it's a good idea to be prowling around father's office at night like this?")

Another useful technique is the use of a sound effect to accomplish your transition. An example of this would be having two characters discuss taking a plane to visit their uncle in Vermont; this is followed by the sound of an aircraft, which gradually fades down and under the dialogue that follows.

A third method, one which is steadily gaining more acceptance, is the use of a cross-fade, a technical term for overlapping the sounds of two different conversations, for instance, one fading down while the other fades in. This is similar to a dissolve in motion picture or television scripting.

Tracks. This is a term a radiodrama scriptwriter doesn't actually need to know, but that comes in handy in understanding the process of producing a script. And it never hurts, when a producer drops a phrase like "We're laying down the first track tomorrow," to be able to smile and know that he or she isn't going to be spiking rails all morning.

To lay down a track simply means to record something. A radiodrama is recorded and assembled in three stages. First comes a voice track for your dialogue. Next, the sound effects are recorded in the sequence in which they will be used. Then a music track is put together, and finally, all three tracks are mixed together and recorded onto a fourth, or "master track."

Parenthetical directions. Since your audience can't see the actors shaking their fists or nodding their heads, there aren't a whole lot of directions you can give your cast in terms of physical action. All you can indicate is how the lines should be delivered. You can, for example, specify that the lines following your parenthetical direction should be spoken in an *angry, sad, breathless, shocked,* or *happy* tone of voice. In many cases, if a line is to be delivered with a light touch, the direction given simply says, *A smile.*

I know that sounds peculiar, but don't laugh. You can *hear* a smile. Maybe it's subliminal, but there is a definite change in a speaker's tone of voice that occurs when the speaker smiles and means it. Try it yourself. Snag yourself a volunteer, put the sucker—I mean, the assistant—in one room, and you go into another. Then deliver the same line or lines twice: once with a straight, sober face, and the next time smiling in good humor. Nine times out of ten, the other person will be able to pick out which was which.

About the only other parenthetical directions for the actor's use are indications of time. If you want a certain line emphasized, you can flag it by calling for a *beat* or a *pause* right before the line. The only real difference between the two is that a pause is generally acknowledged to be a second or so longer than a beat.

Sound effects. Another important element of a well-structured radio script is the proper use of effects, commonly abbreviated as *SFX*. Doors opening and closing, sirens, gunshots, ray guns, footsteps—all fall under the heading of sound effects that in conjunction with dialogue and narration paint a mental picture of the events taking place. You should always choose your effects carefully, plug them in whenever and wherever they are actively needed (don't overload your script with them), and describe them as briefly as possible. For example, an indication for a door opening and closing would be written: SFX: DOOR OPENS/CLOSES. Two people walking on a gravel-covered driveway would be written: SFX: FOOT-STEPS ON GRAVEL x 2.

Vocal effects. Anything done to alter an actor's voice to accommodate a need in the script is called a vocal effect, abbreviated as VFX. In most ordinary circumstances, there are only two vocal effects radio scripters will ever have to call for: a *reverb* and a *filter* effect.

Reverb is shorthand for reverberation. If your character is shouting in a cave, for instance, or in any other enclosed space, there normally would be some sort of echo or reverberation. This effect can be electronically duplicated in the studio.

A filter is used whenever you want to establish that your characters are speaking over the telephone. This is accomplished by electronically attenuating the voice of the actor who is supposed to be speaking through the telephone receiver, which effectively eliminates the lows of the voice and gives it the flat sound you normally get over the telephone.

If you want to get really artsy, you can use a filter to intercut from one speaker and location to another within the same scene. This is accomplished by alternating which voice gets filtered. It also helps if you can establish some kind of background noise behind one of the speakers. This makes the intercutting more audibly understandable because the background noise suddenly becomes louder when we cut to that speaker, whose voice also is no longer filtered.

Any vocal effects beyond those two are used infrequently. In science fiction radiodramas, a device called a vocodor is used to give a weird, alien texture to the speaker's voice. (A vocodor is basically an electronic synthesizer, the difference being that you're running a voice, instead of music, through it.) Other effects are often simply improvised. In *Alien Worlds*, a syndicated radiodrama series, my producer wanted to simulate the effect of two people speaking across space via a radio. But nothing seemed to give it an authentic texture. In the end, he solved the problem by purchasing a small CB radio set, with the transmitter in one studio, the receiver by a microphone in the control room, and the second actor beside a standard microphone in a second studio, wearing a headphone that piped in the other voice. In order to do some intercutting, the producer had the actors exchange places and go through the scene again. Later he spliced together portions of each track, giving the effect of switching from one speaker to another as they communicated via radio.

(The only times this became a difficulty were either when the actor didn't understand that you're supposed to let go of the *Talk* button *after* you've finished speaking, or we started picking up voices that had nothing to do with the script. In fact, on one occasion the receiver refused to pick up the signals from a transmitter that was only as far as the next room—which, in a studio that prided itself on having state-of-the-art equipment, led to much gnashing of teeth and chewing of furniture.)

So:

Having covered the various creative and technical elements a radio scripter needs to have at his or her command, we'll take a look at how all this comes together on the printed page.

Formats

Unlike telescripting, which utilizes four different script formats to accommodate differing technical requirements, there are only two standard radiodrama formats, and of those two, one is fading in popularity while the other rises. Since neither of these formats has a formal appellation, we will refer to them here as either *blocked* or *indented*.

The blocked format was modeled after—some say actually adapted from—the script format used in playwriting. This format was used during radiodrama's earliest years and is still in use today, although its popularity is decreasing. The advantage of using a blocked format is that it makes the dialogue easier to read, since the lines are all double-spaced. The disadvantage is that the pages all look exactly the same: There's no indentation to mark the different portions of dialogue, and the pages thus have a tendency to blur together after a while—particularly during a live reading—and it's sometimes difficult for an actor to find his place on the page again if he's been distracted. In addition, there are no provisions in the format for individual scene notations. There are only transitional devices, which can become confusing if there are a number of different scenes in your script.

Here, then, are the typographical requirements for a radiodrama script written in blocked form:

NAMES are typed in all caps, and appear 10 picas from the left edge of the page.

Sound effects, music cues, and transitional devices are all placed 10 picas from the left, and are written in the following fashion, with each entry underlined: SOUND: A PAIR OF FOOTSTEPS; MUSIC: A DRAMATIC STAB; and TRANSITION: MUSIC or TRANSITION: SOUND OF AIRPLANE UNDER MUSIC.

All dialogue appears between 23 and 75 picas and is written in upper- and lower-case letters. If there is more than one paragraph in a speaker's dialogue, the next paragraph is not indented. You simply move on to the next double-spaced line and continue.

The first page of your script begins with the title of the series written IN ALL CAPS in the center of the page, 8 spaces from the top. The *Title* is underlined, written in upper- and lower-case letters, and appears 2 spaces below the series title, to differentiate between the name of the episode and the series in which it appears.

The first actual line of your script begins 10 lines below the episode title. Each page thereafter begins with the first line of dialogue 8 spaces from the top of the page. The page numbers appear 4 spaces from the top at 75 picas.

If a line of dialogue or any part of a speaker's line is carried over to the following page, it is indicated by writing (CONT'D) at the very end of the last line of dialogue appearing on that page. On the next page, (CONT'D) is written again in the space normally reserved for the first actual word of dialogue.

Having established the typographical parameters of a blocked script, we'll now take a look at how that translates into a typed page, after which we'll use the blocked format in bringing our scene between Frank and George to life. (See Fig. 18 through 20.)

And there we have it. In managing the transition from the largely visual to the exclusively auditory, we've now killed old George off in both television and radio.

The indented format owes much for its development to two-column telescripting, and looks very different from the blocked format. One reason why it seems to be becoming the industry standard is that it's simply easier to work with. The written material is clear, uncluttered, easy to read, far more efficient, times out to one minute a page more consistently than the blocked format and, well, it just *looks* niftier. The only real disadvantage to an indented format is that all the dialogue is single-spaced, and if your cast is limited to an unrehearsed reading it might lead to a few slips.

The typographical rules for an indented format are somewhat more complex than the blocked version, and adhere to these dimensions:

NAMES are capitalized and placed 8 spaces from the left margin. An indication for a NARRATOR is also capitalized, but placed at 13 picas.

Dialogue, when spoken by any of the characters, is written in upper- and lower-case letters and appears between 35 and 75 picas. In order to separate it from the rest of the dialogue, narration is written in all caps.

Sound effects are enclosed by parentheses, using a mixture of lower- and upper-case letters in a pattern like these: (SFX: PNEUMATIC DOOR opens right/closes) and (SFX: Single female FOOTSTEPS enter). The key here is to capitalize only the essential element(s) in your direction. If your script calls for several effects in a row, then you single-space between each direction.

Music cues are placed at 13 picas, blocked by parentheses, and

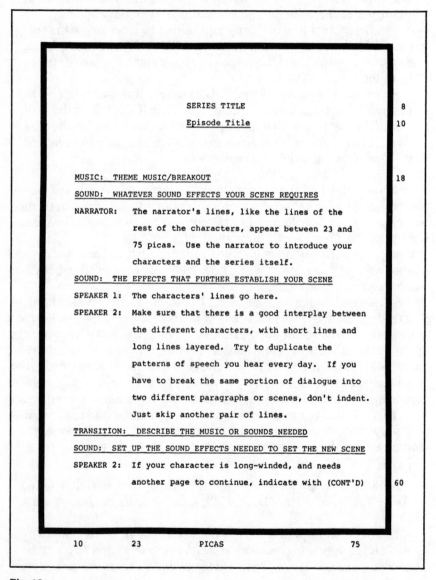

Fig. 18

written in standard upper- and lower-case letters, as in (Dramatic Music Open) or (Theme Music Up and Out with a Flourish).

Double-space between any given sound effect and any music cue.

Triple-space between lines of dialogue from two different characters, between dialogue and sound effects, and between dialogue and music cues.

The first page begins with the series title capitalized, centered on

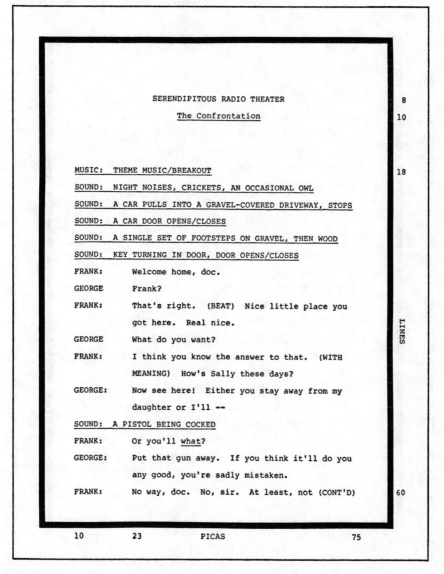

```
                    SERENDIPITOUS RADIO THEATER                    8

                         The Confrontation                        10



        MUSIC:  THEME MUSIC/BREAKOUT                               18

        SOUND:  NIGHT NOISES, CRICKETS, AN OCCASIONAL OWL

        SOUND:  A CAR PULLS INTO A GRAVEL-COVERED DRIVEWAY, STOPS

        SOUND:  A CAR DOOR OPENS/CLOSES

        SOUND:  A SINGLE SET OF FOOTSTEPS ON GRAVEL, THEN WOOD

        SOUND:  KEY TURNING IN DOOR, DOOR OPENS/CLOSES

        FRANK:  Welcome home, doc.

        GEORGE  Frank?

        FRANK:  That's right.  (BEAT)  Nice little place you

                got here.  Real nice.

        GEORGE  What do you want?

        FRANK:  I think you know the answer to that.  (WITH

                MEANING)  How's Sally these days?

        GEORGE: Now see here!  Either you stay away from my

                daughter or I'll --

        SOUND:  A PISTOL BEING COCKED

        FRANK:  Or you'll what?

        GEORGE: Put that gun away.  If you think it'll do you

                any good, you're sadly mistaken.

        FRANK:  No way, doc.  No, sir.  At least, not (CONT'D)    60
```

LINES

```
        10      23       PICAS                          75
```

Fig. 19

the page, underlined and placed 8 lines from the top of the page. The episode title appears 3 spaces lower, at 11 lines.

The first actual line of the script begins 17 lines from the top of the page.

Acts and scenes are indicated and numbered in sequence. These indicators are placed at 8 picas, written in upper- and lower-case letters, and are underlined. Two spaces below the act/scene indica-

---

Confrontation   2   4

FRANK: (CONT'D) just yet. First, me and Sally, we're   8
              gonna have us a little fun. Just like old
              times, y'know?

GEORGE: You lay your stinking hands on my daughter one
              more time, and I'll kill you, I swear it!

FRANK: (LAUGHING) Right. You're gonna hurt me. What
              are you gonna do, doc? You figure on turning
              into a man overnight?

GEORGE   Why, you --

FRANK: Stay back! I'm warning you!

SOUND: A GUNSHOT

GEORGE: (A GASP)

SOUND: A BODY FALLING TO THE FLOOR

TRANSITION: A SHORT STAB, THEN DARK, MOODY MUSIC

SOUND: A POLICE RADIO MURMURING IN THE BACKGROUND UNDER

SOUND: SEVERAL PEOPLE MOVING AROUND, MUTTERING, ALSO UNDER

OFFICER: Then after you arrived, what happened?

SHEILA: Well, officer, I opened the door behind us and
              there on the floor -- (SOBS) -- my father --

OFFICER: I know this isn't easy, ma'am, but we're going
              to need this information if we're ever going to
              figure out what happened. Now, did you notice
              if anything was missing -- jewels, cash?

SHEILA: No. Everything seems to be here.   60

            10   23   PICAS   75

Fig. 20

tor, you briefly describe the location, which is written in upper- and lower-case letters, and blocked by parentheses. Single-space between the location description and a subsequent sound effect, and double-space between it and a music cue, should it follow immediately.

Each subsequent page begins with the page number in the upper right-hand corner of the page, 4 spaces from the top at 75 picas. A condensed version of the title—preferably only one or two words—appears in all caps, 4 lines from the top at 8 picas.

The act/scene indicator is also placed at the top of each subsequent page at 8 picas, 8 spaces from the top of the page. This shows that the scene is continued onto the new page, and would be written as *Act 1, Scene 2 (cont)*. If your scene begins at the top of the page, then don't bother with the (cont). Three spaces below the act/scene indicator (11 spaces from the top of the page) your first line of the script per se begins.

I know, I know . . . it sounds confusing as hell. Actually, though, when you see it written out, it isn't all that scary-looking.

In order to facilitate this, we'll put the prologue and teaser of "Encounter at Twilight" into the indented script format. (As a footnote, it might be worth mentioning that the script was originally sold using the indented format.) As you read the narrator's lines, it might profit you just a little to imagine the words being spoken by Richard Basehart, since he was the one cast in that role. (See Fig. 21 through 24.)

A few notes on the script:

First, a teaser in radiodrama is not at all like a teaser for television. Rather, a prologue is most like a television teaser (and all three of them are least like a giraffe). A radiodrama teaser is played by the individual station throughout the day to entice unwary listeners into tuning in the program that evening. It is separate from the program itself, and need not be heard in order to fully understand the actual program. (A good teaser also gets the *producer's* attention, so while not required, a teaser can be included to help make the sale.)

Second, the prologue does a number of important things. It reintroduces the audience to the mysteries of the sea. In this way, it sets up a nice tension, because the listener just *knows* that whatever happened to those early ships is going to happen again tonight: *Somebody's* gonna catch hell, and it'll probably be the *Trident*. The prologue introduces the ship, gives its location, tells what kind of sub it is, and so forth. It paints a word picture, with the help of a couple of simple sound effects, of the ship moving through the water. Later, through use of a filter, it places the listener in the control room, where he or she is listening in to the observer's report from the ship's deck.

This is one of those nifty things about being a writer: somehow finding a means of conveying information without being expository. Peters is stationed on the sub's deck for the sole purpose of reporting what he sees. So when he begins to describe the strange wall out on the ocean's surface, it's natural, and it doesn't sound like "Here is the author telling you what's happening." Instead, we have a character who is quite naturally describing something extraordinary. That is the imperative thing to re-

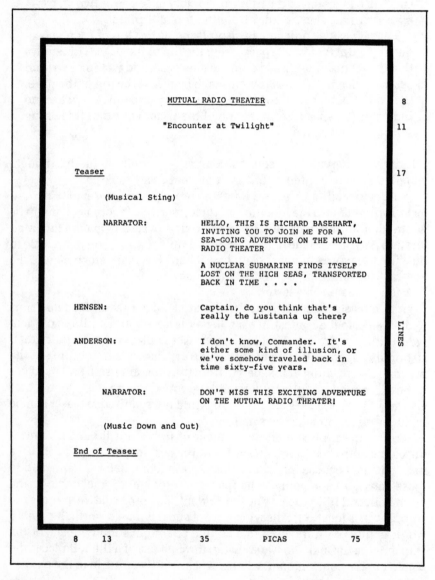

```
                    MUTUAL RADIO THEATER                        8

                   "Encounter at Twilight"                     11


        Teaser                                                  17

              (Musical Sting)

                  NARRATOR:            HELLO, THIS IS RICHARD BASEHART,
                                       INVITING YOU TO JOIN ME FOR A
                                       SEA-GOING ADVENTURE ON THE MUTUAL
                                       RADIO THEATER

                                       A NUCLEAR SUBMARINE FINDS ITSELF
                                       LOST ON THE HIGH SEAS, TRANSPORTED
                                       BACK IN TIME . . . .

              HENSEN:                  Captain, do you think that's
                                       really the Lusitania up there?
                                                                           L
                                                                           I
              ANDERSON:                I don't know, Commander.  It's      N
                                       either some kind of illusion, or    E
                                       we've somehow traveled back in      S
                                       time sixty-five years.

                  NARRATOR:            DON'T MISS THIS EXCITING ADVENTURE
                                       ON THE MUTUAL RADIO THEATER!

              (Music Down and Out)

        End of Teaser


       8      13                35            PICAS              75
```

Fig. 21

member about using characters to paint a scene—they only discuss the unusual. What does Peters say about the surrounding sea prior to the wall's appearance? "Same old sea." Nothing more is needed. If he were to describe the whitecaps, the clouds, the birds and so on, it would not only sound artificial, but Caulder, being the good officer he is, would cut Peters off abruptly.

Finally, the prologue sets up the presence of the two main characters,

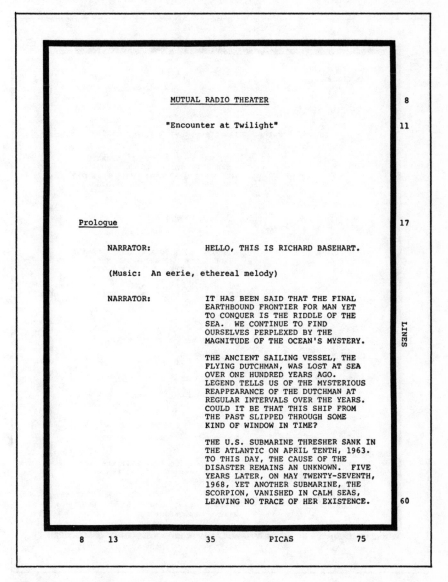

```
                        MUTUAL RADIO THEATER                    8

                        "Encounter at Twilight"                 11



        Prologue                                                17


            NARRATOR:           HELLO, THIS IS RICHARD BASEHART.

        (Music:  An eerie, ethereal melody)

            NARRATOR:           IT HAS BEEN SAID THAT THE FINAL
                                EARTHBOUND FRONTIER FOR MAN YET
                                TO CONQUER IS THE RIDDLE OF THE
                                SEA.  WE CONTINUE TO FIND
                                OURSELVES PERPLEXED BY THE
                                MAGNITUDE OF THE OCEAN'S MYSTERY.

                                THE ANCIENT SAILING VESSEL, THE
                                FLYING DUTCHMAN, WAS LOST AT SEA
                                OVER ONE HUNDRED YEARS AGO.
                                LEGEND TELLS US OF THE MYSTERIOUS
                                REAPPEARANCE OF THE DUTCHMAN AT
                                REGULAR INTERVALS OVER THE YEARS.
                                COULD IT BE THAT THIS SHIP FROM
                                THE PAST SLIPPED THROUGH SOME
                                KIND OF WINDOW IN TIME?

                                THE U.S. SUBMARINE THRESHER SANK IN
                                THE ATLANTIC ON APRIL TENTH, 1963.
                                TO THIS DAY, THE CAUSE OF THE
                                DISASTER REMAINS AN UNKNOWN.  FIVE
                                YEARS LATER, ON MAY TWENTY-SEVENTH,
                                1968, YET ANOTHER SUBMARINE, THE
                                SCORPION, VANISHED IN CALM SEAS,
                                LEAVING NO TRACE OF HER EXISTENCE.  60


        8      13              35        PICAS        75
```

Fig. 22

Captain Anderson and Commander Hensen, by mentioning them, and further heightens the suspense by having Peters say he has an uneasy feeling about whatever's out there. This is what's unofficially known as the "Uh, ohs": The audience, having been primed for something to happen, sees the protagonists hurtling headlong into the upcoming peril, and collectively mutters "Uh, oh!" When the narrator caps the whole thing off with the declaration that the *Trident* is definitely heading for big

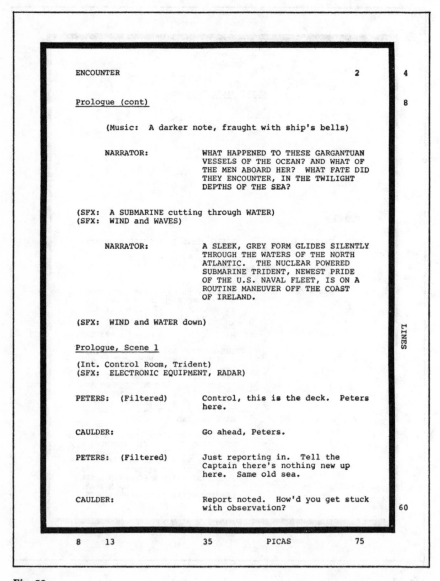

ENCOUNTER   2   4

Prologue (cont)   8

            (Music: A darker note, fraught with ship's bells)

            NARRATOR: WHAT HAPPENED TO THESE GARGANTUAN
                                   VESSELS OF THE OCEAN? AND WHAT OF
                                   THE MEN ABOARD HER? WHAT FATE DID
                                   THEY ENCOUNTER, IN THE TWILIGHT
                                   DEPTHS OF THE SEA?

(SFX: A SUBMARINE cutting through WATER)
(SFX: WIND and WAVES)

            NARRATOR: A SLEEK, GREY FORM GLIDES SILENTLY
                                   THROUGH THE WATERS OF THE NORTH
                                   ATLANTIC. THE NUCLEAR POWERED
                                   SUBMARINE TRIDENT, NEWEST PRIDE
                                   OF THE U.S. NAVAL FLEET, IS ON A
                                   ROUTINE MANEUVER OFF THE COAST
                                   OF IRELAND.

(SFX: WIND and WATER down)

Prologue, Scene 1

(Int. Control Room, Trident)
(SFX: ELECTRONIC EQUIPMENT, RADAR)

PETERS: (Filtered)   Control, this is the deck. Peters
                                 here.

CAULDER: Go ahead, Peters.

PETERS: (Filtered)   Just reporting in. Tell the
                                 Captain there's nothing new up
                                 here. Same old sea.

CAULDER: Report noted. How'd you get stuck
                                 with observation?   60

      8   13   35   PICAS   75

Fig. 23

trouble—and that that's only the *beginning* of their troubles—you've created a situation in which the audience is stuck. They can't leave. You've hooked them, and now they're in for the duration . . . provided that the remainder of the script is worthwhile.

The satisfaction of pulling off a scene like this, of knowing you've crafted a neat little spiderweb of dramatic action, is one of the most attractive things about radiodrama. You really have to use all your wits to

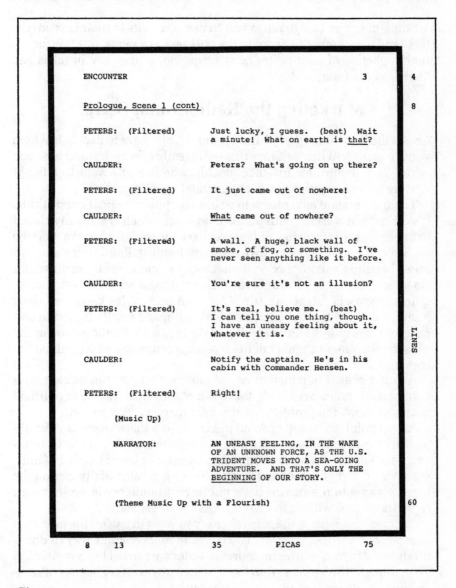

Fig. 24

successfully con an audience into thinking they can see something that isn't there, and doing it well is frankly an awful lot of fun. Radiodrama is simple yet challenging, as vast as the imagination, less technical than television, and free of television's heavy-handed bureaucracy. As we'll discuss a little later, it's something you can even do on your own, with a modest degree of competency. It's a vibrant, exciting medium, and one in which you've got to have your wits about you if you want to make a go of it.

Something else that requires you to use your wits to their best advantage (and this is what's known in the business as a *segue*, folks) is the actual marketing of your radiodrama script. So, as they say in rehearsal, "Let's take it from the top."

Marketing the Radiodrama Script

One of the first things that you as a radio scripter have to decide is whom you are going to write for, since this will greatly affect what and how you write. You should, for instance, decide whether you want to attempt writing for commercial or noncommercial (public) radio.

There are several advantages to writing for public radio. For one thing, it's easier than working with public television, which is generally closed to freelance scriptwriters—unless you have the soul of a bookkeeper, the patience of a saint, and your own source of funding. Public television is a mind-bogglingly complex system that, to quote radio scriptwriter Douglas (*Hitchhiker's Guide to the Galaxy*) Adams on a similar topic, requires proposals "signed in triplicate, sent in, sent back, queried, lost, found, subjected to public inquiry, lost again, and finally buried in soft peat for three months and recycled as firelighters." Public radio, on the other hand, offers a number of freelance opportunities with minimal bureaucratic red tape.

Another benefit of noncommercial radio is that you can tackle topics commercial radio wouldn't touch—metaphysical themes, political points of view, the problems of the handicapped, and so forth.

A final point to remember about public radio is that a writer isn't firmly locked into a particular structure. Because there are no commercial interruptions, you can divide the script into a greater or lesser number of individual acts, and you need not work quite so hard at initially getting the listener's attention, since the basic public radio audience is familiar with radiodrama and willing to give it a chance to get started.

Once you've defined the general area you want to try for, the next step is to select a particular series. The best and most obvious way of doing this is to listen to whatever radiodrama series are carried in your vicinity. First, though, you've got to find them, which might either be easy or rather difficult, depending on the circumstances.

Ideally, you should start by glancing through your local newspaper. Many daily papers carry radio log listings that provide information about what stations carry radiodrama, and what times and days they're aired. Should this lead to a dead end, call up the reporter who normally covers television and radio, and find out if he or she knows offhand of any stations carrying radiodrama in your community. In most cases, such a person will generally be able to point you in the right direction. Should this *also* fail to pan out, then you'll have to exercise a little ingenuity, and work backwards for a while. For instance, you might just decide to track down *CBS Mystery Theater*, which would require finding out which radio station in your area is a CBS affiliate, and then calling the station or listening to it regularly until you bump into the show, or a promo for it. The same technique may work for any other radiodrama series that you know is networked, including public radio series. If a series is syndicated rather than networked, your best bet is simply to write the series' main office (assuming you can find it) and ask for the list of stations carrying the program.

One factor that might be of some assistance to you both in marketing and writing is the tendency for radiodrama series to cluster around a specific genre. If, for example, you have a flair for mystery or suspense, concentrate on the aforementioned *CBS Mystery Theater*. If you've developed several ideas for dramas set in the American Southwest, *Enchantment Radio Theater* might be right for you. Should you wish to adapt a literary classic to radiodrama, contact public radio's *Masterpiece Radio Theater*.

The last means of finding a radiodrama series open to freelancers is to check *Writer's Digest* magazine and *Writer's Market* on a regular basis. The former contains new listings published whenever they come in; the latter is updated yearly.

Once you've targeted a series—particularly if you've done so on your own, without recourse to the publications just mentioned—you should immediately attempt to answer these questions:

After listening to several episodes of the series, do you find the same writer or writers being repeated? If so, there's a good chance the show is staff-written. This doesn't mean you have no chance at all, but it does mean you should be prepared for a rougher ride.

Is it an anthology series, or does it utilize a set of running characters who populate each episode? If so, study the characters and make sure you catch all those little nuances of characterization in your own script.

Does the series revolve around a particular theme, such as mystery, science fiction, adventure, or Old West topics? If so, submit your script accordingly. Don't send a science fiction script to a producer who only wants dramas set in Nevada in 1897.

Does the program use a lot of special effects and music (the sure sign of a high budget) or a bare minimum? If it's the former, you have a lot more latitude in what you can call for in the script; if the latter, use restraint.

Is the program locally produced? Many are, and more are starting every day. Should this be the case, slant your script toward the community, with the script's action taking place at spots well-known in that community. A sense of regionalism never hurts when dealing with local radio-dramas.

Does the program have an "old radio" sound to it? If so, it's a fair bet the producer uses the blocked format. (Another good indication is the producer having been in the business for a number of years, if you recognize his name from your research in old radio.)

Is the series a Writers Guild signatory? If it is, then expect a little more resistance than you might encounter otherwise, since as a rule, WGA signatories can use only Guild writers. However, they can use a non-Guild writer once—provided he joins the Guild at that time—so don't give up hope. Happily, most radiodrama series are *not* Guild signatories, which is good news for the beginning freelancer. (Note: You can only find out whether the series is a signatory by querying the producer.)

After you've answered these questions, you should have enough information to begin putting a few ideas together. As you do this, it's important to keep your developing ideas within the parameters of what your target series usually produces. This is called common sense. At the same time, however, make sure that you are *actively interested* in the idea gestating somewhere in the back of your mind. If you're slipping a moral into it somewhere, be sure it's something that you believe in. If you're just putting in a moral to be Socially Relevant . . . forget it. It'll sound preachy and obvious. At the same time, don't write something commercial only for the sake of writing something that will sell, because that's how schlock is produced. Write what you know, what you believe in, what you *want* to write. This is called not selling out. More than that, however, it's necessary for your creative impetus that you want to write the script you've selected. If it isn't something you're enthusiastic about, then the task of writing will be just that, a task, a weight, soemthing you *have* to do whether you like it or not. This is not a Good Thing, and it will leave you feeling frustrated and unhappy with your lot.

Besides . . . what's the point in being a writer if you don't *enjoy* what you do? Put very simply, that's dumb. Period.

When you've finally settled upon an idea that looks good, go ahead and write a treatment (just as we did in the television chapter) and the *first two acts* of the actual script. Do not write more than that. Here's why: Writing the first two acts gets you going, it gets you well into the story, and assures you that you will be able to finish it at a later date. (Trust me—if your idea is going to crap out on you, it will do so well before the end of the second act.) You don't have to write more than that because in most instances the producer won't want to see more than the first two acts and a treatment for the whole program, so why put in that much time on something that, if he decides not to go with it, won't be produced?

However, if—knowing the risks—you *want* to go ahead and finish the script rather than wait until later, I won't hire a sniper to crouch in a tree outside your window to stop you. Any writing you do will, in the long run, be good for you, which is why writing even the first two acts is beneficial to you as well as to the producer.

When you've completed your first two acts and treatment, the next step is contacting the producer. This can be done simply by calling the local station that carries your target series and asking the program manager for the address of the production company, and the producer's name (if it isn't aired during the regular broadcast). Armed with this final bit of information, you now come to the actual, physical marketing of your script.

In brief, it's time to write your query letter.

A query letter to a radiodrama producer is similar to the query addressed to a television producer. It should state, in no more than a single page, your familiarity with and appreciation of the series; your knowledge of radiodrama formats and technical requirements; the fact that you have written two acts of a finished script, and a treatment that covers the entire episode; and that you would appreciate the opportunity to send the script and treatment along for his or her examination on a speculative basis. Once again, do not put your concept into the query letter, because of the possible threat to the producer of a plagiarism lawsuit. Not only that, but the surest sign of an amateur—and I use that word in the worst possible sense, to convey a certain kind of alleged mentality—is a letter that says basically "I've got this neat idea, here it is, now how much do you want to pay me?" Your letter may not read in exactly that fashion, but the inclusion of your idea is enough to trigger the knee jerk response to amateurs found in most producers and their assistants.

In closing your query letter, you might also want to inquire whether there is a preferred script format used by the show (be prepared for a retyping if so); and if a release form is required when submitting manuscripts (they usually are), would he please forward one for your use. (Most radio release forms read the same as the general purpose one used in this book, so when you receive the release, you might want to check it against this one just to make sure what you're signing is legitimate.)

As you write the query letter, and throughout the waiting period that follows—usually two to three weeks—keep repeating the following to yourself: *Radiodrama needs new writers.* Not only will that keep you sane during the intervening weeks, it's also true, which is better than just being reassuring.

How desperate are producers for original material?

Glad you asked.

Earlier in this chapter, I mentioned *Alien Worlds*, a nationally syndicated science-fiction radiodrama series carried on more than 200 stations across the United States. The producer of *Alien Worlds* grew so desperate for new material that he undertook a massive nationwide search for scriptwriters. He took out advertisements in newspapers and magazines, he gave interviews, he hustled, he had meetings, he gave talks, he looked high, he looked low . . . you get the idea.

Now, I had heard of *Alien Worlds*, but had never listened to the program. For that matter, I had never written a radiodrama script in my entire life. Like many writers, I thought the medium had gone on to join the furry goldfish in communal extinction. But when I heard the producer was looking for new writers (I was not a Guild member at the time, and they were not Guild signatories), I sent off a query letter, figuring I had nothing to lose, and probably wouldn't hear anything anyway.

In my letter, I expressed my intimate familiarity with the medium of radiodrama and specifically with their show. To read my letter, you'd think I had never missed a single episode of the two-year-old series. Admittedly, that was slightly less than factual. I may have exaggerated just a little. Well, maybe more than just a little.

Anyway, less than two weeks later, I heard from the producer, Lee Hansen. He wanted to see a sample script, using the continuing characters that appeared weekly in *Alien Worlds*.

Let me tell you something—you don't know the *meaning* of the word *panic* unless you've seen a budding scriptwriter, foot entrenched solidly in mouth, desperately scrambling to lay his grimy little paws on any available copy of *Alien Worlds* that could be begged, borrowed, taped off the air, or swiped.

Making a long story short: More than 200 writers, myself included, submitted material to *Alien Worlds*. After the producer eliminated those who did not have a grasp of radiodrama techniques, those who couldn't tell a reasonable story, those whose dialogue was stiff and rancid, those whose ideas of science fiction hadn't progressed past the 1950s and those who didn't understand the characters, only two writers remained. Of those two, only one ever sold any scripts to *Alien Worlds*.

Me. I went on to make nearly half a dozen sales to *Alien Worlds*, became a Guild member, then went on to write for the Mutual Radio Network and others. And just for the record, what eliminated nearly all of the potential scriptwriters from consideration was that while they may have known how to write a television script, they did not understand what went into a radio script, which is precisely the predicament we mentioned at the start of this chapter and the gap this book is attempting to close.

(How did *I* pull it off, you ask? By having a close friend or two who *did* know what went into a radiodrama script, and by simply flat-out bluffing my way in. Then, after getting in the front door, I worked as hard as I could to learn all that could be learned about radiodrama, so that no one would ever catch on to the fact that for the first scripts I was only guessing at what was later to become my craft.

(Luckily, the early scripts were good, because frankly, sheer bravado is *never* enough. All the *chutzpah* in the world won't compensate for bad writing. For the record, I do *not* recommend this approach to anyone else.)

End of example, and end of confession.

When you finally hear from the producer, you will receive one of two answers: yes or no. *No* usually can mean: no, we don't take freelance scripts; or no, we're booked up right now, and don't need any scripts for a while (in which case you should try again at a later date); or no, and we're not going to say any more than that, get what you can out of our form rejection letter. Those are the worst rejections, and should you receive a form rejection, stick it up on your dart board, think ill thoughts about the producer's lineage, and move on to the next series.

Yes means: *Yes,* but don't get your hopes up. It means that you should send along your script and treatment—unless the producer specifically asks to see only the treatment—and wait as patiently as possible.

When the producer finally responds to your manuscript submission, there are a number of possible replies, including:

A form rejection. Get your dart board out again.

A not-quite-for-us rejection. This is an open door. Write the producer, stating that you'd like to develop another idea and send it along, if that would not be an inconvenience. If he says that it is, then don't push the matter. If not, then go for it.

An it-doesn't-quite-ring-true rejection with suggestions for improvement. Again, this is an open door. Write the producer immediately, informing him you will rewrite your script to incorporate the suggestions made in his letter, and then resubmit it. If he likes the general idea, he'll say okay. If not, and he still thinks you're just a little off-target, he'll tell you to forget the original idea and develop another. Do so.

A sorta-kinda rejection. This is where the producer says he likes your writing style, your flair with dialogue and characterization, and suggests that although the present story is not quite right, he would be happy to look at another script. This is an even-wider open door. Leap through it.

A conditional acceptance. He likes the first two acts, and the treatment seems solid. So he will most likely suggest that you go ahead and finish the script on a speculative basis. If the rest of it lives up to the expectations raised by the first two acts, he'll buy it. If not, he'll probably buy the idea—giving you story credit—and suggest you try another script. Either way, you've got a sale.

A complete acceptance. You receive a check in the mail for the first two acts, and a few suggestions for the rest of the script, with the balance payable upon completion of the script. Your response: Xerox the check, cash the original, and go out to dinner with your Significant Other. Then get straight home and get to work, because you've just been handed a marvelous opportunity.

Those are the parameters of response, from worst possible scenario to the best. If you get rejected, don't take it personally. Try again, and/or try elsewhere. If you get accepted, well, here are a few things you should know about and prepare yourself for.

First, be advised that most radiodrama scripts are purchased as a *work for hire*. This means the produced script is copyrighted in the name of the production company, and the company owns all the radio rights. Most work-for-hire agreements mention ancillary rights only briefly, and should you, for example, later desire to write a short story, play, or telescript based on your radio script, there usually isn't much of a problem in this. In most instances, you need only secure the producer's permission, although occasionally, depending on the terms of your agreement, the producer may require a percentage or fee. This is, however, the exception to the rule.

What follows is the text of a standard work-for-hire contract. If your producer purchases scripts on such a basis—and again, not all do—you will be asked to sign a contract similar to this one. If the particular agreement you receive specifically places all other rights beyond just the radio rights in the producer's hands, and if you would like to do a version of your story for another medium at a later date, then the best thing to do is simply tell your producer this, and see if you can work out an amendment permitting you to pursue your intention. My own experience has indicated that in most instances both sides can be accommodated.

Here, then, is the text of a standard work-for-hire agreement for a purchased radiodrama script:

Assignment of Radio Rights

This Assignment is made and entered into as of this _____ day of _____, _____ by _____ (herein "Writer") and _____ (herein "Producer").

WHEREAS, Producer is the sole creator of that certain original concept, format and idea for and the individual producer of a series of dramatic plays (hereinafter sometimes referred to severally, collectively and singly, as the context may require, as the "Program(s)"); and

WHEREAS, Producer has the exclusive license to use, deal in and exploit all, but only, the Radio Rights (as hereinafter defined) in and to the Program(s) (said Radio Rights include the right to produce, broadcast, advertise and exploit one or more radio programs or radio program series based on or suggested by the Program(s)); and

WHEREAS, Writer (has been and) currently is employed by Producer as a writer in connection with certain episodes of the Program (such episodes of the Program which Writer (has written or) may in the future write are hereinafter referred to as the "Episodes", which Episodes are now and will in the future be works made for hire under the United States Copyright Act; and

WHEREAS, pursuant to the License Agreement, Producer owns and shall own all rights, titles, and interests of every kind and nature in, to, and with respect to the Programs, as aforesaid;

NOW, THEREFORE, for good and valuable consideration, receipt of which is hereby acknowledged, Writer agrees as follows:

1. Writer hereby assigns to Producer, with respect to his Radio Rights, all said rights, title and interest in, to and with respect to the Episodes, any and all thereof, and any and all parts thereof, including, without limitation, all material, works, writings, ideas, "gags," dialogue, and characters, written, composed, prepared, submitted or interpolated by Writer in and in connection with the writing, preparation and production of the Episodes (hereinafter sometimes referred to severally, collectively and singly, as the context may require, as the "Material").

2. Writer acknowledges and agrees that, subject only to the Radio Rights licensed by Producer as aforesaid, Producer owns and shall own all the right, title, and interest in, to and with respect to the Episodes, the Program(s) and the Material, any and all thereof, and any and all parts thereof, all of which are automatically and shall automatically become the property of Producer.

3. Any and all of the rights assigned to Producer pursuant to this instrument shall be and are fully transferable and assignable by Producer, in whole or in part, without any restriction whatsoever.

4. Writer hereby represents and warrants that:

(a) He has the full right and authority, subject to the Radio Rights licensed by Producer, as aforesaid, to transfer and assign all of his rights, title and interest in, to and with respect to the Episodes to Producer;

(b) The Episodes are in all respects wholly original with Writer;

(c) The exercise of any of the rights granted pursuant to this Agreement or the use of any or all of the Episodes or any parts thereof will not in any way infringe upon or violate the copyright, common law right, or literary, dramatic, or other rights, or constitute a libel, defamation, or invasion of the rights of privacy of, or unfair competition with any person, firm or corporation;

(d) Subject to the Radio Rights licensed by Producer, as aforesaid, he has in no way assigned, conveyed, granted or hypothecated any rights of any kind or character in or to the Episodes, or any part thereof, to any person, firm or corporation other than Producer; and

(e) He is not presently a member of any union, guild or any collective bargaining unit which will require any payments to be made by Producer for or on account of this Assignment (other than the payments made by Producer for Writer's services in connection with the Episodes as aforesaid).

5. Writer shall defend, indemnify and hold harmless Producer and Producer's assignees, successors and transferrees, and each of them, if any, from and against any and all claims, demands, damages, obligations, costs, expenses, liens, actions and causes of action (including attorneys' fees, whether or not litigation is actually commenced) of every kind and nature whatsoever, arising out of a breach or alleged breach of any of Writer's representations or warranties contained herein.

6. Writer acknowledges and agrees that the compensation paid to Writer by Producer shall be full and complete compensation for Writer's services in con-

nection with the Episodes, and that Producer shall have no obligation whatsoever to pay Writer or any other person, firm or corporation on Writer's behalf (including, without limitation, any union, guild or other collective bargaining unit) any amounts for or in connection with the Episodes or any exploitation or use thereof. Further, Writer agrees that Producer has and shall have no obligation to utilize all or any part of the Episodes or to make, produce, release, distribute, advertise or exploit the Programs, the Episodes, or any other play or program based upon or which uses in any manner the Episodes or otherwise.

7. The provisions of this Agreement shall be binding upon Writer, his heirs, executors and administrators.

8. This Assignment shall be construed and interpreted pursuant to the law of the State of _____.

9. This Agreement contains the full and complete understanding between the parties hereto, supersedes all prior agreements and understandings, whether written or oral, pertaining thereto, and cannot be modified except by written instrument signed by the parties hereto.

IN WITNESS WHEREOF, Writer and Producer have executed this Assignment on the day and year first written above.

WRITER_____

PRODUCER_____

If that sounds extraordinarily complex, well, that's because it *is* extraordinarily complex. The upshot of it all, however, is simply this: That you wrote the episode, that you own all non-radio rights to it, that it won't get the producer dragged into a lawsuit of some sort, and that the producer owns all radio rights to your script. This particular agreement is ideal, since it specifically deals only with the radio rights, and thereby puts the writer in the position of someday turning out a version of the script in another medium. (This was the case with Arthur Kopit's *Wings*, which was commissioned as a radio play for the BBC, and which later went on to become a considerable success on the legitimate stage.)

The amount of money you are likely to receive from the sale of a radio-drama script can vary considerably. The range can go from $75 to $900 for a half-hour script, and from $1,000 to $2,000 for a one-hour script. The extent of your payment is almost always a function of the overall budget for the series. It it's a national program, whether syndicated or networked, you can usually count on receiving a fairly substantial amount. If, on the other hand, the show is based at a local station—and there are more and more of these popping up daily—then the odds are pretty good your payment will be less. The important thing to remember, though, is that at first, the amount of money isn't important. That some sort of compensation is made, preferably of a financial nature, is important, yes. But the *most* essential thing is to get that first production under your belt. Once that's been done, and as you've learned more about radio-drama as an art form, then the more prepared you'll be, and the easier it'll be, to move on to the higher-paying markets.

Besides, even if they can only afford to pay you in used tea bags, the greatest joy of all is in actually hearing your radiodrama come to life before your very eyes . . . er, that is, your very ears.

In addition, after you've made your first sale, that same producer is very likely to come to you again for more scripts, and will often refer you to other producers while recommending your services to them. Remember, radiodrama writers are scarce, and when someone discovers a talented writer, it seems that everyone starts beating down his door for material, sometimes on rather short notice. (I once had a producer wave a substantial amount of money in front of my nose for a radiodrama script, provided I could write the whole thing, from start to finish, in two-and-a-half days. They needed it to fill a hole caused by another script that turned out to be unusable. He got his script.)

Once the script has been sold, the agreements signed, and the check deposited in your bank account, there come the usual revisions, discussions, debates over characterizations and cast members, and so forth. You should participate in these and add your own suggestions as often as permitted, without getting obnoxious about the whole affair, and using the opportunity to learn what problems confront the producer, and where you as a writer may be able to minimize them in the future.

Finally, for the scriptwriter who wants to learn as much as possible about radiodrama production, preferably from a hands-on perspective, there is a last alternative that should be considered.

Self-Production

As mentioned at the beginning of this chapter, by the financial standards of television and film, radiodramas are relatively cheap to produce. Assuming you have written a script that does not call for a lot of complex effects and musical scores, it is altogether possible for you to produce your own script. The only ingredients you need to pull this off are the desire to do so, a few talented voices, a multitrack recorder, a tape editor, a good engineer, four or more microphones, and a collection of sound- and music-effect records.

So let's take this one step at a time.

To start with, why would you want to produce your own script? For one thing, it familiarizes you with the problems any producer faces in giving life to a typewritten script. More than that, however, it gives you, as director/producer, complete control over the way your script is interpreted by the cast. It also lets you more fully understand the complete process of radiodrama production, giving you a better idea of the limitations of the medium. It is tremendously exciting. And it is of substantial help when you approach a producer of a syndicated or networked series. He feels more confident utilizing your services since you have established a foothold in the medium, and you have a finished dramatic tape to use as a sample of your work.

After you have decided to go ahead with your own production, you must confront two vital questions: Where will I record it, and who will I get to perform in it? Although those may seem like intimidating questions, the solutions really aren't that difficult.

If you want to spring for the drama yourself, you simply go to any recording studio in your area and tape there. Studio time, at its cheapest, goes for anywhere from $25 to $50 per hour. (You supply your own recording tape.) If you have a cast that's properly rehearsed, and you've already set up your sound effects and music cues in the correct order, you can be in and out of the studio rather quickly. For a half-hour script, you'll probably incur one hour to an hour and a half for the voice track. After the tape has been edited—something you should do away from the studio, with the assistance of someone who knows the process and can help create a finished voice track—you go back in for another two hours or so and lay down the music and sound effects. Total time: three to four hours, again depending upon your state of preparedness.

(We'll get into the technical aspects of producing a radiodrama after we explore the different options for a tape location.)

If your plan is to do a whole series of radiodramas and syndicate them on a barter syndication basis (which we'll also explore later), you might be able to convince the studio to waive a recording fee altogether, provided you promise that if you get a series going after your initial production, you will continue to come to that studio with your business, thereby killing two birds with one microphone: You get a free demonstration tape, and they get the prospect of a steady future customer. (You really have to be a fast talker to pull this off, though.)

If you're not a fast talker, and if you don't have the ready cash to spring on a production, don't despair. There is one remaining alternative: college radio.

College radio stations exist to provide students with experience in radio techniques, and it's been my experience that most of them welcome the opportunity to try something a little different. Since just about every college of substantial size has some sort of radio station—even if it's only one that broadcasts over a two-block radius or through a cable system—you shouldn't have much difficulty finding one in your area. You will admittedly have to deal with college disc jockeys, who tend to be some of the most, ah, unique characters in the broadcasting industry, but at least you'll have a fair number of volunteers able and waiting to work on the project, and a complete studio to work with.

To persuade a college radio station to go along with your project, simply contact the program manager/director—usually a student him- or herself—and explain that what you have in mind is an educational opportunity and all that. Moreover, it will be a credit on the resume of whoever helps out in the project, with said credit also given on the finished tape. Given that broadcasting is a hard industry to crack, and that any credits whatsoever can help someone's prospects after graduation, you probably won't have much of a problem getting a go-ahead. You may, however, have to share producer credit with someone at the station, since some college radio stations insist all productions be under the name of the students using its facilities. But . . . that's show biz.

(Depending upon just *how* fast a talker you are, you might be able to talk a local commercial station into letting you use their facilities, provided that—like the college station—they have the right to broadcast it first, upon completion. This is exceedingly difficult, however, and as such is not wholly recommended here.)

After deciding where you are going to produce your script, the next step is to secure what's known in the industry simply as "The talent." You've got to find your cast members. Peculiar as this may sound, this is probably the *least* of your worries as a producer/director/writer.

To a performer, the single most important thing in the world is the chance to perform, to stretch his or her abilities, to learn, and to acquire a credit or two that might prove helpful in future aspirations. For this reason, many—if not nearly *all*—aspiring actors are willing to perform for no pay at all in community theaters and so forth. You will find this to be the case with your radiodrama production as well. More so, in fact, since the end product of your combined labors will be a tape that the performers can then give to agents, directors, and producers, whereas a credit in a local theater is basically an uninformative paper credit. So you can get a full cast of actors for your show (which should, however, use a minimum of performers) for virtually no money whatsoever. As a personal note, though, having worked with actors and having acted myself, I would highly recommend you dig up some sort of recompense for their labors. Paying for the gasoline they use to and from rehearsals is always a good gesture, and providing each cast member (free of charge) with a cassette recording of the finished show is not only desirable, but essential to keeping good relations with the theatrical community.

After securing your cast and the studio, the single most important element for the production of a decent-sounding radiodrama is the presence of a skilled engineer. I cannot overemphasize the importance of this person. This is the guy who sits at the control board during your taping and should sit at the editing table after the taping, who makes the whole damned thing come together. You must work closely with the engineer and make sure you communicate exactly what you want—how the cast's voices should sound; if you want any electronic effects that can be done during production, like a filter or reverb effect; when you want the voices to fade down or fade up, and so forth. If you explain exactly what you want, and if you have a solid engineer, nine times out of ten you'll get just what you want.

The best way to secure a good engineer is to ask around at the studio or college station. Look for someone who can react quickly, who has worked on live broadcasts, and who has some familiarity, however rudimentary, with radiodrama. When you've found such a person, work hard to persuade him or her to do the tape editing with you as well. If this turns out to be impossible, use the same criteria to find someone skilled at editing tape.

The ancillary equipment, microphones and such, come with the facility you're using. As a rule, it doesn't take much equipment to produce a radiodrama. In fact, I once knew someone who put together a respectable twenty-minute production using a home multitrack recorder, a few microphones, and a handful of friends who volunteered their services as performers and live sound effects people. The result was credible, if simplistic. I recommend this to you only if you happen to own a multitrack recorder, have a lot of talent as an engineer, and come equipped with five arms and six eyes.

Finally, you have to secure your sound effects and music cues. This is also relatively easy. Assuming you've already written the script—a necessity—and you know what effects and music are called for in the script, as well as which ones can be done live as opposed to being edited in later, you need only pay a visit to your local, well-stocked record store and rummage through their sound effects records. Usually, you can find sounds that range from atomic blasts to fly buzzings, and mood music intended for use in radio productions, and therefore free from royalty requirements. (Warning: If you opt to use music from established soundtracks or commercial records, you run two risks. First, you risk the possibility that your listener, recognizing the cut, will be distracted by the memory. Second, should your production ever be aired over a commercial radio station, you may be dunned for royalties for using someone else's music in your show.)

Having attended to all these production-oriented needs, you are now ready to undertake your first radiodrama production. To get started, I recommend the following sequence of events:

1. Select your cast carefully, so that they sound like the people who inhabit your script. Choose them from local theater groups by placing audition notices, and from local colleges the same way. Be gentle, but firm. Don't let anyone you're not really sure of get into your show, because you'll regret it later, I promise you.

2. Rehearse, rehearse, rehearse. Even though your cast will be able to use their scripts during the taping, it's absolutely essential that all the glitches are eliminated before you go into the studio, because each delay during taping will raise the cost of the production, and every flub must be removed during the editing process.

3. Time the script, and be prepared for rewrites. When you do a run-

through of the script with your cast, have them put in the pauses needed by the sound effects and music cues the script calls for. It's necessary for you as the director to know exactly what's needed, and how long each effect will run. If, after a complete reading, you find that the script runs too long, and you can't move the cast through it any faster, start cutting. Cut anything that isn't absolutely necessary to the action, and rewrite where possible those lines the cast members just can't say without tripping over their tongues. Rehearse until you can go through the entire script without a single slip-up.

4. Tape the voice track. Go into the studio, explain to the engineer what you want, and then start the tape rolling. Be ready for flubs, though, no matter how well prepared your cast might be. Remember, it's one thing to read a script in your living room, in the company of friends, and quite another to do the same thing staring at a microphone. Be patient with your actors. Instruct your cast that if a mistake occurs, they should pause silently for two beats, and the person with the flubbed line should back up one or two lines and start again. This eliminates the need to stop and then restart all the recording equipment.

Important note: Be sure the erring cast member goes back to a line that hasn't been "walked on" by someone else. By this, I mean if, in the first run-through, the previous line ended with two people speaking at once, it will severely handicap your efforts to put things together later when you discover you have two different versions of the same line: one with a single speaker, another with two.

5. Edit out the glitches in the voice track. Eliminate the over-long pauses, the stumbles, the flubbed words. This is done by playing the tape on an editing machine and, when you come to the piece of tape containing the error, simply cutting out that piece and splicing together the two remaining ends. When you've finished this—and as someone who's made his fair share of goofs at the editing machine let me reaffirm the importance of a good editor working with you—time the finished tape. If it runs over, you'll have to go back and cut any spoken lines that can possibly be removed without ruining the tape or crippling the drama. It'll hurt, but do it.

6. Put your sound effects in their order of appearance in the script, and transfer them to tape. Do the same for your music cues. Then, when you go back into the studio, you have two options: First, you can record both the voice track and the sound effects onto a separate tape, cuing up each effect as needed, and then later, onto a fourth tape, lay in the music on top of the voices and effects. The problem with this is that each time you re-record a voice, it loses some of its audio quality, and this step requires recording the same voice through two generations. The second option, should you have a really sharp engineer, is to lay both the sound effects and the music cues in simultaneously, so that the voices have been recorded onto only one other generation of tape.

7. Have your finished tape transferred from reel-to-reel to cassette tape, and provide a copy to each of the cast members and the engineer, being sure that everyone's credit has been included on the tape.

8. Throw a party and relax. You're finished.

Well, sort of.

If your only intention was to produce a tape or two for your own experience and education, and for use as a sample of your work, then your efforts stop here. If, however, you have big plans for your show, and want to make a series out of it, you want to take the process one step further, into an arrangement known as *barter syndication*.

The principle behind barter syndication is this: You, as writer/producer, create a half-hour program that runs 24 minutes dry, thereby leaving 6 minutes for commercials. You then approach a sponsor, preferably one with a national product. You tell the sponsor that in return for underwriting the cost of production, he can have all 6 minutes' worth of commercials, which are then pressed on the record along with the radiodrama itself. In exchange, you syndicate the series to a substantial number of radio stations, which broadcast the program and commercials.

The benefits behind this are obvious: For the sponsor to purchase 6 minutes of air time on all the stations that air the drama would cost far more than the cost of simply producing a half-hour show. He saves money, in other words. The participating radio stations get a strings-free radiodrama that they don't have to pay for. And finally, the writer/producer gets a salary, his show is syndicated, and he has the financial capacity to move on to new projects.

This system works with half-hour, one-hour, and even 5-minute radiodramas. (The latter are starting to come into prominence, usually as short comic sketches, but it remains to be seen whether or not the trend continues.)

Those of you who are less adventurous, yet wish to give this technique a whirl, might start with a brief program supported by a local sponsor.

Although barter syndication is usually something a writer/producer gets into only after having been in the radiodrama business for some time, it merits your attention because most of the new radiodrama programs coming down the audio pike these days appear to be functioning on a barter syndication basis, and it would profit anyone entering this business to be aware of this growing trend.

And speaking of growing trends. . . .

A Look Ahead

Judging from current indicators, it does not seem as if the medium of radio will, like television, undergo any radical changes in the coming years . . . except in the following respects.

Because of ever-increasing technology, the ability of radiodrama producers to make their programs sound authentic will continue to grow. Stereo effects and multichannel recorders, synthesizers and vocodors are daily becoming a bigger part of radiodrama production, and given the growing number of audiophiles in the United States, this certainly won't hurt the radiodrama field.

Radio as a medium is also undergoing a subdued revolution, thanks to the cable industry. Just as coaxial cables carry a large number of television channels, they transmit an impressive number of radio channels, too. Many of these stations are willing to experiment and to provide a variety of entertainment options. As the number of stations increases, and the specialties of each become more distinct, it is only natural in the next few decades to expect a significantly higher number of stations providing opportunities for radiodrama.

One of the most promising developments lurking in the future of radiodrama is a distant relative of pay television. As of this writing, an experimental system going under a variety of names—CodeArt in California, for example—is being tested and marketed in selected portions of the United States. The system will allow the direct purchase of audio programs through the use of a cable decoder and tape recorder.

The system works in the following way: A given program—a spoken copy of the day's *Wall Street Journal*, a record, or a dramatic presentation—is scrambled and sent down through a cable to local subscribers. Each program is cablecast at a different time, usually at night when everyone's sleeping. The subscriber chooses what programs he wants to record, sets the decoder to receive only that program or programs, and goes to sleep. The next morning, an audio cassette containing that program is all ready for playing.

The benefits of this system are enormous: It allows program collectors to put together an entire library of audio tapes. Since the decoder monitors which programs are recorded, at a given fee per program, royalties can be paid out of the purchase price to the producer, writer, and cast of a given radiodrama. It is possible to develop programs *only* for this system, called audiodramas, that continue to feed back royalties in the same fashion as a published book.

For these and the other reasons mentioned at the start of this chapter, radiodrama can be expected to see continued growth and expansion, once again becoming a viable part of the entertainment community. Although it will never again be as important, as crucial, as dynamic an entity as it was during the early days of radio—there's no going back, folks, sad as that may be—it will reemerge as a definite source of artistic expression in the coming years.

And freelancers, educated to the basic requirements of radiodrama, will be a very big part of that auditory renaissance.

You have to remember that as soon as you hand in a finished script, the producer says to you, "This is a great script!"
Then they hire two guys to rewrite you.

—Mario Puzo
The Godfather

It's easy to sit at your desk and write in the script, "The desert. Dawn." But five months later, you're waking up at 3 a.m. in a motel outside Flagstaff, wondering what the hell you're doing there.

—Marshall Brickman
Co-author, *Annie Hall*

3.
MOTION PICTURES

It's insidious. It starts in childhood and progresses through adolescence into the adult years. It grows with each hour spent sitting in darkness, hands gripping a tub of buttered popcorn or a box of Raisinets, while the mind—aloft on celluloid wings—travels to a seedy bar in Casablanca, to a freshly opened tomb in Egypt, to a lightning-fraught laboratory in Europe where a massive creature breathes and opens a dull yellow eye, to an otherwise empty room where Fred Astaire is bringing a coatrack to life, and to the unknown reaches of deep space.

It is an abiding fascination with the process of putting pictures on film and, frame by frame, bringing them the gifts of movement and sound. And most of all, it is the thought—rarely expressed for fear of eliciting unintentioned laughter—that says simply, but with conviction, "Someday, *I'm* going to do that!"

If the conviction is strong enough, some—a number that seems to double annually—actually make the attempt. Actors strive to become the next Robert Redford or Diane Keaton, novice directors dream of the day they do the next *Citizen Kane*, and writers, well, writers write. Some of these aspirants fail, often by not realizing that the industry already *has* a Redford and a Keaton, and that *Citizen Kane* has been made by Orson Welles as well as it will *ever* be made. A few others succeed.

And that's the important thing to remember about breaking into the motion picture business. Success and failure are equally possible, and equally indefinable. A writer may sell his scripts, but if they don't say what he wants to say, has he really succeeded at his craft? Another writer's script may be rejected by every studio, year in and year out, but one day someone comes along and sees in that script something precious, something vital, something that by god has *got* to be produced.

Without doubt, the film industry is the screwiest segment of the entire entertainment business, filled with more pitfalls and traps than can possibly be imagined. Yet if you can navigate that maze, the rewards are phenomenal. The thing to remember is that it *can* be done, if you're willing to invest the time, the patience, and most of all, the talent. Newcomers break into the field every day, it seems, and there's no reason why anyone possessing these three qualities should not try and, with the fourth factor—luck—succeed.

This chapter will set forth a few signposts in hope of creating a map of the motion picture industry and show how a gifted writer can become a part of that industry.

Even more than for television and radio, an understanding of the medium's history is vital to making a successful entry into the movie business. The curious and often incomprehensible practices engaged in by people in this business are the *direct consequence* of its history, and if that fact is not understood and implemented, all that follows will be less than meaningless.

So before we sketch a map showing where we are, let's sit down for just a moment and figure out how in the world we got here in the first place.

A Family Tree in Celluloid

The age of motion pictures is generally conceded to have started at the end of the nineteenth century with the invention and subsequent patenting of a device called a Kinetoscope, developed by Thomas Edison. This device allowed a substantial number of photographs to be recorded onto a single strip of negative film. When developed, printed, and replayed at the original recording speed, it created a moving picture. Prior to this time, most examples of motion pictures known to the general public were available only in penny arcades, and consisted of machines that would flip a series of still photographs one atop the other at a rate sufficient to create the illusion of motion.

Naturally, as soon as the process of making motion pictures had become relatively bugproof, the entrepreneurs moved in. Soon there were nickelodeon chains around the country—storefront machines similar to their still-photograph predecessors, but using Edison's newly developed technology. In order to get around paying substantial prices for Edison's contraption, however, many of these entrepreneurs built variations on the camera equipment he pioneered, pilfering and taking advantage of his work by using his techniques without paying any royalties—or the least attention to the patent laws. These shady characters comprised only about a third of the producers of the age. Many of the rest discreetly chose *not* to go this long, involved, and circuitous route. They simply went and flat-out *stole* the equipment.

Such is the nature of progress.

But prosecution under the law is another element of progress, and Edison took *everyone* who violated his patent to court, and usually won. In the face of this legal onslaught, not a few early filmmakers decided to leave town—meaning the East Coast—and head west to avoid inspection by Edison's agents or government officials. Since California was pretty much as far west as they could travel without getting their equipment wet, that's where many of these filmmakers decided to set up permanent camp. In time, many legitimate filmmakers also took the westward trek, lured by the tantalizing prospect of making films all year long, thanks to California's sunny climate and mild winters.

Soon a flood of silent movies were being shipped out of California. Most of these were westerns, for obvious reasons: Given that vast portions of California were still undeveloped, a filmmaker didn't need to construct sets. All he needed was a horse, a star, a wide-eyed palpitating heroine, and a few hills and he was in business. In fact, many filmmakers simply purchased vacant lots, set up a few rudimentary sets, and called the result a studio. (Hence the reason motion picture studios are called lots to this day.) The first four-walled studio deserving the name was constructed by director Francis Boggs in 1909. His efforts were so well received that he was promptly shot and killed by a nearby Japanese gardener who took exception to the racket caused by Boggs's filmmaking.

By 1910, actors were being paid the hefty sum of $5 per day, and generally worked without on-screen credit. Many were professional actors who couldn't find work elsewhere and were ashamed of appearing in what some referred to as "galloping tintypes." Despite the performers' feelings about the quality of their work, a large market soon developed for it. A huge number of films were being produced—often one each week by each studio—and the number of studios proper (or improper) also swelled. Anyone who could afford to buy a camera and enlist the support of a few good performers headed west in the hope of starting his own cinematic empire.

The second gold rush was on.

A large number of silent films were ground out during this period, and many were, of necessity, rather bad. But a respectable portion managed to achieve a degree of quality. These films were the work of men like Cecil B. DeMille, William Fox (the creator of what is now Twentieth Century-Fox), and Adolph Zukor, who founded Paramount Pictures. The nation was virtually afloat on a sea of westerns, love stories, comedies, and Egyptian sagas, which were very much in vogue then. These were the banner years that gave us Chaplin and Lloyd and Fairbanks and Clara Bow and Theda Bara and so many others.

Interestingly enough, while performers and directors became widely known and respected for their cinematic efforts, writers were almost an invisible collective entity. In a sense, screenwriters didn't even exist. The director knew what he wanted in a scene, and performers knew how to stage a fight or fall down a flight of stairs upon demand . . . what else was needed? The only real writing that went into these early silent films were the continuity cards inserted at critical moments to advance the plot, and which were usually slap-dashed off by the director or a company flunky. One director of the time termed writers "more or less useless," and doubted if the written word would ever play a substantial role in filmmaking beyond simply setting up the general idea and the rough scenario or progression of events.

It is worth noting here that the filmgoing audience of the day was used to a vastly different environment from today's. Many theaters boasted what were called traveling tabloid performances, or simply "tab shows." In addition to the main bill, audiences were treated to two or more orchestral pieces, a musical dance number, an occasional recital, a newsreel, a short subject, and whatever else the theater owner could think of to throw into the batch.

The entire film industry underwent a major change with the arrival of sound movies. In three successive years, Warners Films made movie history by introducing the first picture with a synchronized musical score, *Don Juan*, in 1926; the first film with spoken dialogue, Al Jolson's *The Jazz Singer*, in 1927; and then, in 1928, they released the first *all*-talkie, *The Lights of New York*, with Brian Foy.

Many producers of the day called the breakthroughs nothing more than gimmicks that would never catch on. But like it or not, a new era was upon them, and it won the appreciation of audiences throughout the United States.

With the advent of sound movies, writers suddenly became important. The studios went out and actively solicited writers, with varying degrees of success. Many established writers of the period looked at motion pictures with disdain, and generally opted to have little to do with them, at least officially, although some contributed material under the table. With most of the established figures unavailable, the studios turned to other sources, one of which was vaudeville. It was through this route that many vaudevillians, including W.C. Fields, became involved with the film business, first as a writer and then as a performer.

While the search continued and more and more writers were put under contract to the various studios, other careers were destroyed by the arrival of sound pictures. Many silent film performers could not adapt to the change; even vocal lessons could not help some performers, including one actress whose voice, in the words of a director, sounded "like an audible hangover." Audiences frequently found themselves distracted by the realization that the Egyptian queen had an accent distinctly Bronx in origin.

Thus the sound era signalled an entire new beginning for the film industry, complete with a legion of new performers, writers, and directors. It also led to a prosperous period for the studios. During the thirties, the studios wielded an influence unlike anything comparable today. They owned chains of theaters across the United States, often dictating what films each of these theaters would show, regardless of actual box office potential. (This was done by pairing a grade B film with a slightly more profitable production and promoting it as a double bill, a process known as block booking.) They had huge numbers of writers, performers, directors, and crew members under contract.

Although the contract system left much to be desired as far as writers were concerned—they lacked creative control, lacked respect, made but modest salaries and no backtalking allowed—there were, admittedly, some benefits. The contract system provided opportunities for novice scriptwriters, who were taken under the studio's wing and taught the techniques of movie-writing. In addition, the writers worked on a variety of films in different genres, whether they liked it or not, and therefore received useful experience in writing mysteries, love stories, musicals, adventures, gangster movies, and so forth—an uncommon situation today, when writers tend to specialize in one, or at most two, genres. (When was the last time you saw a science fiction film by Neil Simon? Or a musical comedy by Ray Bradbury?)

Many writers refer to those years—the thirties and early forties—as the "good-old/bad-old days." More films were made during each of those years than at any time since. The studios developed concepts that they felt would do well in the motion picture marketplace, selected a cast from among their contract players, and then assigned one of their staff writers to actually write the film. (Sometimes, however, a staff writer would develop an idea of his or her own, and follow the project through to completion.) And thanks to block booking, the studios could rest assured that none of their films would fail to bring in at least a modest return.

Overall, it wasn't a bad deal.

Until 1948, that is.

Following a Supreme Court antitrust decision, the federal government issued "consent decrees" requiring the studios to divest themselves of their theater chains, a crushing blow that led to the elimination of the contract system.

As if this wasn't bad enough, the film industry also had to deal with something they'd hoped would simply go away if they ignored it long enough: television. Once only a toy with—in the industry's estimate—limited audience potential, television had been steadily eroding the box office, the film industry's foundation. What's ironic is that television did so by doing just what filmmakers had done in the early motion picture business: They invested heavily in genres. Westerns, crime dramas, comedy and variety shows peopled by performers stolen from radio—all these and other genre pieces were daily television fare. Why, audiences wondered, should they pay money to see a western at a movie house when they could see essentially the same thing in the privacy of their own home? Nor was content the only factor to be considered; television was a marvelous, bright and shiny toy, and like any toy, its early years saw a lot of use by its purchasers. The American public was fascinated by the one-eyed newcomer to their home, and spent as much time as possible playing with it.

The impact of the antitrust decision together with the popularity of television was devastating. Between 1948 and 1955, movie attendance dropped from 90 million to 46 million per week. In response, the studios, no longer sure of a return on their productions, made fewer films. The smart studios looked analytically at television and set out to produce films that offered something different—exotic locations, long and involved plots, popular stars, and high-paced adventure. Other studios, unable to change and adapt to the new demands of the world around them, went into bankruptcy and oblivion.

In the midst of all this confusion, the studios also had to contend with the fact that the star system was replacing the contract system, and with the growing influence of unions. By then, the actors, writers, and directors had formed collective bargaining organizations (writers organized the Screen Writers Guild, which later became the Writers Guild of America) that applied pressure for higher salaries and increased creative input.

Taken together, these overwhelming elements led many studio executives to wonder if there were any open windows still available on Wall Street. But they persevered—by lowering the number of films they produced, by gearing each film to a specific audience, by featuring big-name stars with box office draw, by working where possible only with established writers, and by offering audiences such incentives as a 1957 sweepstakes trip to the Academy Awards ceremony. Although audiences continued to decline in number, reaching an all-time low of 36.6 million in 1958, the studios were surviving, and that was the important thing.

During this period, however, yet another player was preparing to step onto the stage and grab the spotlight: the independent producer, who proved to be a boon to novice screenwriters.

Because independent production companies were small entities that lived literally from film to film, they needed less substantial returns on each production than the studios did to survive. Sensing a gap created in double bills and B movies by the lowered output of the major studios, the independents churned out a phenomenal number of quick, low-budget pictures for drive-ins and small theaters across the country. Because their organizational structure was less monolithic, they could respond quickly to changing audience demands, particularly the demands of teenagers, who frequented drive-ins for reasons that were not always honorable. Thus were born youth-in-rebellion movies, five-dollar-budget science fiction movies, and other cinematic creations of the *I Married a Teenage Biker from Outer Space During Beach Blanket Bingo* genre.

Independent producers were mavericks who worked outside the studio system. Because of minimal production budgets, they were unable to afford established writers and performers. As a consequence, they turned to the vast pool of talent that was available and willing to work cheap in their search for The Big Break.

And what were the overall results of the development of independent producers?

Audiences, particularly those seventeen to twenty years old, swallowed the low-budget films whole and came back for more. The films provided them with an excuse to get out of the house, a place to gather with their peers, topics not dealt with by the major studios, and films directed specifically toward their tastes and attitudes. From a sociological perspective, it was largely the impact of independent films that helped shape and define the growing group-consciousness of youth in the fifties and early sixties. For good or ill, these films encouraged group identification determined by age, and helped sow some of the seeds of disaffection that led to the generation gap of the sixties. It was only one factor, to be sure, and there were many others more powerful—the draft and an unfortunate interlude in Southeast Asia—but the youth rebel films of those years, which posited an us-versus-them mentality, certainly influenced this growing sociological schism.

Theater owners found these films a godsend. They could once again boast double bills, and new drive-ins sprouted like weeds across the country.

Novice writers and performers were finally able to see the fruits of their labors up on the screen, and with the steady amassing of credits they were eventually able to move on to the more established production companies. This constant turnover resulted in a steady flow of opportunities for newer talent eager to get into The Industry. And the independents were eager to give them this chance, since every star or writer who went on to recognition lent more credibility to the producer's efforts—and meant more money at the box office with each re-release of the early film.

And the major studios? Well, they fussed and fumed and crabbed and muttered and generally carried on cranky whenever a reporter brought up the subject. Their public stance was that the independents were pandering and lowering the cinematic art form. But deep inside their cash-register hearts, the studios were not entirely displeased at the success of the independents, although they certainly could have used the income the independents were generating. For one thing, these mavericks were producing the films that the majors either didn't make any longer—grade B cheapies—or wouldn't touch with a ten-foot boom mike. But most important of all, they recognized that the independents were inculcating the movie-going habit into a whole new generation of potential audience members.

In short, movie attendance was on its way up again.

By the mid-sixties, and on into the seventies, the movie industry regained its financial legs. More films were produced, although the number never again reached the pre-1948 level. The independents continued to cater to specific audiences with their quick-buck films, while the major studios went on making films with big-name stars and steadily growing budgets. In time, the two sides formed a workable, if sometimes uneasy, alliance. In not a few cases, an independent filmmaker would produce a film on a *negative pickup* basis. This meant that the producer would raise the money himself and make the film on his own, after which he would bring the completed project to a major studio. The studio would then repay anywhere from 50 percent to 100 percent of the film's cost, depending upon what percentage of the profits the producer wanted, in exchange for ownership and distribution rights. In this way, the studios always knew what they were purchasing, didn't have to worry about the project suddenly going over budget, and had a finished product that was ready to distribute under their name at minimal risk.

These two practices—bigger-budget films and negative pickup deals—became more consistent trends during the seventies and the first part of the eighties. Confident that audiences could be induced to leave their homes only if a bigger-than-life epic awaited them at the theater, budgets continued to skyrocket. Whereas once a film could be made for $1 to $3 million, the budgets of individual films now soared to the range of $6 to $30 million. This trend entailed a number of risks, however. The higher the budget, the more the film had to recoup at the box office in order to show a profit. It soon became evident that a film with a $25 million budget couldn't be *just* successful; it had to be a blockbuster, and if it wasn't, the studio people who had approved the project were often asked to retire. This made studio executives understandably twitchy, and frequently they placed the question "How commercial is it?" before "How *good* is it?" in their decision to produce or not produce any given property.

Over time, this led to the production of fewer films, because the money that could have produced, say, four or five medium-budget films usually went into one big-budget extravaganza. By 1981, however, the studios had been burned by big-budget flops in sufficient number that it's safe to say the trend is starting to reverse itself. There is now a growing emphasis on securing medium-budget properties.

In expanding the number of negative pickup deals, the studios have become almost more like financiers than production companies: They are approached to put up production money for a film, and the individual producer goes off and makes the film himself, hoping to bring it in within the allocated budget. Many times, in fact, the executives who approve the deal never see the film until it is virtually completed. Their only input is an occasional visit to the shooting location, where the producer generally tries to get rid of them as fast as possible. One unfortunate consequence of this has been the rise of executives who can package a deal, but who know little about the actual craft of filmmaking, and are therefore unable to pick up on the subtle signs that the person in charge of the film isn't carrying on in a responsible fashion.

An alliance has also been made in recent years with that once-terrible enemy: television. Studios are now able to recoup at least some of their production costs by preselling films to television, often before they are released to the theaters. (This development presents a double-edged danger: If the film is a surprise success, the payment the studio receives will probably be less than could have been secured after the film's release. On the other hand, if the film is expected to do well, gets a sizeable purchase from a network, then bombs at the box office, the studio will have gotten far more than the picture was probably worth.)

Some studios, particularly those that own both television and film divisions, have recently developed a standing policy on their films: If the film has screen quality, and looks like it will do well, it will be released as a feature. On the other hand, if its appeal is limited, it will be released as a television movie. In some cases, as mentioned in the chapter on television, should a studio's television division come up with a surprisingly popular television movie or series, the company will often release the project overseas as a feature film.

All these factors, and others that will be mentioned later, have led to the creation of a contemporary film industry that is extremely complex. The routes leading to production can be confusing and intimidating to the newcomer, with the degree of complexity varying with each route. But the key point here is that there are more routes now than ever before. Whereas the fate of a script once rested with a handful of people, now there are a variety of resources available to the scriptwriter.

Having established some of the oddities inherent in the film business, as well as some of the inanities thereof, we shall proceed to the next obvious question: Why would anyone in his or her right mind want to get involved with the film business in the first place?

The Benefits and Drawbacks of Screenwriting

In nearly a decade of semiprofessional, and then professional writing, I've never met anyone who *wouldn't* like to be a part of the film industry, in one capacity or another. People from all walks of life have become hypnotized by the buzzwords and catchphrases of H*O*L*L*Y-*W*O*O*D: Package deals. The cinema. Cannes. Westerns, adventures, romances, horror, and science fiction. Grade A's and grade B's; PG's, R's, G's, and X's, the whole alphabet soup of morality in filmmaking. Flicks and photoplays. Movies and moguls. The silver screen. Hey, baby, loved your last flick, have your secretary call my secretary and we'll take lunch some time.

They're cinematic buzzwords that boil down to one thing: big bucks in Tinseltown. To some, they're phrases voiced with the same fervent reverence as Hindu mantras, recipes for aphrodisiacs, and the Pledge of Allegiance at a VFW convention.

Hollywood. It's a word that has become associated around the world with a fast-lane-only galaxy of high finance, nonstop excitement, fame, fortune, and mind-wrenching glamour.

And the surprising thing, folks, is that half of it is true.

At its best, the film industry represents the single best chance for a writer to come away with an almost intimidating amount of money in a relatively brief period. At its worst . . . well, we'll get to that in a moment or two.

The first benefit is one of the biggest attractions of screenwriting: the heretofore-hinted-at financial rewards. Depending on the film's budget and the writer's reputation, a screenplay can bring in anywhere from $16,000 for a new writer working on a low-budget film, up to $500,000 or more if you're Mario Puzo and you're working on a big-budget flick. And that's only the initial fee; *then* there comes a salary during production, so the writer can be on hand for revisions, a percentage of the profits (called *points*), as well as a percentage of any ancillary rights, including book sales and other merchandising attempts. When you figure in a sale to television, and any residuals through reruns, as well as the possibility of a series based upon the script—which is becoming more of a trend these days—you're talking about an awful lot of money. Now, not *every* deal will include each of these financial factors; if you're new to the business, you may not have the clout to demand two or three points off the film's net profits, for instance. Even without all the fringe benefits, though, the sum paid is far beyond what most writers could expect to receive writing for any other medium—unless, of course, you happen to be a James Michener or a John Irving, and can churn out one bestseller after another. The money looks better yet when you look at the amount of actual work involved. To illustrate:

A motion picture screenplay runs anywhere from 100 to 130 pages. Upon purchase, the very least a writer can expect to make right off the top is anywhere from $30,000 to $40,000, assuming the film's budget is over $1 million (and films coming in under that figure are steadily becoming rarer). That is a minimum figure, and payment can and often does exceed that amount. If the film does reasonably well, and you've got a point or two on the profits, that means $10,000 to $25,000 or more, depending upon any costs after release and actual attendance—figuring in for inflation, of course. (Production costs never end with the final cut of the film. Added on is the cost of making prints for all the theaters where the film will be showing—anywhere from several hundred to a thousand dollars apiece, particularly in the case of 70mm Dolby Sound prints—as well as publicity, press junkets, repair of ripped prints, print replacement, and so forth.) In any event, you're assured of a potential $40,000 to $65,000 at the end of the film's history, once all the payments have been tallied.

A book publisher, on the other hand, pays an average advance of anywhere from $1,000 to $15,000 for a first novel, which often can run 300 to 600 pages. Royalties of 10 percent to 15 percent of the net price for each book purchased can bring in a fair hunk of change, but it takes a lot of years, and you don't see any of that money until after the publisher recoups the advance. In screenwriting, payment is not made against the film's eventual profits. You get a fee, free and clear, and possibly a percentage of the profits—a better deal for less per-page work.

Two related benefits: Selling one screenplay makes you a very attractive prospect to producers who figure you must know what you're doing, and you need only sell one screenplay each year—if that many—to live comfortably. Your output needn't be as great, or as hurried, as a nonfiction article writer's, so you can take your time and try to do a better job.

A strange Hollywood paradox makes it wholly possible to make almost as much money by being a failure as by being a success! It's like this: On one hand, we have many writers who churn out a disquietingly large number of screenplays annually. These are knowledgeable writers producing scripts they believe in, and/or scripts that are highly commercial (i.e., topical). These scripts are then marketed and optioned on by one of the major studios. An option, as we'll discuss in more detail in the marketing section, is a fee, usually around $5,000 or so, paid by a studio in return for movie rights to the script for a year or sometimes two. They haven't bought the script, but are holding on to the property until they make up their minds, or until the script becomes commercial. At the end of the option period, they may either renew the contract under similar terms, or fail to do so, which means the writer can take the script to another studio and do the whole thing all over again. In this way, he may never have his scripts produced, but he is making a living by screenwriting, usually $10,000 to $25,000 annually.

On the other hand, the studios ask reliable scriptwriters to do adaptations. For instance, a studio may purchase movie rights to a popular book, but they don't want the author to do the script. So they give the assignment to a scriptwriter who can give them an idea what the book will look like as a screenplay. Often, they discover it just won't work as a movie and give up on the project. But the screenwriter got paid, and has another credit to his résumé, even though his work was never produced!

Like I said . . . it's a screwy business.

Another benefit of screenwriting is less tangible, but important nonetheless. It has to do with prestige, both inside the industry and outside among the general public. It is a simple reality that screenwriters' names are more easily recognizable than the names of television or radio writers. In these latter media, the writer's name rolls by once, and that's about it. But motion picture credits are listed in newspaper advertisements, on television and radio ads, in reviews, on theater programs, and of course, on the screen itself. Not a small part of this is the result of the Writers Guild *insisting* that writers' credits get equal space in advertisements.

In addition to popular recognition, there is another intangible benefit of screenwriting: The characters who populate your script are entirely of your own invention. You don't have to worry about tailoring the characters to fit the preconceptions of someone else, as you must with a television series and certain radio programs that use continuing characters. For as long as the script is in your typewriter, the only person you have to please is yourself. (What happens after the script leaves your typewriter we'll discuss shortly.)

Finally, a good screenplay—or, more realistically, several good screenplays—can be your route to producing or directing your own films. A substantial number of film producers and directors started as screenwriters, and most now direct or produce their own scripts. Steven Spielberg, Francis Ford Coppola, George Lucas, John Carpenter, George Romero, Woody Allen . . . these are only a few of the better-known writers who have gone on to produce and direct as well as write films. An old film industry adage is that if you've written an exceptionally hot property, you can name your price and, in a fair number of cases, expect to get what you asked for.

No one, for example, wanted Sylvester Stallone to star in *Rocky*, which he'd written specifically with an eye toward portraying the main character. The studios argued. They pleaded, thundered, grumbled, and complained. Stallone wasn't a box-office name, and they felt that without the presence of a name star, the film wouldn't do well financially. But Stallone stood firm. He dug his heels into the dirt, crossed his arms and faced into the wind, knowing that he had something they wanted, and that sooner or later, if they wanted it badly enough, they'd cave in.

They did, and the rest is history.

All of these things, then, are the nicenesses that inhabit the world of a screenwriter. But be advised that this is not the whole story: There is a flip side to the film business, and if you ignore the darksome aspects of screenwriting in deference to the tinsel-and-cute-little-bunny-rabbits image the industry tries to project, you will be inviting grief into your home.

So let's backtrack, and take each point one at a time.

Yes, the financial rewards of screenwriting are considerable. As a consequence, after seeing the latest weekly box office receipts listed in *Variety*, new screenwriters can sometimes be convinced to take a smaller fee up front in return for a few percentage points of the film's net profits. If you ever receive such an offer, then I and every other writer who's ever been involved in the film business can offer only one piece of advice: Don't take it.

The reader is to be reminded here that the motion picture studios are in the illusion *business*. They deal in applied creativity, and this creativity does not always stop at the bookkeeping office. By tacking on little costs here and there, both during and after production, these necromancers can make even the most successful film look like a failure. The film, as far as they're concerned, will always be in the red, which means that anyone waiting for a percentage of the profits will have a long wait ahead of him.

This is nothing new. It's been going on for decades. Neither is it entirely illegal, since it involves cross-dealings between different branches of the same production organization, each arm billing the other arm for its services. But there is hope this practice may change during the next decade. As of this writing, nearly a dozen cases are in litigation as writers and directors and performers try to get a percentage of what is rightfully theirs and to open the studio's books to an examination by their attorneys.

So always be wary of anyone who tries to sell you on taking a smaller salary and fee in return for a few points—unless you're dealing with a respected figure whose credibility cannot be challenged. George Lucas is such a person, and *anyone* who works at Lucasfilms, including the guy who sweeps the floor, is given, and *receives*, a percentage of the profits. In most other cases, the producers or studios know they can juggle the figures so the film appears to be a loser, or they know it will never make enough money (after they take out their own fees) for there to be enough to worry about anyway.

When it comes to dealing with independent producers, the waters are *filled* with sharks. You see, in order to claim that he or she is a television producer, the individual in question must be under contract to a network, and will have worked on any number of television series. But *anyone* can, with a few bucks, rent an office on Sunset Boulevard or even right at the corner of Hollywood and Vine, come up with a snazzy name for the template, and announce that he is an independent producer. If challenged by anyone wanting to know what he's done in the past, he can simply shrug and say he has several deals "in development" with major stars and directors. That statement is nearly impossible to refute, since just about everybody in Hollywood has something in development, and the principals he claims to have involved are usually next to impossible to locate for verification.

These are the people to beware of. They are the fast talkers, the ones who answer questions in generalities, who know almost nothing about the film business and are therefore bound to fail—usually taking someone else down with them. Hollywood is filled with horror stories about unwitting writers and performers who got involved with shady operators and are still recovering from it.

Here's one of those stories: A friend of mine was contacted by an independent production company I shall refer to as the DoubleCross Corporation. He had a few produced plays under his belt and was thrilled at the prospect of being in the Movie Biz. So he agreed to and signed a contract for one percentage point of the profits, and what was then Guild minimum for a screenplay. But the payments were to be made on a deferred basis, the terms of which are given here verbatim: "Producer agrees to pay Employee the sum of $14,000, which shall be distributed in the following manner: Ten percent on the date whereon the budget for the motion picture is allocated to the Producer; forty percent on the date of the Employer's commencement of principal photography of a motion picture based on said property; and fifty percent to be paid on the last day of actual photography. In addition to this fee, Producer agrees to pay to Employee one percent of the net profit from the motion picture. Producer agrees to use its reasonable efforts to effect production of a motion picture based upon said property. In the event, however, that Producer is unable to begin or complete production of the Photoplay, Producer shall provide to the Employee the compensatory sum of $1,000." (This kind of arrangement, by the way, is patently forbidden by the Writers Guild.)

"It was," my friend has said on many occasions, "the biggest mistake I ever made in my entire life." Here's what happened: The DoubleCross Corporation was never able to receive financial backing for the project, since the alleged producer had never worked in the industry before and was recognized as a less-than-reliable character. That took care of the $14,000. So the writer tried to get his $1,000 kill fee. But the producer had an out, a loophole: The contract specified that the kill fee only went into effect after all reasonable efforts to secure production of the script had been made. So whenever my friend tried to get his money, all the producer had to say, truthfully or otherwise, was that he had shuttled the script to yet another studio, and that they were looking at it. This constituted a reasonable effort. Translation: It would be impossible for the writer to ever get his kill fee, since the producer could claim indefinitely that reasonable efforts were being made to produce the screenplay. And since no time limit was attached, the reasonable efforts could go on forever.

The result of all this? The writer wrote a very good script, for which he never received a single penny, and probably never will. He cannot market the screenplay as is, because even though he was never paid for his work, it contractually belongs to DoubleCross. Now, he could probably—almost certainly—break the contract in court, given the circumstances, but the producer, along with the DoubleCross Corporation, long ago vanished. Telephone disconnected, no forwarding address, and a solid year of work down the drain.

The writer, of course, has said that he harbors no grudges. "But if I ever find that guy," he added in a recent conversation, "I'm gonna chew on his eyes."

Moral: Whenever dealing with an independent production company, check them out with the Writers Guild and the Better Business Bureau—unless, of course, they have some kind of track record or are known personally by you. Do not sign *any* contracts until you have talked to an attorney, and have compared them to the standard contract supplied in this book. A little caution can save you years of heartbreak.

Sharks aside, other potential drawbacks lie in wait for the dedicated screenwriter.

Once you've turned your script over to a director, a producer, and a cast, your words can be changed in a thousand different ways. Admittedly, for most original screenplays—as opposed to an adaptation of someone else's work—you are given the right to do the first rewrite, and to be on hand for revisions, but other changes can still be made. After you've done the first full rewrite, the studio has the right to bring in a second writer to totally rewrite your material. A director can opt to change lines, and will almost certainly change your camera directions. Cast members will grouse that they can't say the lines as written, or that the lines don't mesh with the character (who they, of course, know better than the writer, who created the characters in the first place). If the cast members have enough clout, they can change the lines.

Even if your lines are preserved pretty much as-are during production, they're *still* not safe. Writers have seen the entire thrust of a script turned inside-out as the film is edited. Lines can be juggled, dubbed, looped, or cut out altogether, thereby subtly changing the nature of the film. Often, a writer's contract will specify that he is allowed a say in the editing process, and can view the finished version, or "final cut," as it's usually known. But the right to actually do the final cut almost always rests with the director, who is the final arbiter.

Of course, if the film succeeds, everybody will claim it was successful *in spite* of the script, and if it fails, it will be entirely *because* of the script.

Those, then, are the essential benefits and drawbacks to screenwriting. Although some of the information might belong in the section on marketing, I believe it's terribly important for you to know up front exactly what kind of world you'll be dealing with as a screenwriter. In the interest of objectivity, I should also state that although many screenwriters tell endless horror stories about their misadventures, there are also those who manage to avoid the pitfalls, who always get paid on time, whose words are not significantly changed, and who have never been on the wrong end of a bad contract.

The interesting thing about all this is that despite the hazards, the attraction of screenwriting lives on. Even the most battle-scarred screenwriter is willing to give it another try, given the choice. Why? Why do salmon swim upstream? Why do lemmings rush off cliffs into the sea and drown? Why? Frankly, it beats me. I've talked to more writers, directors, and producers than I can count, and none of them had a really good answer to that question. To tell you the truth, I don't even know why I do it.

Except.

Except that maybe—sharks, warts, pitfalls, fast waters, six-foot-tall man-eating rabbits and all—it's still a chance to be part of the Movies; to see, for a brief moment, your name flickering across the silver screen of cinematic immortality.

And maybe Ethel Merman was right. Maybe there really is no business like show business, and as long as there's an actor waiting for the words that will give life to a character who will seize the collective unconscious and imaginations of moviegoers around the world, who will enliven them with the realization that they have just seen a little of The Truth in their local cinema, then there will always be people willing to write those special words, no matter what the risk might be.

On second thought, I think that must be it.

Now, if I could only figure out the one about the lemmings. . . .

Let's move on.

The Art of the Screenplay

Putting together a screenplay differs in many ways from writing a telescript. Probably the most obvious difference is the length involved. A screenplay can run anywhere from 101 pages, as for the 90-minute movie, *The Producers*, to 160 pages, which was the length of the original shooting scripts for *Network* and *The Empire Strikes Back*. (The only form of telescripting that approaches this length is, of course, the television movie.)

Because of this length, a screenplay is a complex creature that requires considerable forethought, planning, and a large chunk of time devoted to the actual writing process. Never undertake the writing of a screenplay without a complete belief in its importance. If you do—and I've seen this happen more times than I can count—you'll lose interest, your enthusiasm will wane, the project will suddenly become overwhelming, and you'll get bogged down halfway through. A screenplay written under such circumstances will rarely be completed, and that makes it harder to start the next one.

Writing a screenplay also requires, by virtue of its length alone, a certain degree of craftworthiness. You've got to have a genuine feel for the development of a script, for the pacing, the proper length of a scene, transitional devices, realistic-sounding dialogue, and so forth. *Anyone* who attempts to sit down at his desk and, as his first venture into scriptwriting, produce a complete screenplay, is just *asking* for an ulcer. Now, mind you, I'm not saying that it's impossible to complete a screenplay under such conditions. What I *am* saying is that the writer involved will finally catch on to the right techniques about two-thirds of the way through, then have to go back and do the whole thing over again.

Before you write a screenplay, there are two ways to prepare yourself for the undertaking. While some writers prefer one means over another, I heartily recommend both, for the following reasons.

First, the cardinal rule of all scriptwriting: Read as many examples of the particular medium as you can find. Happily, it's considerably easier to locate published film scripts than it is to secure television or radio scripts. Major studios sometimes release screenplays through a publishing company, usually accompanied by stills from the movie. So keep a sharp eye on the movie section of your local bookstore for these releases. (Ignore the novelizations, however. A movie based on a novel is one thing, but a novel based on a movie is rarely more than a pale imitation of the original product, written under contract by someone associated with the studio who, if he had any talent whatsoever, would be out writing his own novels instead of putting *Highway Pickup Girls* into prose for the general irritation of the civilized world.)

Probably the best recent publications of screenplays have come through Ballantine Books. I refer specifically to their publication of *The Art of Star Wars, The Empire Strikes Back Notebook,* and *Raiders of the Lost Ark: The Illustrated Screenplay.* These large editions contain not only the complete produced scripts, but other production information as well, including a hefty number of production drawings and storyboards—sketches that illustrate the action that occurs around the written word. I cannot recommend them highly enough to the writer trying to figure out what a screenplay involves. (I am confident that, as the other seven episodes of Lucas's *Star Wars* triple-triptych are released, more of these editions will be published.)

If you're interested in studying movie screenplays of the past, a number of publishers are actively engaged in publishing such scripts. Among the most prominent of these is the Wisconsin/Warner Brothers Screenplay Series, published by the University of Wisconsin Press. These clothbound editions are available through most bookstores and contain the scripts for *The Jazz Singer, Treasure of the Sierra Madre, To Have and Have Not, White Heat, The Corn Is Green, The Big Sleep, Arsenic and Old Lace,* and thirty-one others (as of this writing).

Another invaluable source is the MGM Library of Film Scripts, published by Viking Compass Books. Available through this publisher are *North by Northwest, Ninotchka, Adam's Rib, Singin' in the Rain, A Night at the Opera,* and *A Day at the Races.* What's truly nifty about this series is that in some cases, specifically the last two scripts mentioned, the book contains both the original script and the script as it finally ended up on the screen. This provides a remarkable insight into what changes a "finished" screenplay can undergo after it leaves the writer's hands, and it's often amusing to sit back and imagine the process that led to some of the more bizarre changes.

As a subset of this cardinal rule, it's imperative that you see as many movies as your finances can support. See current films for an understanding of where the medium is now and what's currently considered marketable and see as many old films as you can, preferably uncut, at whatever theaters in your area (if any) showcase film classics. Make it a point to see the good films, the films that garner the Oscars and the best reviews, as well as the real stinkers. There's a reason for this. A wellcrafted film will stay in your mind as an example of the best the medium can accomplish, and though you may not be able to pinpoint *exactly* what it was that made it a winner, somewhere in the back of your mind the various elements will be categorized and filed away for future use. Upon seeing a really bad film, however, it's remarkably easy to pick out where it failed, and where you, as a writer, could have made it just that much better a film by changing this character or heightening that plot element. In some ways, you can almost learn more about good writing by seeing a really bad film than by seeing a good one.

Barry Schneider—the somewhat reluctant and abashed screenwriter for *Harper Valley PTA* and *Take This Job and Shove It*—observed in a recent conversation, "Once you've decided to become a screenwriter, you can never again go out and enjoy a movie. Give it up, you're finished, you know? Because if it's a good movie, your basic screenwriter will get depressed, confident that he'll never be able to turn out something that good. A really good film makes the rest of us feel like shmucks, even though there may not be any valid reason for that feeling. On the other hand, if you see a bad film, you come down with high blood pressure thinking, 'How come *that* piece of dreck got produced, when my stuff is still sitting in a trunk in Toledo?' It'll make you crazy, it really will."

As yet another step in preparing to write a screenplay, it's a good idea first to write one or more one-hour dramatic television scripts, or at least two or three half-hour scripts in film format. The benefits of such a practice run are twofold: First, it gives you a feeling for dramatic structure, dialogue, and all the other elements we mentioned earlier. Once you've done it a few times, in abbreviated form, the prospect of writing one hundred plus pages of film script becomes less intimidating. As a second benefit, the finished scripts are samples of your writing, should you ever approach an agent or a producer who first wants to see some of your work.

In considering some of the other creative aspects of screenwriting, it's worth remembering that there are distinct, if subtle, differences between the topics covered in a movie, and those examined in a television series or telefilm.

Your basic television series usually centers around one of two themes. It is either character-oriented, as in most situation comedies and a few family-oriented dramatic series, or it is action-directed, as exemplified by police dramas, rescue programs, detective series, and the like. In the former, the premise of each episode is built upon the interrelationships of the characters. In the latter, the characters are frequently flat and the action elements take greatest prominence in each episode. (There are, of course, exceptions, but these are usually just that—exceptions.)

A motion picture, on the other hand, must balance both aspects if it is to be worth anything. You can't rely on the audience coming to know your characters over a prolonged period: You've got an average of two hours to make your audience feel they really know the characters who populate your script. At the same time, however, beyond just sketching out your characters, *something* must be happening onscreen. That something needn't be bombs exploding or machine guns barking; it can be the tension that grows steadily within a family on the verge of disintegration, or a character teetering on the edge of madness. But if there isn't something going on to hold your audience's attention, you've failed.

Television movies, on the other hand, tend to combine characterization and action. The difference is that most telefilms are issue-oriented, to wit: A network executive or a telescripter sees a topic of considerable controversy, be it nuclear power or the women's movement, and then goes out and either finds or creates a character to build a story around, and so examines the issue. Some network executives have staff members who do almost nothing but go through stacks of newspapers, sifting through the passions of the day for stories that might lend themselves to a telefilm format.

Motion pictures intended for general release can also be issue-oriented, but the percentage is considerably smaller than is the case with telefilms. There are two reasons for this. First, films that deal predominantly with issues can be risky at the box office. If the film's point of view runs counter to public attitude, the studio runs a chance of taking a financial bath; as a result, they are understandably leery of such endeavors. The Oscar-winning film *The China Syndrome* probably would never have been made without the box office security the studios had in the presence of such name performers as Jane Fonda and Jack Lemmon.

The second reason is also directly related to the constantly changing current of popular opinion. If a studio produces a film that capitalizes on a popular issue or media trend, it is very likely that the film will be outdated by the time it's released. Remember, it frequently takes anywhere from one to three years for a film to be made, from the first treatment to the distributed movie. By that time, what was once a hot property can become little more than a celluloid-wrapped dead fish.

This was precisely what happened to a film by Marble Arch Productions entitled *Can't Stop the Music*, which featured Valerie Perrine, and The Village People in their first starring role. The film was a painfully obvious exploitation of the disco craze then sweeping the country. At least, that was the case when the project was embarked upon. But when the movie was finally released, disco had not only become *passe*, a vociferous backlash had developed against it. Disco records were publicly burned at stadiums and arenas, and the film, released to much ballyhooing by the studio press office, died a terrible death.

(At a subsequent public seminar, Marble Arch Vice President Howard Alston asked the two hundred-plus people in the gallery, "How many of you would have predicted that *Can't Stop the Music* would have died at the box office?" Almost everyone raised their hands, proving again that maybe the public better understands what makes a good film, and what will and won't sell, than do the executives at the major centers of film production.)

Probably the single greatest distinction between telescripting and screenwriting is that a movie is more of a real *story* than a television program.

Consider it. If you were to sit down and, after watching your favorite situation comedy or, in most instances, an hour-long dramatic program, attempt to rewrite the program as a short story, you probably wouldn't have much of a story. Individual episodes of a television series are like separate scenes in a short story or novel. The characters generally don't change much in the process of one episode, and it's only over time that you, as a viewer, really get a strong feeling for the characters and the situation that envelops them. A single episode of *All in the Family* might not—I daresay could not—tell you much about the character of Archie Bunker. You might catch a few shadings of character, depending upon which facet of his emotional make-up the writers decided to stress that week, but you wouldn't get a real feeling for the person. But if you follow the series week after week, year after year, you *do* come to know the character, and you get to understand how he has changed as the result of different events. Television series characters develop and change through time and circumstances, with each new episode adding one more piece to the puzzle of who the character is, and why he or she behaves a certain way.

A motion picture, on the other hand, is wholly self-contained. Like a short story, it has a clearly defined beginning, middle, and end. You must tell your story and draw your characters within those parameters. You can't tack on an epilogue in which you explain why your characters did such-and-such, or what this event over here really means, and what it will lead to. The audience can't come back next week to find out more about the situation, and they can't come to the movie with any previous knowledge of your characters, upon which to build a whole portrait. You've got to tell your story, reveal your characters, and get out cleanly, because once it's released, there's no going back.

The final aspect that differentiates a motion picture screenplay from a telescript is not essentially creative in nature, but it does have an impact on the creative process. In nearly every instance, a motion picture will have a larger budget than a television movie: bigger budgets give screenwriters far greater latitude in determining what action will take place and where. If your script calls for the protagonist to scale the Eiffel Tower, the overseas jaunt will be figured into the overall production cost.

The danger is in letting this more substantive budget get in the way of creativity. You should never throw in an extravagant scene just because it might be kinda fun. Any action or locale used in your script must be necessary to the story. So if your action is to be set in some exotic locale, there'd better be a damned good reason why it's taking place there instead of, say, Cleveland. And the only acceptable reason is that it's happening in this place because it couldn't happen the same way anywhere else. The same applies to action. After reviewing films in print and on the air for something over seven years, I have seen quite enough purely gratuitous car crashes, thank you very much. If there's no need for cars careening into one another at high speed, or for any other such non-plot-related action, drop it. Omit it. Bury it and lose your map. A really good script is as spare as you can make it. Don't let the quality of your script get lost beneath a mass of unnecessary and distracting action.

Which brings me to one important little point I want to get out of the way right here, right now: In every writing class, seminar, or lecture I've undertaken, I've heard such phrases as "the obligatory chase scene," "the obligatory sex scene," and in greater numbers these days, "the obligatory throat-cutting-in-graphic-detail scene." To be totally blunt with you, that is a load of absolute, unmitigated ka-ka.

Nothing is ever obligatory! That attitude of, "Well, this scene is expected, and everybody else is doing it," has forever been one of the forces that cripple what would otherwise be fine films. The only thing you as a screenwriter are obliged to do is tell your story. Period. You don't *have* to follow the standard formula used in X-number of other films, because if you do, then it isn't your script anymore. It's a formula script, and it will never be anything more than that. If you put in one single, solitary, crummy little scene *not* because you think it belongs there, but because you think it's *expected*, then forget it. You've just sold out.

There's nothing whatsoever wrong with a chase scene if that scene is a natural, essential part of your story. But to do it because it's allegedly "obligatory" is just plain dumb. Worse than dumb, in fact, because it's the first step down the road toward losing your integrity as an artist.

And for those who feel that every instant of bloodshed must be splashed in technicolor Type O across the screen, I refer you to the work done by Alfred Hitchcock and Val Lewton, who managed to create a more vivid sense of horror through subtlety and indirection than could ever be realistically recreated and photographed. Remember the lessons of radiodrama and let your audience's imagination do most of your work for you.

End of sermon.

These are the steps involved in the creation of a screenplay. You must come up with a story you feel very strongly about. It must be self-contained. It should not be trendy, unless you can be absolutely sure that the trend will be going on one, five or twenty years down the line. It should be a character story, but something must be happening as well. The action, however, should not get in the way of your characterizations. The action should be fully resolved by the script's conclusion, and the audience should feel that they have grown to know the characters. The action should take place in an orderly, logical fashion. You should be familiar with the techniques of dialogue, pacing, and description, either from studying films, or writing practice television scripts; ideally, by doing both. The script should be as spare as you can make it, eliminating any unnecessary or "obligatory" action. Thus armed with the tools of your craft, and ready to begin transplanting ideas from your imagination to a blank sheet of paper, you can now move on to the actual mechanics of putting together a script, from start to finish.

The Craft of Screenwriting

What your first step in developing a screenplay will be depends a little on how much emphasis you want to put on marketing. As a rule, a screenplay—like everything else—starts out with an idea that, using the criteria established earlier and in previous chapters, you develop into an interesting story that you would like to tell.

If, however, you want to increase the potential marketability of your script, you can select a popular performer and write a script around that performer's *persona*. This happens all the time. Some writers find that it makes writing easier, since by already being familiar with the performer's style and delivery they need only imagine how that actor's *persona* would respond in this new situation. The rhythms, inflections, and attitudes are already there—only the plot has been changed to protect the innocent. The danger with this technique, of course, is that if the performer you pick is too recognizable or idiosyncratic, you may have a hard time placing the script elsewhere if the performer you've selected turns it down.

(For those interested in following this path anyway, let me pass along a little trade secret. Just don't tell anybody I told you. By following the trade papers—*Daily Variety*, the *Hollywood Reporter*, *The Hollywood Drama-Logue* and suchlike—you can find out what performers have signed multiple-picture deals in recent months. If you already know that, a while back, a performer signed such a deal with a studio, you can—with a little persistence—call the studio and bug them into telling you how many films remain in the performer's contract. This will give you a list of performers who not only are available, but are legally obligated to star in a specified number of motion pictures and therefore are actively soliciting scripts. You then pick those performers who are roughly similar in nature, so the character you choose to create as a vehicle can be applied to any of these performers. This simultaneously increases the potential marketplace for your script, and makes it less narrow in its applicability. It's sneaky, underhanded, and while still somewhat risky, it's often effective. (I do not, however, personally recommend this without reservation. The less studios are harassed, the happier they are. Consider this a last resort.)

So: You've got a story you've decided to tell in a screenplay. Your next step is to develop that story through all the stages mentioned previously in the chapters on television and, to a lesser extent, radio. You must transform the idea into a brief synopsis, an outline, a treatment, and then, finally, the script itself. Some of these terms have a slightly different application, however, and *all* of them are equally essential if you intend to produce a marketable screenplay.

The Synopsis

First, you must be able to sum up your idea as briefly as possible, usually about a paragraph or so. A lot of writers find this very difficult, since they are so intimately connected with their characters and their story. But learn to do it anyway. After all, the process is exactly the same as when a friend asks you what the movie you saw last night was about, and you sum up the whole two hours in a couple of sentences.

Having come up with your synopsis, type it up and store it away in the typewriter-paper box along with what will soon be the rest of your property. But first, memorize it until you can repeat it verbatim at a moment's notice. This is vital, because in many cases, before a producer or an agent will even look at a film script or a treatment, they want to know exactly what it's about, in the briefest possible terms. Believe it or not, quite a few films are produced solely on the basis of a synopsis of no more than a few sentences. The science fiction film *Outland* was one of these, although from a critical perspective it really isn't much of a film. The deal for that movie was made on the basis of *one sentence*. Writer/director Peter Hyams went to Warner Brothers and simply told them, "It's *High Noon* in outer space."

Thus was born a motion picture. A deal was arranged on the spot, and preproduction was initiated not long thereafter. The mistake Hyams made, of course, was that he actually stuck to this premise, attempting a transplant that didn't work. The film was full of holes as a result.

On the other hand, writer/producer Gene Roddenberry sold the *Star Trek* series to television by emphasizing the notion "It's *Wagon Train* in outer space," but at least had the common sense, once the network had given him approval to go ahead on the series, to make it a lot more than a simple rehash of another writer's ideas.

Moral: Never underestimate the value of a good synopsis.

We press on.

The Outline

When it comes to motion pictures, outlines can be peculiar little critters. No two writers do them quite the same way. Although there is general agreement on the length of an outline—anywhere from four to ten pages—there is some disagreement about its complexity. A substantial number of writers—I will take my life in my hands and hazard to say a majority of them—prefer the narrative prose format associated with the television and radio treatments presented here earlier (see the TV and radio chapters for samples.). Others prefer to fill out their outlines with specific camera directions, transitional devices, blocking directions, and so forth.

Speaking from personal experience and remarks made by other writers, producers, and directors, I recommend sticking with the narrative prose format. Don't worry about camera angles and the like until you get into your treatment and script; concern yourself primarily with telling your story in as cogent and undistracted a fashion as possible.

An outline is usually sent along either by you or an agent after a producer's attention has been hooked by the synopsis. Since an outline doesn't cost as much to photocopy as a treatment or a script, multiple copies can be shuttled to a variety of producers, and because of its brevity, a producer can respond with interest or a lack thereof in far less time than he could with a screenplay—often sending back word within a day or so.

Because producers often don't like to read, you should keep a "just the facts" attitude when writing an outline. An outline should be written in uncluttered fashion, using short story techniques. Do not include any asides, long-winded explanations, or lingering descriptions of scenes. Just tell your story. If it's an interesting idea, you won't need artificial adornments. If it isn't, then all the asides and marvelous prose descriptions in the world won't help you.

Once your outline is completed, you come to a point where you have to make a decision. Some writers feel that the writing process should, for the moment, end at this juncture. They choose to market the outline alone until they find an interested producer who wants them to write a treatment and a script based on the outline. The benefit of this tactic is that if no one seems interested in the idea, they can turn to another project and abandon the first one without having wasted the long hours and days and weeks required to write a screenplay. The danger is that if the writer is new and unproduced, and the studio decides it likes the idea, it may opt to buy the idea flat out and assign the story to another screenwriter, rather than chance losing time and money by assigning an unproven writer to write a script that may prove wholly unworkable.

I recommend that you *do* go ahead and write the treatment and the screenplay before you begin the marketing. There are several benefits to this. First, if a studio shows interest in your outline, they can immediately look at the screenplay and decide if it's what they want, thereby increasing the chances not only that they will buy your idea, but buy your services as a writer. Second, to repeat an earlier premise, no time spent behind the typewriter is ever wasted. If your first script doesn't sell, at least you will have finished it. You actually will have written a complete screenplay, and that makes the second one easier to write. Finally, a complete screenplay, even unproduced and unsold, can be given to an agent as a sample of your work, thereby securing his representation, and it can be shown to a producer with the goal of possibly getting you an assignment on some other project.

Besides, just because a script doesn't sell the first time out doesn't mean it won't ever sell. Having it on hand for the future is never a bad idea.

So we are decided. We move on to the next step.

The Treatment

A treatment can run anywhere from 15 to 45 pages, and includes each scene that will appear in your screenplay.

Probably the single best way to organize a treatment, and later your screenplay, is to start by briefly describing each scene on individual

3x5 index cards. Each card should contain the location of the scene in terms of exterior or interior settings, an encapsulization of the action that takes place, and a few snippets of dialogue to jog your memory when it comes time to actually script the scene. Each scene should be numbered, roughly in the sequence in which it will appear in your script. Write each number in pencil in the upper left-hand corner of each card, since it may well develop that after looking over the finished order, you'll want to shuffle the sequence of events.

For purposes of illustration, let's say we're writing a screenplay about the adventures of an unsuccessful Lothario—a comedy about a man who is perpetually striking out before he ever gets to bat. We've decided the action will take place in a small Midwestern town, where his reputation, or lack thereof, is widely known. In order to immediately introduce the audience to our character—whom we'll call Walter—and his plight, the first scene will be an attempted seduction in his car following a date with a rather vacuous woman. The index card for that first scene would look something like this:

---

1 EXT. ESTAB. SHOT/INT. WALTER'S CAR—NIGHT

Walter is nervously trying to strike up a reasonable semblance of a conversation with Melissa. Nothing takes off. She wonders how he got her phone number. He hedges, then admits it came from a men's room wall. "Which one?" she asks. After explaining and winning her confidence, he begins making his moves, which start to be successful until he surprises her with a rubber duck. She stomps out of the car in indignation. He squeezes the duck. It squeaks. "Oh, shut up," he says, then drives off.

Once you've transferred each of your scenes to individual index cards, you'll want to determine roughly how much space you will give each scene in your treatment. If it's not an important scene, you'll want to use only narrative description and not get into any dialogue. About a paragraph will suffice for these. For an important, pivotal scene, you may want to spend as much as a page or a page-and-a-half. It's not a bad idea to lay out the cards in sequential order on the floor or on a large cork board so that, with one glance, you can see the progression of scenes. If you have several scenes in the same location, for instance, you may want to combine them into one scene to do the work of several. This helps move the story forward a little faster, eliminates one extra scene and a little of the time the audience may have to spend in the same location. With this done, you are ready to undertake the treatment itself.

Typographically, the format used in a film treatment is much the same as in an outline. The content appears between 10 and 75 picas; NAMES,

TRANSITIONS, CAMERA ANGLES (if necessary) and EFFECTS are capitalized throughout. (After first introducing a character, however, you can cease capitalizing the entire name.)

The title appears in all caps, centered on the page 8 vertical lines from the top. Two spaces below this is your name, followed 2 lines later by the date the treatment is being written. Six spaces further down, you type the words FADE IN in all caps at the far left margin. Double-space again, and then you begin your first line of the treatment.

Here is what the first scene of our amorous friend's misadventures look like in treatment form. (See Fig. 25 and 26.)

The treatment continues in this fashion until the entire story has been told. A good point to remember is to include only your strongest and best-crafted pieces of dialogue, thereby giving the reader a feeling for your writing at its best.

When your treatment is complete, give it to someone you know and solicit criticism. Make sure it's someone who will tell you what he *really* thinks of your work. Do *not* go to your mother or your father. Your sister or brother, maybe. Siblings are notoriously ruthless.

After getting feedback on your treatment, if anyone points out any holes in the plot, any stiff dialogue, or problems in structure, consider the advice carefully and, if you agree, make the changes in your treatment.

With your revised treatment finally in hand, you are ready for the final step in the development of your property.

The Screenplay

Some writers, having followed their story through the developmental stages of synopsis, outline, and treatment, find the task of writing the screenplay a bit anticlimactic. The story, as far as they are concerned, has already been told—why retell it all over again, for the fourth time? This is understandable. One of the primary forces that make a writer write is an internal pressure, an inner drive that won't rest until the tale has been told. Once this has been done, some people's interest wanes. Norman Mailer once said, "I think it's bad to *talk* about one's present work, for it spoils something at the root of the creative act. It discharges the tension."

At this point a screenwriter must develop a highly tuned sense of discipline, a willingness to write and rewrite the same story as often as necessary, to polish it until it is as hard and bright as a diamond.

As you begin writing your screenplay, it may be helpful to remember that to a certain extent the whole story has *not* been told. The treatment has conveyed the events, names, and places that make up the high points of your story, but the characters remain largely unexplored. Oh, there have been glimpses here and there, certainly. But it's only within the body of the screenplay that you have the opportunity to really develop your characters.

Your treatment should be looked upon as a road map through the maze of your story. It will keep you on the right track as you move from one place and one event to another. But like anyone visiting a foreign country, never pay so much attention to the road map that you miss all the scenery. Your characters are the scenery in this case, and for as long as you know where you are in your story and what should come next, never be afraid or reluctant to linger for just a moment here and there, so that

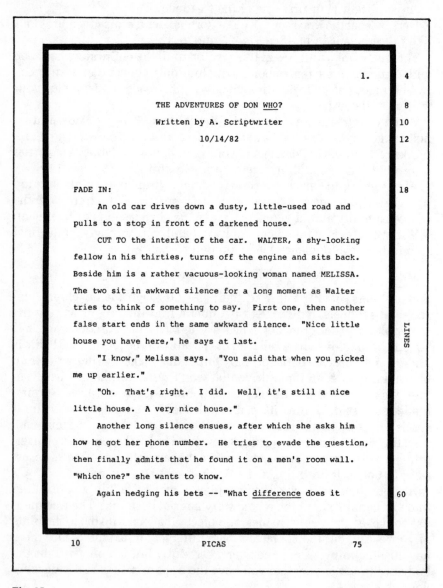

```
                                               1.        4

            THE ADVENTURES OF DON WHO?                   8
            Written by A. Scriptwriter                   10
                    10/14/82                             12


FADE IN:                                                 18
      An old car drives down a dusty, little-used road and
pulls to a stop in front of a darkened house.
      CUT TO the interior of the car.  WALTER, a shy-looking
fellow in his thirties, turns off the engine and sits back.
Beside him is a rather vacuous-looking woman named MELISSA.
The two sit in awkward silence for a long moment as Walter
tries to think of something to say.  First one, then another
false start ends in the same awkward silence.  "Nice little    L
house you have here," he says at last.                          I
      "I know," Melissa says.  "You said that when you picked   N
me up earlier."                                                 E
      "Oh.  That's right.  I did.  Well, it's still a nice      S
little house.  A very nice house."
      Another long silence ensues, after which she asks him
how he got her phone number.  He tries to evade the question,
then finally admits that he found it on a men's room wall.
"Which one?" she wants to know.
      Again hedging his bets -- "What difference does it        60


        10                  PICAS                   75
```

Fig. 25

you and your audience can get a close look at just who these extraordinary people really are.

Here are some other hints that may prove useful in writing your screenplay:

Avoid long, potentially tedious monologues. A single speech that runs as much as a page or more can slow down the pace of your screenplay to a torturous crawl. Handled improperly, long monologues can be deadly to

---

2.   4

                                                                    8

make?" -- he finally admits that it was the YMCA. "The
YMCA?" she asks. Then, memory strikes. "Oh, the YMCA!
Gee, they remembered!" Walter decides to make his move.
He kisses her fully on the lips, then pulls away, awaiting a
reaction. "The YMCA," she says, oblivious to everything.
"Who would've thought it? Gosh, they're such sweet guys."

     CUT TO: An OWL perched on a tree limb just outside
Walter's car. He blinks once at the car, then twice.

     CUT BACK TO: The interior of Walter's car. They are
both out of sight beneath the dashboard. We hear the
occasional SOUND of moaning and fumbling -- then a squeak.
"It's nothing," Walter hurriedly says off-screen. "Nothing."
It happens again. Melissa sits up, clothes in slight dis-
array, coming up with Walter and a squeezable toy duck.
She squeezes it. It squeaks. "I can explain that," Walter
says quickly.

     She throws the duck at him, storms out of the car and
slams the door behind her. "You're disgusting, you know
that? Absolutely disgusting." She stalks toward the house.

     Walter picks up the duck and squeezes it. It squeaks.
"Oh, shut up," he says. He then starts the car, throws the
duck into the rear seat, and drives off into the night.

     DISSOLVE TO: The interior of Walter's bedroom as a
phone solicitor tries to sell him ten "free" dance lessons.   60

LINES

10   PICAS   75

Fig. 26

an otherwise well-crafted script. If it's essential that a lot of information be conveyed during a single scene, try to break it up with occasional remarks from the other person or persons in the room. Even if the remarks only amount to observations of shock or astonishment, use them anyway. (And be honest—how often in real life are any of us allowed to speak at length without someone or something—a ringing telephone, a solicitor at the front door—interrupting the flow of things?)

Now, on some occasions, you might *want* a long-winded monologue, to say something about the character involved. If the speaker is long-winded himself, or pompous, you can use the monologue as a device to reinforce this detail. If you desire, you can heighten this effect by having other characters *try* to get a word in edgewise, and fail. A long monologue can also be used in the context of a sermon or a broadcaster's delivery of the day's news. Paddy Chayefsky's screenplay for the motion picture *Network* is filled with such speeches, each brilliantly crafted to tell us about the characters involved. Thus monologues function on two levels: they convey information overtly through the spoken word, while covertly telling us something about the person doing the talking.

Should you decide to go ahead and use the device of the long monologue, use it sparingly. I cannot help but think of a classic scene in *The Great Muppet Caper* wherein actress Diana Rigg delivers a long, involved monologue filled with more information than anyone could possibly care to hear. After the speech, Miss Piggy (manned—or perhaps pigged—by Frank Oz) asks, "Why are you telling me all this?" Rigg simply shrugs and says, "It's exposition. It has to go *somewhere*."

In addition, it's always a good idea to break up any scenes that, taken sequentially, form a static image. If there are several inactive scenes in a row, you might want to throw a more active scene into the middle, even if it's only the character driving toward the place where the next scene is set. By the same token, avoid using the same set too many times in a row, and try to layer your exterior and interior scenes as evenly as possible.

You should write almost exclusively in master shots. That is, number each scene, tell where it is, when it is taking place, describe it briefly, and then let it go. Use camera angles and shots only when necessary to your story. Not only can an abundance of film terminology prove confusing to the less-than-cinematically-informed reader, but it will inevitably be ignored by the director. One director that I know makes it a point to take a felt pen and black out all but the most essential directions on any script he chooses to direct. "What writers must remember," he explained, "is that they are responsible for the story, yes. But the director is responsible for the *look* of the film. There are a dozen ways at least that any shot can be filmed, and it is the director's responsibility, using his experience and training, to look at the finished set, the dynamics of the performers, and a thousand other factors, and decide which would be the best shot. To do less than that is to abnegate one's obligations as a filmmaker."

Along these lines, you should indicate specific transitions only when necessary. You need not write CUT TO after each scene. That's understood. Only call for such transitions as a dissolve if it is your intention to indicate an interlude in time, or a wipe (the introduction of the new scene by having it "wipe" across the screen from side to side, or from one corner to the other) if it is your intention to convey the feeling of an old movie, since this device was used frequently in the late silent film era, and for such serials as *Buck Rogers.*

Try to start your screenplay on a strong point, a hook that will get the audience immediately interested in your story. In other words, something that will get the attention of an audience that just paid five dollars or more per ticket and wants to get its money's worth from the moment the lights go down and the projector grinds to life. Naturally, your script should also end on a strong point, and there should be a number of smaller crests—similar to hooks in television and radio writing—to help sustain the audience's interest.

Until you are secure with the techniques of screenwriting, it's often best to stick with a linear plot. Unless handled properly, jumping all over the place in time and space, and the excessive use of flashbacks, can confuse and, in some cases, actually irritate an audience. Woody Allen's *Annie Hall* is a good example of a nonlinear plot properly handled, as are his *Stardust Memories* and *Interiors.* Vonnegut's *Slaughterhouse Five* (adapted by Stephen Geller, directed by George Roy Hill) is another prime example.

Finally, when it comes time to resolve your story, be sure the resolution comes naturally. It should be organic, growing out of what went before. Dropping in a sudden, unexpected solution—the poverty-stricken mother of eight suddenly winning the Irish Sweepstakes, the *real* murderer confessing out of compassion—can get a hostile response from an audience that feels it's been cheated of a solid, well-crafted story. The *deus ex machina* school of thought may have worked for the ancient Greeks, but in contemporary society it's bound to have your audiences demanding their money back. It is often wise if your characters are personally responsible for the film's resolution. You don't send a hot-shot New York cop to track down a murderer only to have the case solved by a street cop we've only seen for five minutes. Let your main characters work their own way out of whatever dilemma you've put them in.

Or, as someone once said, "The practice of drama is to get your character stuck up a tree, and then throw rocks at him." It's no fun to have someone else come along and take the rocks away. Your character has to save himself on his own.

Beyond these basic requirements, the form taken by your screenplay is largely a function of your own interests and attitudes, and the kind of story you've chosen to tell. The only other requirement to consider is the typographical format used in motion picture scripts.

The screenplay format is virtually identical to the format for television movies and for other programs produced on film.

Scene numbers are placed at 15 and 75 picas.

All dialogue and scene descriptions are single-spaced and written in upper- and lower-case letters.

Double-space between two different sections of dialogue, and between scene descriptions and dialogue.

When used in direct conjunction with dialogue, the NAMES of characters are capitalized and typed at 40 picas.

Dialogue directions, and indications for inflection, appear at 35 picas.

Dialogue itself appears between 30 and 60 picas.

The page number appears at 79 picas, usually 4 spaces from the top of the page.

The first page of your screenplay begins with the title, all in caps and underlined, centered on the page at 7 lines from the top of the page. Five spaces below that, at 12 lines, the words FADE IN: appear, with the first numbered scene appearing 2 lines further down, at 14 lines.

Each subsequent page begins with the page number in the upper right-hand corner at 75 picas, 3 lines, and the first continuing scene indicated 7 lines from the top of the page.

The bottom of each page should have the word CONTINUED in all caps at 68 picas if that scene carries onto the next page.

Using these format requirements, let's see what the first few pages of our treatment would look like in screenplay form. (See Fig. 27 through 31.)

A few notes on the sample screenplay:

In translating the treatment into a script, I used a funnel approach to make the audience immediately aware of where they were. An opening shot of a 1950s car cruising down a series of old country roads establishes both a mood and a period. The focus narrows further by having the car pull into the driveway in Scene 2. This connotes that whoever is driving the car is returning after being away for a while.

The small awkwardnesses and hesitations in Scene 3 tell us that Walter and Melissa don't know each other very well and create a sense of immediate familiarity. Everyone, at some point in life, has been in a situation like the one Walter is trying, rather badly, to handle. It tells you something about Walter, to wit, that he's so desperate for someone to go out with that he resorts to the old telephone-number-on-the-men's-room-wall route. That Melissa's number was on the wall in the first place, and that she can easily recall the questionable circumstances that led to its placement, tells you something about her as well.

Scene 4 provides a smooth transition in time. We needn't see how Walter manages to accomplish his move. (Probably, she didn't even notice.)

We have the bird's wide-eyed reaction. It also saves time by cutting down on the dialogue.

Scene 4 serves another purpose, in that it breaks up a scene that would otherwise be static, taking place entirely in the car, without a break. The diversion is a momentary one, it acts as a transition, and provides a brief, visual relief from the same static scene.

Scene 5 picks up in the car, but the direction calls for ANOTHER AN-

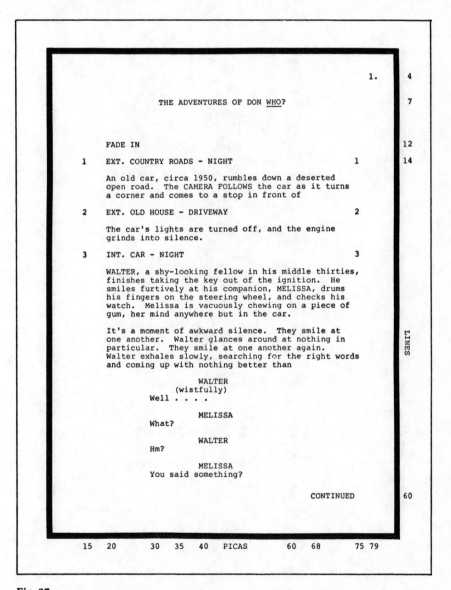

Fig. 27

GLE. This indicates to the director that a different perspective might further break up the static action without telling him precisely how it should be done. For example, Scene 3 could be shot by having the camera peeking in through the window on the driver's side, or by alternating from side to side, or by simply shooting through the front windshield. If the director chooses the first possibility, Scene 5 could be shot, say, from over the back of the seat, with the camera positioned where the rear seat

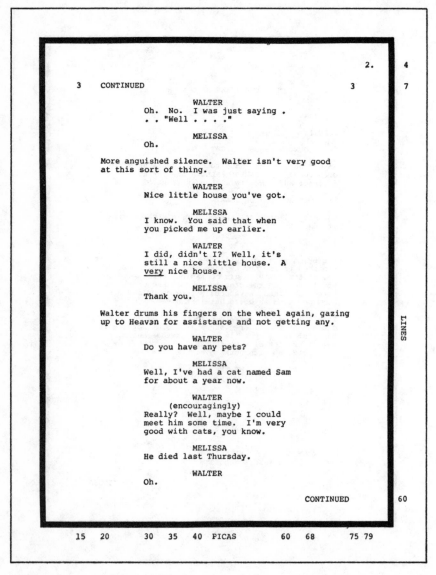

Fig. 28

would be. Failing that, he could also use any of the other options we described above.

Finally, Scene 6 accomplishes a transition in time. The morning sunlight is dazzling after the night scene, and tells the audience that this is Walter the next morning, trying to deal with yet another of life's little annoyances, a telephone solicitor.

So when making the transition from the index card to the treatment to

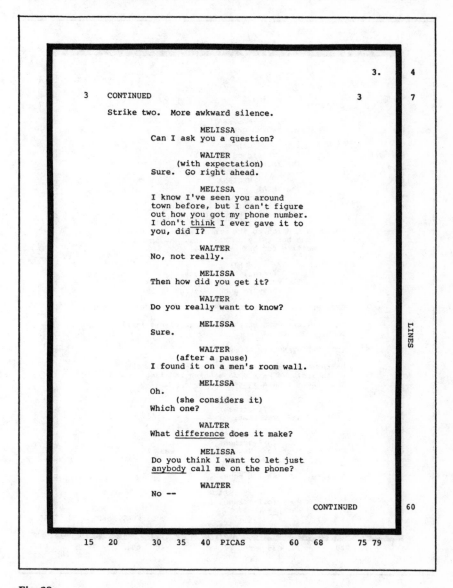

Fig. 29

the script, we've actually turned one scene into five, using what we know about the craft of film to keep the action moving and as nonstatic as possible.

The rest of the script continues in this fashion, using all your ability to produce something you would like to see in a motion picture.

Then, once finished, there are several questions you must ask yourself.

Is it too long or too short? If so, then eliminate any scenes that are not

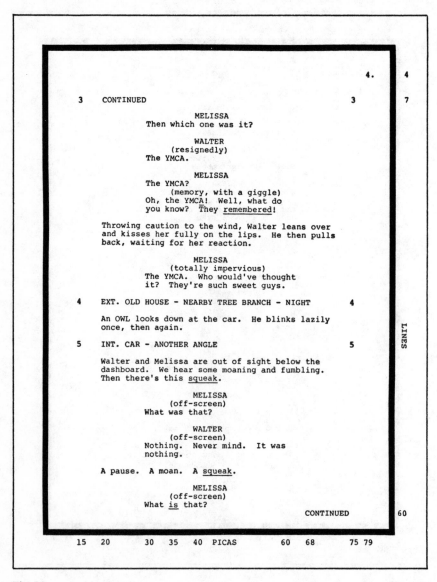

Fig. 30

truly necessary, or fill out your script with more characterization or more active scenes.

(In deciding if your script is too short or too long, remember that some scenes that might take only a paragraph to describe, last several minutes on film. Likewise, a scene which takes a complete page of careful description might require only a few seconds on film. Bear these facts in mind, and compensate for them in your reading.)

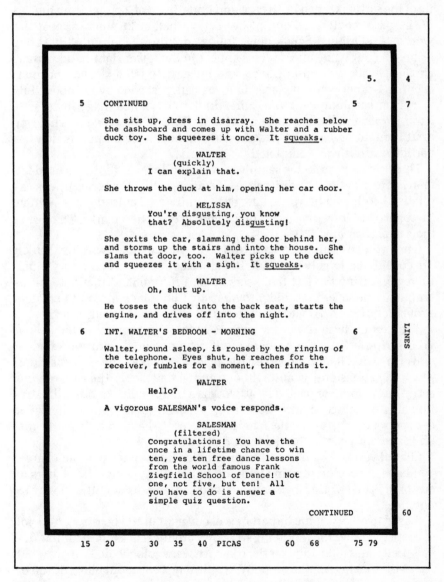

Fig. 31

Does the script say what you wanted it to say? Is it dull?

Ask yourself honestly if the script would do better as a television movie or a feature film. If you finally decide it might not have the special magic that would qualify it as a feature film, go ahead and market it as a television movie.

When you have done this, you are ready to put your screenplay together. The first step is to write a title page. A title page is very simple. The title of the script is typed in all caps and underlined at 22 lines from the top of the page, centered. Four spaces below that, at 26 lines, appear the words "An Original Screenplay" followed 2 lines later with "By (Your Name)." Your name and address appear in the lower right-hand corner, single-spaced, written in upper- and lower-case letters. If you have an agent, his or her name is placed here instead, preceded by the note, "Literary Representation:". If it is a first draft, this is noted in the lower left-hand corner in all caps and underlined. (This is the case for whatever draft it might be.) Single-spaced below this is the date upon which the particular draft was completed.

This title page format, a sample of which follows, is the same used for television or radio. The difference, of course, is that the series title is capitalized, followed two lines later by the individual episode title, written in upper- and lower-case and bracketed by quotation marks. The rest is the same. (See Fig. 32.)

Once you've completed your title page, you come to two steps which are considered largely optional. But since both have become very much in vogue during the last five years or so, I recommend that both be attempted whenever possible, provided that both be handled to create a professional look. Amateurism here can only hinder your efforts.

The first of these is a cover page. A cover page consists of the title of your script, artistically rendered, with the potential addition of some clever artwork. It helps to have a friend who knows a little about calligraphy and can tastefully, and without undue flair, letter the title of your script onto the cover page. The artwork is a line drawing or other illustration of a critical scene from the screenplay, or one that captures the flavor of the screenplay as a whole. It helps here, too, to have an artistically gifted friend who can be bribed with dinner.

Should you know no one who can provide this service without charge, you have the option of going without it altogether, using press letters to create the title, or finding someone who can do it for as little money as possible.

(I used to discount the importance of cover art until I began seeing a lot of it, and was told the following story by a producer at a large studio: "We had pretty much decided on the films we were going to do that year, but were still looking for one more. Well, one day, I got about half a dozen or so scripts which had been forwarded by the readers. I was a bit tired that day, but because a decision had to be made soon, I decided to start reading immediately. As I looked them over, I came across one that had a fancy-shmancy cover. I admit that it was a trifle overdone, but it intrigued me. The drawing was well done, and it got my attention. Besides, I figured that if the writer had gone through enough trouble to do a cover like that, then the least I could do was to read it. So that was the one I read first. As it turned out, I liked the script, and we decided that we'd do that

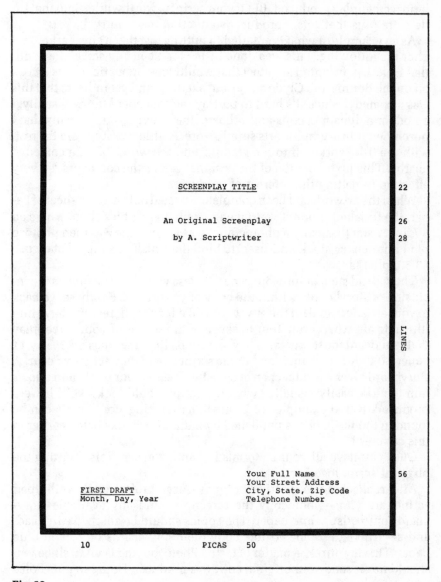

Fig. 32

one as our last project. Now, as it happened, I later came upon another script in the same batch that is also producible, but by then our quota was filled. If the property is still available next year we'll probably take an option on it, or just go ahead and produce it. The only difference was that I just happened to read the other script first, because it caught my eye."

(Note that the script they decided to produce was good, it was worth producing. No amount of fancy graphics will *ever* result in getting an inferior screenplay produced. But if your script is worthwhile, then that little extra plus that gets a producer's attention never hurts.)

As an example of what is entailed in putting together a cover art page, I offer the following. This was done by me for a comedy screenplay entitled *Hold Up*. I wanted an effect that would look dramatic (it was a take-off on the Bonnie and Clyde story) and exciting, and yet indicate that this was a comedy. Since it's hard to portray the concept of *funny* visually, I opted for a dynamic, cops-and-robbers line drawing, one of many that I purchased from a graphic arts supply store. A little presstype did the rest, with the title worked into the graphic, and the words ". . . a comedy" nearby. This juxtaposition of the criminal versus the comic proved very effective in getting the interest of producers.

When the artwork had been completed, pasted onto a 4 by 5 sheet of paper, the finished product was taken to a photo/graphics shop, where an 8½ by 11 stat (basically a photograph) was taken. This was then photocopied onto cover stock and used to bind the finished script. Total cost: $3.50, plus tax.

The second step, helpful but generally less vital than the first, is the inclusion of storyboards within the body of your script. For these, go back to your artistic friend, or the guy who'll do it for a small fee, and have him illustrate anywhere from four to seven of the scenes of your screenplay that you deem most crucial. They should be line drawings on 8½ by 11 paper, so they can be included in the script where they actually occur. A storyboard gives a producer an even better feel for your work, and allows him to more easily visualize what the script would look like if it were produced. (Good examples of professional-looking storyboards can be found in the script books published by Ballantine Books listed earlier in this chapter.)

Once you have all your materials in hand, you can finish putting the physical script together.

After rechecking your script for typos—neat, professional, well-typed scripts are *vital*—photocopy the screenplay and any available storyboards onto crisp white paper. The copies should be sharp, easily read, and unwrinkled. (Some writers copy their storyboards onto light-blue paper. This is entirely a matter of taste.) Photocopying is vital, since you should never send your *original* copy to a producer. Doing so puts holes

in the original, and any wear and tear will show on future copies. For this reason, keep your original in a safe place. Besides, lost scripts are not uncommon occurrences.

Next, have your cover sheet (with optional artwork) copied onto a heavier stock of colored paper. A 60 lb. bond is usually preferred, using gray, deep-blue, or cream-colored stock. Make sure the backing sheet is the same stock. Then punch three holes along the left-hand edge of the script, binding the whole thing together with brass paper fasteners.

Finally, hold the script in your hands and heft it a few times. Go ahead—every writer does it. A finished, bound, snazzy-looking script is a joy to behold. You shouldn't feel the least bit sheepish if you stand there, a silly grin on your face, hefting the script, glancing through it, holding it at a distance for a better look, and generally carrying on. Why not? You've put in an awful lot of work, and a little aesthetic appreciation is small enough reward.

Besides, now comes the hard part. It's time to go back to work.

Marketing the Screenplay

At long last, you've got a finished screenplay for a feature film in your hands, ready to go. The question now is, what to do with it? One possibility is to use it to get an agent, a process discussed in more detail in the appendix dealing with agents. For our purposes, though, we will confront the actual process of selling your screenplay entirely on your own. Now, mind you, it'll be difficult. I cannot reinforce that strongly enough. At the same time, it is not impossible, either. It simply requires persistence and an adherence to the rough guidelines that follow.

The first thing you'll want to decide is to whom to send your screenplay. Part of this decision-making is estimating, in your own mind, the approximate budget for the screenplay should it get produced. Nothing specific, mind you; you don't have to say it'll be around $6 or $7.5 million. Just realistically decide, as closely as you can, whether it will be a big-budget film or a small-budget film. If it calls for a lot of exotic locations, special effects, or very extensive sets, you can probably assume it will require a large budget. If it needs but a small cast, simple locations, and minimal effects, you could safely classify it as a low-budget film. Within the filmmaking community, a low budget is anything under about $4 million dollars, although for its own purposes in deciding what a writer should be paid, the Writers Guild defines a low-budget film as anything below $1 million.

Making this decision will start pointing you in the direction of a likely producer. If you've written a high-budget film, most independent producers probably couldn't handle the overwhelming costs. By the same token, you'd have a better chance placing a low-budget film with an independent producer than with a major studio, at least as of this writing. (I have good reason to believe that this trend will reverse itself, and the major studios will soon begin looking for more low-budget films to produce and distribute.) So writing a low-budget film gives you greater flexibility, allowing you the choice of approaching either a major studio or an independent producer.

It's usually easier for a screenwriter who hasn't previously sold a script to sell a low-budget script than a high-budget screenplay, simply because the producer won't risk as much should the property fail to take off. Remember—as the risks of production are minimized, the chances of production are maximized.

Although it's not required—in fact, you needn't even consider it a wholly recommended option—some writers actually include a complete script breakdown with their screenplay. A script breakdown is a page-by-page analysis of the physical requirements contained in the script. It does not contain an exact cost breakdown, since these shift with inflation and a dozen other factors. But breakdowns do help give the producer a more precise idea of what the script actually involves in terms of supplies, locations, manpower, and so forth.

Should you desire to include a script breakdown with your screenplay, here is a blank sample for your reference. Each page of the breakdown deals specifically with one given location.

Moving from top to bottom, you would fill in the name of your script, the set that would be required (don't worry about the sequence—that's something that's filled in during preproduction), the time period in which the story is set, the season, whether the action takes place during the day or the night, the surrounding location, and the total script pages required for that one location.

For example: Let's say part of your story takes place on an old ranch in Nevada. Scenes 3, 5, 7, 14, 29, and 74 all take place on that ranch, just outside the horse stable. After filling in all the preliminary information listed above, you would go to the section marked *Scene Numbers & Synopsis* and write each scene number individually, followed by a brief synopsis of what happens during each of those scenes. Under *Cast* you would provide the name of each major character who appears in those scenes, the bit players called for (those who have one or two lines of dialogue), and the type and number of nonspeaking extras needed. If the scenes require any special effects or special camera processing, this is also indicated and described. List any incidental music needed during the shoot or during postproduction as well as any specific visual props, action-oriented props (exploding bombs and that sort of thing), and any animals that may be needed.

The completed script breakdown is then numbered and included with the screenplay at the rear of the packet. For your own purposes, you can either have the following script breakdown page photocopied and enlarged, or type your own, following the example given on the next page. Either way, continue to bear in mind that including a script breakdown will not sell your script for you. It will, however, give the producer even more confidence that you know what you're doing, and will help him to determine whether the budget is within his capacity to handle.

It's a nice little extra, but it is *not* absolutely needed. Use your own discretion on the question of including it or not in the completed screenplay.

To further illustrate the purpose of a script breakdown, a second page is included with the appropriate information filled in for a movie western. (See Fig. 33 and 34.)

Once you've determined whether to approach a major studio or an independent producer, the next step is to narrow down the possible alternatives to specific production companies, and to find out where they are.

You can use a number of resources to get a list of current film producers. First, you can turn to your daily newspaper and check the movie listings to get the names of different production companies. This is not an all-inclusive list although it *will* tell you what individual producers have presented in recent months, and what they are likely to look for in the future.

There are quite a few publications that provide far more extensive lists of producers. Among these are:

Boxoffice, a monthly trade magazine aimed at movie distributors. This magazine provides a good deal of information about what the studios are currently producing. This is particularly true of its annual Buyer's Guide Directory, which is published in August. The address is 1800 North Highland Avenue, Suite 316, Hollywood, CA 90028.

Pacific Coast Studio Directory, a quarterly directory that has been called the "bible of the entertainment industry." This slim volume contains the names, addresses, and phone numbers of virtually *every* production company in Los Angeles, San Francisco, Arizona, Hawaii, and ten other states. In addition, it includes the same information on talent agencies, publications, industry craftspeople, the different unions, advertisers and film/television bureaus in each state listed. If you want to contact a major studio or a small, independent producer, you'll probably find them listed here somewhere. Of course, you have to know the name of the company before you can look it up. Write to 6331 Hollywood Boulevard, Hollywood, CA 90028.

The Hollywood Scriptletter, a monthly newsletter that features interviews with writers and producers, trend analyses and some market listings. Write to 1626 North Wilcox Avenue, Suite 385, Hollywood, CA 90028.

ScriptWriter News, a biweekly publication that features market listings, screenwriting tips, trend analyses, and contest information. Available from Writer's Publishing Company, 250 West 57th Street, Suite 224, New York, NY 10019.

The *Hollywood Reporter Bluebook*, an annual volume that contains hundreds of listings of different production companies and their needs. It's particularly useful for a scriptwriter, and it makes a good companion volume to the *Pacific Coast Studio Directory*. Write to 6715 Sunset Boulevard, Hollywood, CA 90028.

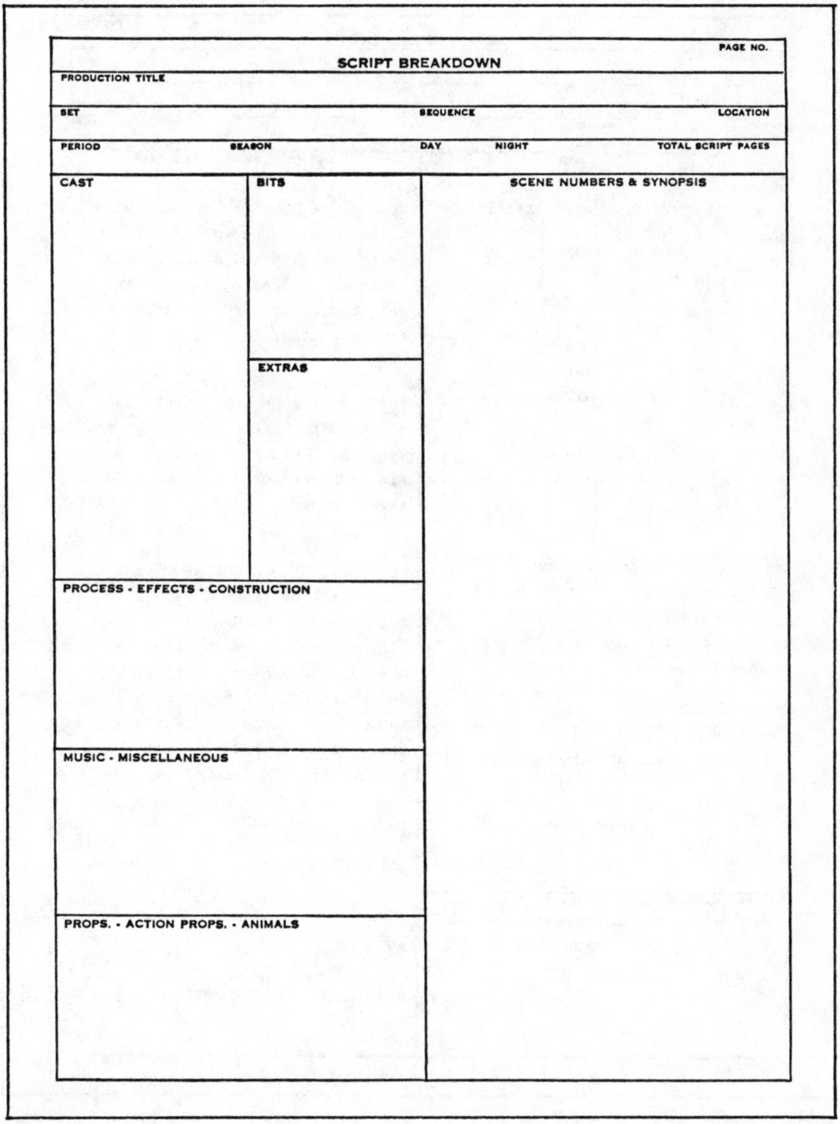

SCRIPT BREAKDOWN

PAGE NO.

PRODUCTION TITLE

SET | SEQUENCE | LOCATION

PERIOD | SEASON | DAY | NIGHT | TOTAL SCRIPT PAGES

CAST | BITS | SCENE NUMBERS & SYNOPSIS

EXTRAS

PROCESS - EFFECTS - CONSTRUCTION

MUSIC - MISCELLANEOUS

PROPS. - ACTION PROPS. - ANIMALS

Fig. 33

Daily Variety, 1400 North Cahuenga Boulevard, Los Angeles, CA 90028, and *The Hollywood Reporter,* 6715 Sunset Boulevard, Hollywood, CA 90028, are both excellent sources of information on current trends in filmmaking, and the former publication publishes a regular film and television production chart, complete with telephone numbers. Write for current subscription and individual prices.

A listing that contains the most reputable and long-lived film produc-

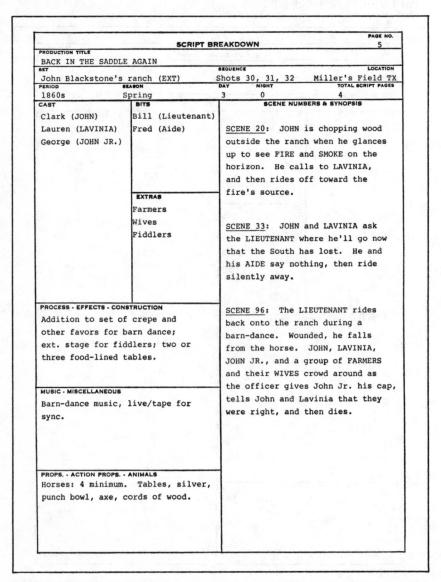

Fig. 34

tion companies can be found at the rear of this book.

Using these resources, pick out a handful of production companies that you believe might be appropriate for your screenplay. Rank them in order, from the largest to the smallest company, or from the most receptive to the one you imagine will be least receptive. You must also decide whether you want to approach all these producers simultaneously, or if you would prefer to market your script to one producer at a time. A case can be made for and against both these routes. Marketing your script to one producer at a time can be very time-consuming. But many producers like to think that they—or at most one or two others—are the only ones who have seen the script. So sending your script all over Hollywood in a massive assault may alienate some producers—and sending out five or ten scripts can be an expensive proposition. However, if you manage to get two studios interested in your script, you can have them bid on the property, thereby raising the ceiling on what you'll get up front.

My personal feeling is that you should market your script on an individual basis or, at most, to two producers simultaneously. Any more than that and you're risking trouble.

Having selected the first producer you intend to approach, you must then invest a little more money in a telephone call. Call the specific production company you're interested in and ask for the story department. (Because it's not at all uncommon for as many as a dozen production companies to be situated on the same lot, using the same switchboard, be absolutely certain that the switchboard operator knows which production company you want. If the production company has its own direct outside line, then this isn't a problem.)

Once you've been transferred to the story department, ask for the name of the story editor. Don't ask to speak with the person, just get the name, thank the answerer for his or her time, and hang up.

To understand why this bit of information is important it is necessary to first explain a little about how a production company works.

In some respects, a production company is not unlike a book publishing company. Each is literally flooded by a steady flow of manuscripts, solicited and otherwise, and each employs a large number of professional readers charged with the responsibility of wading through the dreck and finding the occasional jewels. There are several ways studio readers differ from the readers at a book publisher. First, they are all members of a union, specifically the Story Analysts division of the International Alliance of Theatrical Stage Employees (I.A.T.S.E.), Local 854, 7715 Sunset Boulevard, Los Angeles, CA 90046. Second, many of these readers are retained on a part-time basis, and may work for several different studios. Finally, not a few of these readers (when you speak to them, call them story analysts, or they'll get rather distant on you) are, themselves, writers. Some of them are Writers Guild members, but a majority are beginning writers who want to learn something about scriptwriting firsthand, and or want to slip in one or two of their own scripts along the way. (If you are a resident of the Hollywood/Los Angeles area, and would like to try this route, you should contact I.A.T.S.E. at the address given above and find out what the procedures are.)

One way in which studio readers are like publishing readers is that unless you specifically address your manuscript to someone there, you're likely to have a more difficult time getting anyone's attention. Putting someone's name on the letter of inquiry—instead of simply addressing it to the story department—makes that person at least partly responsible for your manuscript. It also gives the reader the feeling that, if you know whom to approach, you must know what you're doing—and again, that impression is always important in the screenwriting business.

Once you have the story editor's name, write a query letter, because an unsolicited script arriving without prior warning is anathema—just as it is for television and radio producers.

Your query letter, like your script, should be spare and to the point. You should state that you are familiar with the films they produce; that you have developed a feature film screenplay that is consistent with their trends in production; that you have followed this development through the synopsis, outline, treatment, and final screenplay stages; and that the script is currently available for examination. You should also point out that you own all the rights to the screenplay, that it is an original work, and that since it's consistent with popular trends it will likely be a very commercial property. If you have any special qualifications—a degree in an area touched upon by the script, for instance—mention them as well. Do not, however, include any information about what the story is about. This little step will protect both you and the studio.

Conclude by stating that if he or she would be interested in examining the outline, the treatment, or the complete screenplay, you would be pleased to send it along for his or her examination. Also, you should clearly state that you will be enclosing a release form (available in this book) with your submission, but that if there is a specifically worded release form the company prefers, ask that this also be forwarded so that you can include it with your submission.

As a rule, your finished query letter should run about a page long, and certainly no more than a page and a half. It should also be as tightly and well-written as possible. I say this because I've seen a lot of writers who can turn out fantastic scripts, but who slap-dash off some of the crummiest queries I've ever seen. If you've just spent half a year of your life working on a screenplay, then it only makes sense to put a little effort and forethought into your query. You should also be sure to keep a copy of the query for reference in writing future letters to the story editor, and so that you can just retype the thing should you need to approach another studio.

For further assistance in writing a query letter, a sample letter is printed here. (Needless to say, it should not be copied verbatim. It will cause much concern when the story editors get a whole series of identical letters.)

Mr. Leslie Morgan
West Coast Story Editor
Warner Brothers, Inc.
4000 Warner Boulevard
Burbank, California 91522

Dear Mr. Morgan,

I have recently completed an original screenplay that I believe is consistent with the quality and type of film produced by Warner Brothers.

Entitled *The Nightshade Equation*, the screenplay includes many of the elements of supernaturalism that have become popular in recent years, while taking an entirely different approach that is unique unto itself.

While not a member of the Writers Guild, I have been a freelance writer in other media for several years, and *The Nightshade Equation* is partly based on actual research that I carried out in the area of the occult, and which formed the basis for several published articles and short stories. (I still retain all rights to the idea, however.)

In addition to the actual screenplay, a brief synopsis, an outline and a treatment are also available for examination.

I would appreciate the opportunity to submit the script or any other material for perusal by the Warner Brothers Story Department on a purely speculative basis. I will be happy to enclose a standard release form with the submission or, if there is an in-house release preferred by Warners, I will sign and enclose that one instead.

Hoping that I shall hear from you soon in this regard, I remain

Most sincerely yours,

A. Nother Writer

Surprising as it may seem, you probably won't have to wait long for a reply. Usually, you'll get word back from the studio within a few weeks, or occasionally as much as a month after you sent off your query. During this period, you can realistically look forward to one of three responses. The first is that they simply cannot look at any script unless it's first been sent in by an agent. But don't let this discourage you, because there are just as many other producers that don't require an agent. The second is a request to look at the treatment or outline alone. The third is the go-ahead to submit the entire screenplay, although some will ask for you to also enclose the outline or the treatment. In these latter two cases, they may tell you to go ahead and use your own release form, or they will send one along for your use.

If a treatment is ever requested, with or without the screenplay, it is often a good idea to Xerox off the cover art page and use that as the cover for your treatment. It never hurts.

Before sending off anything, however, you should take one more step, largely for your own protection. You should register the script with the Writers Guild of America, west. It's unlikely that anyone will plagiarize your script, but when dealing with the film industry, it's never a bad idea to cover all your bets. The steps for registering a script are simple; just send a copy and the appropriate fee to the WGAw office at 8955 Beverly Boulevard, Los Angeles, CA 90048. As of this writing, it costs $10 for a non-WGA member to register a script, and even though that fee shows no sign of increasing soon, you should contact the Guild and verify the fee. With this done, you can, should you want to do so, write the words *Registered, WGAw* on the title page of your screenplay, directly under the date in the lower left-hand corner. You may also want to include the serial number that the Guild will assign your script, but this isn't really necessary.

With your material finally collected together, and your release form filled in, you can then send the material to the person who responded to your letter. Be sure to refer back to your earlier letter, and to having received his or her responding letter, so the secretary who opens all the mail will know that your property is not coming in unexpected. You should also write the words *Release Form Enclosed* on the outside of your mailing envelope.

Then . . . well, then you wait.

While you're waiting for a reaction to this direct approach, let's consider some of the other, less direct means of selling your screenplay.

As mentioned earlier, you may have decided to write a screenplay for someone under contract to a studio for a number of motion pictures. If so, specifically state this in your query letter. This can further help to move your property along, since the performers who enter such deals frequently put pressure on the story department to come up with the perfect vehicle for their talents, and if such a script comes in over the transom, so much the better.

In addition, should you have a specific performer in mind who may or may not be under contract for a certain number of movies, but who is just perfect for the starring role, you have the option of approaching the performer directly. You can do this by addressing your query letter to the performer in care of the Screen Actors Guild, 7750 Sunset Boulevard, Los Angeles, CA 90046. They will forward the letter, unopened, to the individual performer. (You can also contact any writer—including me—by writing a letter to the person in care of the Writers Guild.) In your query letter to such a performer, you'll want to include all the information included in the query to a producer, and add your conviction that the role is very consistent with the performer's other roles, but also allows for a certain expansion. You can even state that you wrote the entire screenplay specifically for that performer. This may or may not be true, but at least it's flattering, and will get the performer's attention.

If the performer likes the script, then he or she can either option your screenplay directly, or approach a studio with the desire to do your screenplay. This technique, while not always successful, does present a fair chance. In fact, it was precisely through this direct-sale method that Frank Sinatra read, liked, and agreed to star in Von Ryan's Express.

Finally, should you decide, after going through all the trouble of writing your screenplay, that you'd really rather not go through the difficulty of marketing your property, you always have the option of approaching a literary agent with the script—which, if it's good enough, will inevitably be represented by someone. The process for securing an agent is given in the appendix. But it would be wise at this juncture to discuss one of the more recent developments in agenting—the packager.

A number of agencies in recent years have begun following the example set by such monolithic corporations as International Creative Management and the William Morris Agency, and have widened their sphere of influence. In other words, they represent writers, actors and directors. This arrangement puts the packager in a truly novel situation. If a packager agrees to represent a new writer's script, he can then call a studio and offer them not only the script, but an established performer and a director, both picked from the agent's stable. This is what's known in the business as a "package deal."

A package deal occurs for one of two general reasons. First, it could be that the agent has a good script that calls for a large budget, but it's by an unproven writer. By throwing in an established name performer and director, he maximizes the studio's chances of breaking even, and in the process gets his other two clients some work. Second, an agent can, upon spotting a trend, call a studio and promise the studio a certain number of name performers and a director, with the script to be written at a later date. The benefit of all this to the agent is that he not only receives 10 percent of the salaries of all those he finds work for, but also receives a certain percentage of the actual film itself.

(Naturally, such package deals are also the bane of the filmmaking industry. The aforementioned *Can't Stop the Music* was one of these. I can just hear the agent: "Listen, disco's hot right now. Tell you what—how about a film that's *all* disco, you know? We can toss in Valerie Perrine and the Village People, and we'll make it a jazzy, fast-paced, knock-em-sock-em musical. What's it about? Who *cares* what it's about? We'll worry about a writer later." That, of course, was their big mistake.)

Those are the indirect methods. Having established these, we can move on to the consequences, good and not-so-good, of the direct method.

When your script arrives at the studio and is delivered to the story editor, it is handed on to one of the readers, who reads the entire screenplay for the first time. If it is, in his estimate, unproducible, it will be shunted back to you with a brief note stating that it's not their type of film, or they were unable to generate enough interest in it to pursue it further, or suchlike. If, on the other hand, it is producible and looks like a property that might fit in well with the studio's other projects, the reader will do three things: First, he will synopsize the script into a page or two of narrative; he will write up an appraisal of the script, its strengths, weaknesses, its potential audience, and, on occasion, a recommendation of a specific producer; finally, he will send the screenplay back to the story editor with his written commentaries.

The story editor is the next person to read your script. At this point, he may exercise the prerogative of sending the script back to you, or he may opt to bump the script on to the next person in the chain of command, adding his own comments to the reader's.

But when the script leaves the story editor's office things really start to get confusing. Based upon my experiences and those of other writers, and after having spoken with representatives of a dozen major studios and independent production companies, it seems safe to say that there is no clear-cut chain of command. "Every script is different," explained a story editor at Paramount Pictures. "I've never yet seen two scripts take the same route on the way to a possible production. There are often group creative meetings, someone may come in from inside the company and personally take over, or a director might come to us specifically asking to do that particular script. But there's no one person anywhere along the line who can decide that the company's going to do a particular screenplay, with the exception of the president of the company, who has the final word on all projects submitted for our examination."

Here, however, are some examples of what *can* happen, and what frequently does happen:

The script will go from the story editor to an individual producer within the company who the editor believes might be interested in the project. If so, the producer approaches the president directly and, after a long negotiation process, gets the go-ahead to proceed with the film. This is the quickest route.

If the story editor can't come up with an interested producer, the script goes on to any one of the many vice-presidents in charge of production. More people read the script. More appraisals are written, initialed, and shuttled on. More meetings are held. Copies of the script may be sent to outside (independent) producers and directors to solicit their support for the property. If enough interest is developed, the entire project is laid at the feet of the president, who makes the final decision.

The script may find its way into the hands of an inside producer who likes it even though others want to pass on it. In such a situation, he may option the script personally, promising to work with the scriptwriter until the property is appropriate for production. At that time, he will secure producer status for the property.

The script may also be sent on to an executive producer within the company. The executive producer, who carries a hefty amount of weight with the company, may get permission from the president to pursue a development deal. With this, he will assign a producer to the property and attempt to find a director.

There are other possibilities beyond those listed here, and someone may opt to pass on the script anywhere along the line. But if they don't, here are the potential responses that you will get. (The response time, by the way, can range anywhere from a few weeks to several months.)

Again, there is always the possibility of flat-out rejection.

The studio may decide to simply option the script for one or two years. This means that they will agree to pay you a certain fee, usually anywhere from $5,000 to $10,000, for the rights to your script during that time. You, in turn, promise not to market the script anywhere else until the option period has expired. During the period covered by the option, you may be asked to rewrite the screenplay. In addition, the studio will use this time to A) Make up their minds once and for all whether they intend to go ahead with the film or not, and B) Once so decided, put together a development deal and get the film moving into preproduction.

Finally, the studio may opt to purchase the script outright and move directly into preproduction. If this is the case, you will be offered a flat fee, the possibility of a percentage, and a salary. We'll take a closer look at the dollars and cents involved, but for the moment it's important to emphasize two points:

First, even though your script may be optioned or even purchased, this does not guarantee production. Many more scripts are purchased each year than are *ever* produced, and nearly three times as many scripts are

WGA 1981 THEATRICAL AND TELEVISION BASIC AGREEMENT
THEATRICAL COMPENSATION

	Effective 3/1/81-6/30/82		Effective 7/1/82-6/30/83		Effective 7/1/83-6/30/84		Effective 7/1/84-6/30/85	
	LOW	HIGH	LOW	HIGH	LOW	HIGH	LOW	HIGH
Screenplay, with Treatment	15,876	29,845	17,781	33,023	19,737	36,565	21,513	40,000
Screenplay, without Treatment	9,924	20,412	11,115	22,861	12,338	25,376	13,448	27,660
Story or Treatment	5,953	9,072	6,667	10,161	7,400	11,279	8,066	12,294
Original Treatment	8,223	13,609	9,210	15,242	10,223	16,919	11,143	18,442
Screenplay Rewrite	5,953	9,072	6,667	10,161	7,400	11,279	8,066	12,294
Screenplay Polish	2,978	4,536	3,335	5,080	3,702	5,639	4,035	6,147

Low Budget =Photoplay costing less than $1,000,000
High Budget =Photoplay costing $1,000,000 or more

optioned annually than are purchased and produced. But having one script optioned or purchased is a vital first step. You may receive an assignment to write another film for them, and your next original treatment will be given even greater consideration.

Second, either of these two occurrences will allow you to join the Writers Guild and to get an agent. I strongly urge anyone who receives any kind of offer whatsoever from a studio to immediately contact an agent and, explaining that a deal is already in progress, sign a representation contract and have the agent step in and negotiate the sometimes awesome legal machinations that arise whenever one deals with the film industry.

Rates of Pay

Just about any legitimate studio will, upon deciding to produce your script, pay you according to Writers Guild minimums. And as you must join the WGA after making your first sale, it is generally advisable that you do this as soon as you receive the first payment, otherwise you will not be protected by the Guild.

The chart on page 188 shows the prescribed minimum fees for a motion picture screenplay purchased by a studio or independent producer. It is worth mentioning that the amount paid can go up from these figures. Percentages are not required. And it is wholly possible for the studio to agree to purchase your story or your treatment, but assign someone else to write the actual screenplay. (Hence, the credits you sometimes see that read, "Based on a story by. . . .") Figures for this kind of purchase are also included.

No matter what the studio finally decides to purchase—a complete screenplay, a treatment, or a story—you will be asked to sign a contract with the production company. If you're not working through an agent, you may want to bring the contract to an attorney for examination, simply to be sure that you know what rights are being purchased, and what you will receive in return.

Happily, most legitimate studios use a standard contract whenever concluding such an arrangement. A sample contract is provided here. If the contract you receive is substantially different from this one, you should either contact the studio and find out why there is a discrepancy, and/or ask your attorney what it means and how it will affect your rights.

WRITER'S FLAT DEAL CONTRACT

EMPLOYMENT AGREEMENT between _____ (hereinafter sometimes referred to as "Company") and _____ (hereinafter sometimes referred to as "Writer"), dated this _____ day of _____, 19_____.

    1. The Company employs the Writer to write a complete and finished screenplay, presently entitled or designated _____, including the following:

Treatment
Original Treatment
Story
First Draft Screenplay
Final Draft Screenplay
Rewrite of Screenplay
(Draw a line through portions not applicable)

2. (a) The Writer represents that (s)he is a member in good standing of the Writers Guild of America, west, Inc., and warrants that he will maintain his membership in Writers Guild of America, west, Inc. in good standing during the term of this employment.

(b) The Company warrants that it is a party to the Writers Guild of America Theatrical and Television Film Basic Agreement of 1981 (which agreement is herein designated "MBA").

(c) Should any of the terms hereof be less advantageous to the Writer than the minimums provided in said MBA, then the terms of the MBA shall supersede such terms hereof.

Without limiting the generality of the foregoing, it is agreed that screen credits for authorship shall be determined pursuant to the provisions of Schedule A of the MBA in accordance with its terms at the time of determination.

3. The Company will pay to the Writer as full compensation for his services hereunder the sum of _____ DOLLARS ($_____), payable as follows:

(a) Not less than EIGHT HUNDRED EIGHTY DOLLARS ($880.00) shall be paid not later than the first regular weekly pay day of the Company following the expiration of the first week of the Writer's employment.

(b) _____ DOLLARS ($_____) shall be paid within forty-eight (48) hours after delivery of the TREATMENT, ORIGINAL TREATMENT, or STORY, whichever is appropriate, to the Company.

(c) _____ DOLLARS ($_____) shall be paid within forty-eight (48) hours after delivery of the FIRST DRAFT SCREENPLAY to the Company; and

(d) _____ DOLLARS ($_____) shall be paid within forty-eight (48) hours after delivery of the FINAL DRAFT SCREENPLAY.

(e) _____ DOLLARS ($_____) shall be paid within forty-eight (48) hours after delivery of the REWRITE.

4. The Writer will immediately on the execution hereof diligently proceed to render services hereunder and will so continue until such services are completed.

5. On delivery of a treatment to the Company, the Company may call for changes within three (3) days thereafter; if the Company fails in writing to call for any such changes, the treatment shall be deemed approved, and the Writer shall proceed with the first draft screenplay based on such treatment or adaptation.

On delivery of a first draft screenplay to the Company, the Company may call for changes within three (3) days thereafter; if the Company fails in writing to call for any such changes, the first draft screenplay shall be deemed approved, and the Writer shall proceed with the final draft screenplay.

On delivery of the final draft screenplay to the Company, the Company may call for changes within three (3) days thereafter; if the Company fails in writing to call for any such changes, the final draft screenplay shall be deemed approved.

6. This contract is entire, that is, the services contemplated hereunder include all of the writing necessary to complete the final screenplay above described, and this Agreement contemplates payment of the entire agreed compensation.

(Company)	(Writer)
By _____	Address_____
Title_____	_____
Address_____	_____
_____	

A few words of explanation about the preceding contract sample: If this is your first sale, you need not be a member of the Writers Guild, as specified by paragraph 2(a), provided that you do join immediately after you sign the contract, and maintain your membership in good standing.

Section 3(a) is made operative in the case of those writers who are specifically hired to write a screenplay and treatment on assignment.

Section 3(b) becomes operative if you have written a treatment, and the Company agrees to purchase it, or the writer on assignment turns in the first treatment. If you are selling your screenplay sans a treatment, then obviously this payment is not activated.

Section 3(c) is the actual sum paid for your original screenplay should the Company agree to purchase it. This is also the amount paid to the writer on assignment when, having secured approval on the treatment, he or she turns in the first screenplay.

Sections 3(d), 3(e), and section 5 have to do with rewriting. The studio may purchase your screenplay, but upon purchasing it, stipulate that certain changes must be made. (And for the record, changes are almost always made, to varying degrees.)

Frequently, this contract is filled out after the screenplay has been submitted, in the case of an outside submission such as the type described here. In those cases, the contract is retroactive as far as the original, first draft screenplay is concerned, and the application to the rewrites remains the same.

The thing to remember here is that the preceding contract is intended to be an all-purpose agreement, and as indicated in the first part, where it states that those portions not applicable are to be crossed out, may not apply in all ways to your own work. But the gist of it always holds.

It is, of course, fully within the rights of both parties to attach a rider to the contract specifying an agreed-upon salary and a percentage of the film's gross or net profits. (If you have clout, you can get a point or two off the gross. If you don't, you'll probably have to settle for some of the net profit, if so offered.)

Beyond the task of attending to whatever revisions may be called for, the extent of your further responsibilities as a writer will depend on the circumstances of your employment, and the wishes of the producers. You may be asked to be on the production set to make any last-minute changes, in which case you will be given a salary and per diem expenses. (Some producers and a *lot* of directors, however, don't *want* writers lingering on the set.) You may be asked to contribute to the final cutting and editing of the film. You may be asked to stay home and stay out from underfoot. But upon becoming a member of the Writers Guild, you do have two rights—the right to view the final screening, and the right, should revision be necessary, to do the first rewrite. (That's why I stressed the importance, upon selling your screenplay, of joining the Guild *immediately*. Otherwise, if the script needed revisions, the producer could turn it over to another writer for the first rewrite, and you would have no recourse to stop that from happening.)

Sneaking In the Back Way

The bulk of this chapter has been dedicated to the techniques of selling an actual, typewritten screenplay for production as a feature film for general distribution. But there is one more way into the film business. It is, in fact, a route being taken by more writers now than ever before. Many of them find it quite successful.

Do what William Peter Blatty did with *The Exorcist:* Write it as a book and get the damned thing published. If the book sells reasonably well, and has an applicability to a screenplay format, the studios will come to you. They will offer to purchase the screen rights, and you can then hold them up for the right to do the first draft screenplay.

What many writers have found to be the most effective technique is to write both the screenplay and the novelization at the same time. Probably, you'd be better off in finishing the novel first, and getting that out to some book publishers while you're finishing the screenplay.

Two simple facts: If your story is worth some studio's spending several million dollars in producing, then it's got to be worth a publisher's investing several thousands of dollars to publish. And what's more, since the film and book publishing businesses are becoming more entwined every day, publishers are actively looking for novels that have movie potential since they get a cut of the screen rights. So if they know you are also working on a screen version, they will probably be even more disposed toward publishing the book.

You can either wait until the book is published and out on the market before doing anything, or play both ends of the street simultaneously. By that, I mean that you can send the book off to publishers stating that a screenplay is being written and/or currently marketed, and write to the studios explaining that your book, upon which the screenplay is based, is either being considered by a publisher, or is definitely being published by someone. This way, if the book sells first, you can expect more for the screenplay. If, on the other hand, the screenplay sells first, you can demand more for the book rights.

Because producers are not always willing to take chances on untested properties, a story that has either been proven in the book marketplace, or that has been accepted by a major publisher, removes a lot of that fear. As a consequence, it's happening more and more each year. In fact, the movie rights for *Ordinary People* were purchased by Robert Redford while the book was still in its rough typeset (galley) stage—and that, I remind one and all, was Judith Guest's *first* novel.

So when all else fails or might take too long, you can always go in through the back door when nobody's watching.

The Future of Cinema

The filmmaking industry, like any other business, creative and otherwise, has its fair share of doomsayers. When television made its debut, everyone predicted that it would mean the end of the motion picture business, and while it did have a temporary adverse effect, movies continued to be made. This growth continued on through the sixties and seventies, to the point where 1981 was a phenomenal year for the film industry. Theater chains across the country did land-office business.

But the eighties have also brought renewed doubts about the future of filmdom. One predominant reason for this is the rise of cable and video-tape/videocassette/videodisc industries. Another factor is the general decline in service at most theaters: a less refined atmosphere, poor or scratched prints, and multi-cinemas that often cram audiences like sardines into a tin can equipped with sound.

These developments have led many media experts to announce that the film industry is just about to bite the dust in an economic western of its own making . . . and this time John Wayne can't come to the rescue. Why, they ask, should an audience go out of its collective home at night, pay as much as five dollars or more per ticket (not counting the extra bucks for babysitters, munchies, and parking), and put up with less than optimum conditions to see a movie when they can stay home and see a movie on cable, or on a video player? What further compounds the problem is the fact that studios are releasing versions of their films in some video format within an ever-shortening period after the film has been released to the theaters. It is expected that within the next few years, both versions of a motion picture may be released simultaneously—a prospect which does little to reassure theater owners.

But those who mourn for the—in their eyes—apparent demise of the motion picture business are forgetting several important things. First, a videodisc or videocassette player is not yet within the financial reach of every American consumer, and it is doubtful that it ever will be. Just as sizeable portions of the population still don't own stereo receivers or stereo recorders, it's reasonable to expect that these same people will consider a video player to be a luxury that isn't entirely necessary.

In addition, seeing a film on television just isn't the *same* as seeing the same film on a large screen, equipped with Dolby sound. *Star Wars*, for example, can be enjoyed nicely on a small television screen. But it can only be *experienced* when it's presented on a large screen. And that, if you think about it, is really the ultimate purpose of the cinema. It's not just to look at a bunch of pretty colors, see a continuous pattern of pictures, or listen to well-spoken words, although those are certainly parts of the process. I believe that most people go to the movies because they want to *experience* something, to live someone else's life for two hours, to go somewhere and do something that they've never done before. It's the opportunity to block out the real world with cushioned seats and red curtains and live only the film—something that cannot really be done at home, surrounded by reminders of daily life, the bills that have to be paid lying on the coffee table, the dog that wants to be walked and so forth.

Finally, movies are a group experience. They are a chance for a family or a group of friends to get out of the house for a little while. In this respect, films will always be a large part of the social life of teenagers, who want to get away from the house to engage in the traditional courtship behavior of youth.

It is, therefore, reasonable to expect that the motion picture business will continue to be with us for many years to come.

There will, however, be some changes in the scriptwriting marketplace. The studios may begin soliciting safer material that is more likely to turn a profit. In other words, commerciality may become an even greater factor in the decision to produce a film than it is today. But then again, even *that* prediction may prove too pessimistic. We'll just have to wait and see.

In terms of the opportunities for screenwriters, though, it can be stated with some accuracy that the marketplace will increase during the next decade . . . and it will do so precisely because of the cable and video revolution.

By the year 1980, television programs and specials were being produced specifically for cable systems. By late 1981, actual television series were being produced for cable, and preproduction was begun on a number of full-scale motion pictures for exclusively cable use. Nearly 70 percent of the major studios have added divisions to their corporate structure that deal directly with the cable and video corporations. The purpose of this restructuring is to prepare to meet the expected demand by both areas for full-length motion pictures that will be produced for the cable and video marketplace.

It was this very trend toward making movies for video and cable that led to one of the most hotly contested demands of the 1981 Writers Guild strike. The writers, the producers, and the studios all knew that production for the video industry would, within the next two decades, become a potent arm of the entertainment industry overall, and the writers wanted to make sure that a part of the action was given to those who write the words.

As a result, writers who work in tape and film intended for use in the cable or video marketplace not only will receive the standard WGA approved minimums, which was a major landmark in itself, but they will also receive 2 percent of the accountable receipts, which start from the first dollar earned. To placate the studios, the writer will receive a check only after the producers have recouped $1 million per hour for taped productions, and $1.25 million for productions on film. (Those recoupment figures will increase 12 percent on 7/1/82, 11 percent on 7/1/83, and 9 percent on 7/1/84 through 6/30/85.)

The next 10 to 20 years, according to most industry watchers, will see more products aimed at the cable and video industries. Movies will be sold in videocassette or videodisc form just as books are advertised, marketed, and purchased. The same will apply to movies sold to cable for national distribution.

All of which, in conjunction with the continued production of motion pictures for release to general theaters, will mean a host of continued opportunities for new screenwriters. As the need for feature-length productions increases, so will the demand for scripts also grow, and that means that more scriptwriters than ever before will have the opportunity to make their first big break into Showbiz—tinsel, troubles, splendor, aggravation, and all.

See you at the movies.

Try to be original in your play and as clever as possible; but don't be afraid to show yourself foolish; we must have freedom of thinking, and only he is an emancipated thinker who is not afraid to write foolish things. Don't round things out, don't polish—but be awkward and impudent. Brevity is the sister of talent. Remember, by the way, that declarations of love, the infidelity of husbands and wives; widows', orphans', and all other tears, have long since been written up.

—Anton Chekov

Correct often and carefully if you expect to write anything worth being read twice.

—Horace

4.
THE STAGE PLAY

Witness a question that reduces the author to a state of mumbling incomprehensibility: "Given that writing for live theater is less immediately lucrative than working for the electronic or film media, and is generally seen by less people on a per-show basis, why write for the stage at all?"

To answer that, I can only offer—for the moment—the following personal story.

The place: the Marquis Public Theater, San Diego. The time: 7:58 p.m. The date: Friday, April 19. After what seemed like endless weeks of rehearsal, my three-act comedy *The Apprenticeship* was finally set for opening night. The audience had arrived, taking up every available seat. Backstage, the performers were winding themselves up, patting one another on the shoulder, exchanging wishes of good luck, closing their eyes and concentrating. I was sitting in the first row, paralyzed, realizing that my twelve-hour antiperspirant had just expired after one hour. This was to be my twelfth produced play, an even dozen. But the anxiety was there, as always, just as it was for my first production. The heart races, the blood pounds in the temples, breathing becomes rapid and shallow. Nervousness is a physical, palpable thing, with precise dimensions and distinct features. Why? Because it's all happening *right there!* The audience you never see when working for television and radio is occupying the many seats that fill the theater, and the performers usually flattened into two-dimensionality or reduced to faceless voices will be standing right in front of you, looking into your face, speaking the words you wrote, the words that are their only shield against a possibly hostile and unforgiving world. If the play fails, they must continue to speak the words anyway for the two hours to come, agonizing through every moment. And if the play succeeds . . . but you never think about that. Not on opening night. Bad luck.

The house lights dim after an eternity condensed into one single minute, the stage lights and follow spots spring into life, the first actor steps onto the stage, and the first lines fly out into the gallery, looking for a laugh.

And the laughter comes. And the drama follows. And you can see the faces of the listeners as they work their way through the play along with the performers. You yourself hear the lines as if for the first time, a thrill running through every inch of your body similar to being plugged into a heavy-duty wall socket. You hear the reactions of the audience during intermission, and for the first time you allow yourself to think, *It's working! My god, it's working!*

No one leaves during the intermission, a good sign. The play continues relentlessly onward to its inevitable conclusion. You suddenly find yourself wishing that it wouldn't end, that the lines would go on forever. But they don't. There comes the final line, the blackout, the applause and the lights go up on the cast taking their final bows. You join in the applause, exhausted, uplifted, dizzy, frenetic, heart tapping out a flamenco dance against the bones of your ribcage.

In my case, the actress came out at show's end with a bouquet of flowers, reached down into the first row and, with a considerable lack of grace on my part, pulled me onto the stage and handed me the flowers. The light was as dazzling as the fact that I was receiving a squatting ovation. (Some sitting, some standing.) It was a moment of equally distributed trepidation and exhilaration.

And it's always the same, show after show, individual performance after individual performance. Always the same, but always different, varying with the kind of audience, the type of day, the way the performers are feeling, and any other number of factors.

And *that's* why people write for the theater. It's an experience unlike anything else. It is a field in which the writer's contribution is treated with the greatest amount of respect, wherein a talented writer can, in time, make a reasonable income from his words, and that is currently providing ever more opportunities for beginning playwrights.

It's also a medium that requires muscles not usually exercised in other forms of scriptwriting. Its dimensions are different, the techniques that are used in one medium rarely applying to the other. Playwriting requires a new and revised mindset in order to be done properly . . . all of which will be examined in detail in the following pages.

First, though, while knowing something about where theater came from is less vital than it is for television writing or screenwriting, a brief excursion into the history of live drama is certainly worth our time.

The History of Playwriting

The play, in all its varied forms, is probably the single oldest vehicle for dramatic presentation in the long history of civilization. Its origins stretch back to the dawn of mankind, when the hunters of a nomadic tribe would return to the caves and, in mime and simple words, sketch out the events of the hunt, reenacting each kill for the rest of the tribe. Although primitive in form, all the elements of a play were there nonetheless: a stage, a flickering light, a story of life and death, an audience, and a performer. Such have always been the bottom-line requirements of drama, and these basic elements endure.

As the centuries passed, drama became more institutionalized. It was used as a means of conveying news from distant places, to mark the changing of seasons and phases of the moon; in time it merged with ritual and religion, and drama became the means whereby we could understand the activities of the gods.

Early drama probably reached its peak in Greece, where it was used to portray the passions of the gods and the foibles of human beings. Here, drama flourished under the capable hands of Aeschylus, Aristophanes, and Sophocles, to name but a few. Even Aristotle took a few well-aimed shots at explaining precisely what drama was and how it should best be presented. (He maintained that a play is a whole which has "a beginning, a middle, and an end. A beginning is that which does not itself follow anything by causal necessity, but after which something naturally is or comes to be. An end, on the contrary, is that which itself naturally follows some other thing, but has nothing following it. A middle is that which follows something as some other thing follows it. A well-constructed plot, therefore, must neither begin nor end at haphazard.")

What distinguished Greek drama was its use of such clearly defined plot devices as a distinct beginning, middle, and end, and the introduction of a chorus which—being omnipresent and all-seeing—could pass on to the audience information that the characters themselves either did not yet know, or did not know they knew. The chorus was also a handy device for some not-too-subtle moralizing at the play's conclusion.

With the fall of Greece, the flame of dramaturgy was given over to the Romans for safekeeping. (Some historians speculate that the Roman empire embraced drama not so much out of aesthetic appreciation as out of jealousy, anxious to prove that they were every bit as intellectual and artistically oriented as the Greeks.) Plays were soon presented before the general public, and even in the hall of the various Caesars. Interestingly enough, it was in the latter that political drama began playing an increasingly greater role. In many cases, productions were staged before Caesar's court that ridiculed the emperor's enemies and glorified his many conquests. From time to time, the players were even permitted to lightly—

very lightly—satirize the emperor himself, although those who took the opportunity a little too much to heart soon found themselves considering the prospect of an immensely shortened lifespan.

In time, however, Rome also fell, and largely took with it the fate of the live play. In fact, some forms of drama, including pantomime, were banned and their performers exiled by religious decree. Although it would continue to sprout up and enjoy a brief glory in the following centuries, the art of drama was still held in generally low esteem and was even dubbed by some "the Subversive Art." (In China and Japan, though, theater enjoyed and continues—to varying degrees—a healthy life as part religious ritual, part cultural expression, and part celebration.)

Unquestionably, drama in the English language underwent its greatest renewal in the late sixteenth and early seventeenth centuries. These were the years of William Shakespeare and Francis Bacon and England's famous Globe Theater. It can probably be argued that Shakespeare was the one person most responsible for legitimizing and popularizing the play. His dramas were tightly constructed and elegant in form; he worked with the blessings and financial support of the monarchy—but maintained a constant affinity with the lower classes. He wrote of kings and battles, of star-crossed lovers, of madmen caught in the irresistible tide of Fate, of mistaken identities and enchanted midsummer evenings . . . all the things, in short, that the common people loved to hear about. His plays often ran three hours or longer, because this was, for many in his audience, their only entertainment, and he wanted to give them their money's worth.

During the years that followed, dramaturgy—having established a firm foothold—continued once again in its growth, frequently favored by the people and sanctioned by the government. In time, it gave us Goethe in Germany, Moliere in France, and Cervantes in Spain. It is amusing to consider that even as drama became more institutionalized and more respectable with the passage of time, the performers were rarely given much social acceptance. An actor was generally held to be a person of low character and questionable morals, and an actress was looked upon as possessing neither character nor morals, her station in life not very far removed from the street-corner prostitute.

All of which made for a fascinating paradox: It was quite fashionable to be seen at the theater, but to be seen on the town in the company of someone *with* the theater was likely to result in rumors and social repudiation.

This situation did not noticeably improve when drama made its leap across the Atlantic to the United States. More than one American mother during the eighteenth and nineteenth centuries joined in the age-old chant, "Better death or a convent for my daughter than a life in the theater!"

For the record, it's worth noting that playwrights were not always included in the community's roster of disreputable characters. Not all were deemed shady individuals. Some were, in the public's mind, simple alcoholics, and the rest were, well, just a bit *odd*, you know, but basically harmless in the absence of sudden loud noises.

It goes almost without saying (almost, but not quite, so I'll say it anyway) that in nearly every instance, these characterizations had nothing whatsoever to do with the real world. But then, what stereotypes ever do?

Happily, by the time the twentieth century arrived, those who chose to align themselves with the theatrical world were no longer perceived as pariahs. Some of them were even found to be quite interesting, if just the teensiest odd.

Win some, lose some.

During the last several decades, live theater has become an integral and respected facet of American life. It inhabits the bright lights of Broadway and the ramshackle, fire-code-violating makeshift theater in small towns across the nation. At first largely dependent upon the works of Shakespeare and other European playwrights, American theater eventually found its own voice, and thus the world was given Eugene O'Neill, Thornton Wilder, T.S. Eliot, Lillian Hellman, Arthur Miller, and Tennessee Williams, to name but a few.

Today, virtually any community of moderate size has at least one repertory company, and other avenues of dramaturgy have arisen in the larger cities. This has, however, led to a certain theatrical stratification. Working from a playwright's perspective, American theater can be divided up into four categories, each of which arose out of the economic and cultural milieu surrounding and shaping the evolution of contemporary theater.

The first is the small community theater that is really more of a repertory company. It produces low-budget plays that rarely require more than one set, uses a small cast that tends to reappear in one production after another, stages its productions at irregular or limited intervals, and frequently operates out of whatever structures are available at the moment—a church, a public auditorium, or even a high school gymnasium. As a rule, theaters of this sort tend to produce plays by established playwrights because they cannot sustain the economic risk of an untested play by an unknown or little-known playwright. In many cases, they operate on a shoestring budget, somehow surviving from one show to the next, limping along from Ibsen to Chekov to Shaw and, upon occasion, Ionesco. Although such operations offer little in the way of opportunity for new playwrights—except in the rare instance of a local competition for a new play—the contribution of these small theaters to American drama should never be understated, because it is here that most performers cut their teeth on the acting profession.

One step up the ladder are the local theaters that are somewhat larger, work out of a single, stable house, offer a regular season, and are capable of staging more elaborate productions. They frequently operate on a non-profit basis, receiving some assistance from the city, the state, or the federal government in the form of grants and subsidies. In most cases, these theaters offer the usual selection of conventional plays by established playwrights, but are not entirely deaf to the entreaties of new voices, and from time to time—whenever their budgets permit the risk—they will stage a new play by an equally new, and often local, playwright.

Bridging these two venues, and yet always just outside and to the left of both of them, are the experimental theaters. These are the community-oriented organizations that make it a daily practice to fly in the face of convention. The seeds of contemporary drama and drama for all the years to come are sown most prolifically here. These theaters operate out of a love that ignores the figures in the bank account and the threats of countless creditors. They are staffed by marginally paid executives and volunteers who in many cases literally live in the theater. They produce occasional classics (when the accounts drop too low), plays by exotic foreign playwrights, new works by local playwrights, experimental plays, socially-relevant plays, staged readings, ethnic plays, and whatever else they *feel* like producing. They are perplexing, impudent, outrageous, wholly accessible to anyone willing to invest time and effort, and enormously refreshing.

The final category consists of what some theatergoers rather snobbishly refer to as "legitimate theater," as if all the other theaters were somehow illegitimate. Included in this category are the large, well-established community theaters that stage a full season of elaborate productions, showcase theaters that feature national or regional touring companies exclusively, and of course, Broadway itself. The latter two tend to favor new works, but these plays are usually by established writers, and have been proven at a variety of smaller theaters before making their big Broadway debut. (In recent years, the emphasis on a Broadway premiere has been supplanted by debuts on the West Coast, usually in Los Angeles and occasionally in San Francisco.)

Naturally, there are some theaters and dramaturgic organizations that do not readily fall into these four categories. But in most instances, these different outlets comprise the bulk of contemporary American theater. In addition, there are a number of publishers who turn out countless plays, not a few by new playwrights, on a yearly basis.

So the opportunities are there, and the search for new material continues. One of the most frequently asked questions in theatrical circles is, "Where are all the new playwrights?"

Before that question can properly be addressed, however, it would behoove us to examine another question raised briefly at the start of this chapter—*why* write for the theater in the first place?

The Benefits of Playwriting

Besides being an exciting, powerful medium rich in history and tradition, there are several concrete factors that make playwriting an attractive prospect for scriptwriters. One of the foremost of these is the deep and abiding respect given by the cast and the director to the written word. It's a marvelous attitude that makes the very thought of rewriting a playwright's words beyond any serious consideration.

In television, film, and radio scriptwriting, you as the writer are generally working for someone else, and that person therefore has the right to change anything in your script—a right that is frequently exercised, to varying degrees. But when you sit down behind your typewriter and begin committing a play to paper, you are working for no one but yourself. As a consequence, the play must stand or fall entirely on its own merits. If it is worth producing, then those doing the producing are obligated to produce it as is. If there are many things in it that, in their estimation, don't work, then they can simply choose not to produce it. But once committed, they must stage it properly, potential warts and all. They do have the right though—within the boundaries of common sense and artistic integrity—to edit the play for purposes of keeping within certain time constraints or eliminating cumbersome scenes.

That's a very attractive arrangement, one that you just can't beat. In the other media discussed in this book, the written words can be changed to accommodate the performer or the director, but in live theater, the cast are charged with molding themselves to fit the work.

Concomitant with this benefit is the fact that playwrights are generally more respected by the lay public and the entertainment community than any other kind of scriptwriter. Because the other media involve so many compromises and decisions by committee, a play is largely viewed as a vehicle for individual expression, and is therefore considered—rightly or wrongly—to be a purer art form. (I know several television writers who would probably disagree with this. I also know, however, that each of them has at least one unfinished play lurking somewhere in his desk.) The simple fact is that playwrights are more widely known by name than most writers for the other media. The most notable exceptions to this— Larry Gelbart and Paddy Chayefsky—have achieved a fair degree of success on the stage as well as on the screen or the television tube.

A third niceness is the eventual income to be derived from an even moderately successful play. This income comes from two primary sources—the published playbook and performance royalties. As for any published book, the author receives a certain percentage of the cover price, usually ranging from 5 percent to 10 percent. Most publishers also make it a point to turn over a percentage of the performance royalties— generally 25 percent or more of what they get—to the author. These payments can continue to come in for as long as the book remains in print, which effectively guarantees a steady income for many years to come.

It's also a warm, fuzzy feeling to look at your royalty check—broken down into performance and book fees—and, with a little division, figure out that your play, your words, have been given life in five, ten, or fifteen theaters across the United States during the preceding six months. (Every time I get one of those little suckers in the mail, I usually end up wandering around the house for several hours thereafter, wearing a dumb grin that will *not* go away.)

A fourth advantage to playwriting is the greater freedom of expression available here than in most other media, particularly television, with only motion pictures coming close in terms of visual and verbal latitude. If the proper telling of your story requires nudity, profanity, references to peculiar sexual habits or any of those other facets of everyday existence that make life worth living, then you are within your rights to include them in your script, as long as you remember that the racier the script, the less chance of production in the conservative American heartland.

Finally, you as the playwright have the marvelous opportunity to receive feedback from the audience and, in many instances, the cast itself. In the early stages of production, this enables you to tighten any sequences that don't work, and after it's been out in book form, to witness the reactions of an audience purely for your own satisfaction.

Before we can reap any of these benefits, however, it is incumbent upon us to first write the play. To do this requires an understanding of the art and the craft of playwriting, and along the way, an equal understanding of the ways in which plays differ from scripts for any of the other media we've discussed in this book.

The Art of the Stage Play

There are many creative steps to take before actually sitting down and writing a play. We will examine each of these considerations on an individual basis. But before we even begin to touch upon any of them, there is one criterion that must be addressed above all else: You must, must read and see as many different kinds of plays as possible. Such a prolonged study will tell you far more about playwriting than can possibly be conveyed in this or any other book.

What follows, then, is a list of plays that will probably be of greatest value to the scriptwriter who intends to discover what makes a really good play what it is. These are plays lurking in my own library that I make it a point to reread at any given opportunity, learning a little more from each reading. Between them, you have a cross-section of the various kinds of plays, from the comic to the tragic to the absurd and the classic.

Samuel Beckett's *Waiting for Godot.* (absurdist)
Christopher Fry's *The Lady's Not for Burning.* (satiric)
Alan Ayckbourn's *The Norman Conquests.* (comic)
Christopher Marlowe's *Dr. Faustus.* (tragic)
Anton Chekov's *The Seagull.* (tragic)
Peter Shaffer's *Equus.* (psychological drama)
Anthony Shaffer's *Sleuth.* (thriller)
Edward Albee's *A Delicate Balance.* (social drama)
Moliere's *The Misanthrope.* (verse play)
Jean Giraudoux's *The Enchanted.* (light drama)
Simon Gray's *Otherwise Engaged.* (heavy drama)
Harold Pinter's *Old Times.* (heavy drama)
George Bernard Shaw's *Too True to Be Good.* (satiric)
Arthur Miller's *Death of a Salesman.* (dramatic/tragic)
Luigi Pirandello's, *Six Characters in Search of an Author, The Man
    with the Flower in His Mouth.* (surrealist)
Israel Horowitz's *The Line.* (farce)
Jean Paul Sartre's *No Exit.* (existentialist)
Thornton Wilder's *Our Town.* (light drama)
William Shakespeare's *Two Gentlemen of Verona, A Midsummer
    Night's Dream, The Comedy of Errors, Julius Caesar, King Lear,
    Macbeth,* and *Hamlet.* (mixed bag)
Bruce Friedman's *Steambath.* (existentialist)

Although rather long, this list is by no means all-inclusive. There are many other plays that greatly deserve attention from any aspiring playwright. These would include Jerome Lawrence's *Inherit the Wind*, Tennessee Williams's *The Glass Menagerie*, and the many plays of Ibsen, Cocteau, Brecht and Ionesco. But the ones I've listed are those you might best profit from at first; each is an excellent example of the genre it represents. Thus, if you are of a surrealist or humorous bent, you would probably be well advised to go through the list picking out the plays in those categories and see how each playwright handled his theme.

Reading these plays will give you a healthy knowledge of the dramatic devices and techniques that have gone on to shape contemporary theater. Meanwhile, we'll take a look at the many elements that should be taken into consideration when beginning a stage play, particularly those that make writing plays different from scriptwriting for film and television.

Possibly the single most important thing to remember when writing a stage play is that you are dealing with an extremely restricted physical universe. In radio, using the stage provided by the imagination, you can go anywhere, any time, as quickly as you like. A big-budget motion picture has less of a capacity for handling unusual or exotic settings, and television is even more restricted. But in live theater, you must make do with one stage, anywhere from one to four sets, a limited cast and a limited budget.

All this may seem rather obvious, but it's a point where many new playwrights run aground on the rocks of practicality. I've seen many play scripts that call for rapidfire scene changes, with the action continuing throughout. In a film script, for instance, you could have a scene in which George, a frustrated and underpaid accountant, is at home with his wife, discussing his fear of asking for a raise. Finally resolved, he walks out the door. You then cut to the office, with George walking in through that door and confronting the boss. The action is continuous, and accomplished by a simple cut. But in a stage version, such a direction would require stopping the action for anywhere from ten to fifteen minutes while the stage is reset for the office scene. As a consequence, you should try to accomplish as much in each scene as possible, and only indicate scene changes when absolutely necessary. In film, we emphasized the importance of "opening up" the script visually, to include a variety of scenes in order to make the action interesting. In playwriting, you have to do just the opposite, and "close down" the universe of your play to just the absolute essentials.

Also, remember that limiting the number of sets does not by any means limit the possibility for action. You can write a perfectly interesting and exciting play using a single set. In fact, some of the very best plays have been written just this way: *Sleuth, Waiting for Godot, The Line,* and *Steambath* are all one-set plays. *The Norman Conquests* is unique in this respect because it consists of three individual plays, all taking place on the same weekend, but each set in a different part of the same house. One play takes place in the dining room, another in the living room, and the last is set in the garden. The remarkable thing about them is that each of the three plays can be seen individually, without having to see the other two (although I recommend seeing them all, just for the fun of it). Each play is vibrant, exciting and—most important—a whole unit unto itself.

To proceed along similar lines, here's another of those paradoxes-that-really-aren't-when-you-think-about-it. Although it is imperative to limit the physical universe of your play as much as you can, you as the playwright must be constantly aware of everything that is going on *beyond* that limited universe. Let's say that you've decided to write a play that is set entirely in the living room of a house. That's fine. But *where* is the *house?* Remember, you've got to be prepared to indicate dialects and mannerisms. So we now decide that it's in the southern part of the United States. Fine, but which part of the South? Each region is different. Okay, so let be it's in Louisiana. When? The year is very important in terms of dress, social attitudes, and so forth. At last, we decide that the play is set in the living room of a house in New Orleans in the year 1952.

Then, once so decided, you must remember your environment and maintain the atmosphere of that place and that time within the microcosm of your play. Always be mindful of the world that exists just outside the mock front door of your set, because the world you have chosen to create onstage is a part of that exterior reality. Case in point: During a workshop, a student turned in a play set in Victorian England. Within seconds of looking it over, I noticed two critical errors. I illustrated the first by having some of the students read part of the play aloud without telling the listeners where or when it was set. They were then asked to guess at the time and location of the play. Nearly everyone guessed the present, somewhere in the United States, possibly the East Coast. *He had not taken into consideration the different syntax, idiom, and attitudes of the period.* That was his first mistake. His second mistake was in having the protagonist and his fiancee behave in an openly affectionate manner—hugging, kissing, holding hands, and so on—in the presence of casual friends. This is something that, to say the least, would be severely frowned upon because of the repressive sexual attitudes prevalent during the Victorian era.

He had not, in short, done his homework. A play is built upon subtleties, and passing over them can be self-destructive. In contemporary England, for instance, one does not ride in an elevator, visit the rest room, go to a bar, or call a friend. One rides a lift, visits the loo, drops by at a pub, and rings someone up. They're small things, yes, but not paying attention to these details makes the entire work somehow ring false in the ears of the audience.

Another example: In a play of my own (just to show that everyone screws up on occasion) set in the first part of the twentieth century, in New York, I had a character call someone on the telephone by dialing the number. A critic who sat in on the performance took great pleasure in nailing me to the wall with the fact that direct dialing was not initiated in New York until five years after the date of the play's setting. Before then, the caller would tap on the telephone cradle, get the operator, and *ask* for the correct exchange. Again, it was a trivial point, but as a reviewer myself, I can say that critics love to find such oversights and will nail you every time you ignore such details of daily life. (For the record, since it was the play's debut, I was able to write in the line "Emerson three-two hundred, please," and the prop department supplied a nondialable telephone.)

Since we're on the topic of time, it's worth noting that as a playwright you are actually dealing with four separate time zones, a situation which can lead to literary jet lag. These are: *period time*, already discussed. *Real time*, which is the time the audience actually spends sitting in their seats, also known as the running time. *Story time*, is the subjective time required to fully tell your story, which may be weeks, days, months or years. Finally, in *dramatic time*, an hour is condensed into ten minutes, or a minute is expanded to fill an hour's real time. These distinctions are important to bear in mind when doing any jumping around in time. If the first half of your play is separated in story time from the second half by a period of ten years, then you have to deal with the fact that the characters will not, in most cases, act and speak in the same way they did ten years before. They are not the same people. They have lived, changed, experienced joy and sadness and loss and success, have gone through the fire and returned again, perhaps not quite as naive—or even as cynical—as they once were. Your task as a playwright is to keep track of these changes, let them become evident through dialogue, and in time, explain them.

As a sidelight to this, having a person come back after ten years totally unchanged also tells the audience much about the kind of person he or she might be. The only people not changed by life are those who are unaware of it in the first place.

Certain concessions must also be made to real time. In a film, it is possible to show someone receiving an insult, and then cut to a later scene where the person is venting rage at the remark, thereby eliminating the necessity of showing him working up the rage. This doesn't work on stage, however. It is difficult for an actor to go from happiness to anger in a split second (unless the person being portrayed is a psychotic, of course). From a pragmatic point of view, they're caught in the same real time as the audience. They must, therefore, process through from one emoton to the other. Your task as a playwright is to provide the time and the dialogue for this transition.

So when you get ready to write your play, be sure you have a handle on its proposed length, the period you will be using as a background, and the total time subjectively required to tell your story, always allowing sufficient time for the performers to process through from one emotion to another. (I once had a student submit a play for critiquing in which all the emotional changes took place in another room of the house, while the actor was offstage, thereby—in the playwright's mind—taking care of the difficult task of processing through each new emotion. I handed it back and asked that the setting be changed to the other room. It was probably a lot more interesting in there.)

There are other creative decisions that must be made before you can sit down and begin writing your play. You must decide whether your play will revolve around a certain theme or story, or if it is a character study. Any play of quality will have all of these elements present, but in nearly every instance one of the three is dominant. Deciding clearly what your story is about will help keep you on track, and help you avoid going off into territories not necessary to the dominant purpose of your play. Be careful, though, not to overemphasize any one of these elements. Having a certain theme is fine, provided that it does not turn your play into a social or political tract. Story is essential, but it must not reduce your characters to limp two-dimensionality. Finally, you can write a wonderful character study, but if there isn't a story, something that will bring out that character and move the play along, then it will be wandersome, purposeless, and generally, garden-variety dull.

Peter Shaffer's *Equus* is a good example of this principle. The story is based on a news clipping that Shaffer chanced upon, and the resulting play about a boy who blinds a stable full of horses was guided carefully by the facts in the case. This anchor in story is particularly useful when, as is the case with *Equus*, much of the story takes place in the shadowed realm of a disordered mind. It keeps the playwright from getting lost. Although the play slowly reveals *why* he did what he did, the entire thrust of the play remains *what* he did. The incidents of the story form the basis for everything that follows, and those events are the direct result of everything that went before.

You must also decide *whom* your play is really about. While there may be many different characters, all undergoing some changes in status or personality during the course of your play, there must always be one particular character who forms the focus of your play, and the play is *really* about this character. It needn't even be the character who has the most lines. But it *is* the most pivotal character.

For instance, while in the play *Romeo and Juliet* both of Shakespeare's star-crossed lovers share equal billing in the title, and both have a roughly equal number of lines, the focus of the play is unquestionably Romeo. He is the active character, the one who makes the decisions; he chooses to fight Tybalt, kills him, decides to accept banishment, arranges for the couple's planned rendezvous, and is the first of the two to die. Juliet is, by and large, the passive, reactive character. The same rule applies to Shakespeare's *Julius Caesar*. As matters develop, Caesar's time on the stage, both in corporeal and spiritual form, is very limited, and aside from his death (which affects him deeply), he does not change much for the remainder of the play. *Julius Caesar* is actually about Marc Anthony, and the struggle between his conscience and his belief that what he is doing is right for Rome.

Beyond the other elements of drama that are universal and apply equally to film, television, and the stage—a plot that moves the audience from point A to point B, rounded three-dimensional characters, and a climax that resolves the story—the final element that serves to distinguish the stage play from any other form of scriptwriting concerns the question of action. The prospect of half an hour of two people talking on the movie screen or in a television show, without any physical or visual action whatsoever, is considered deadly. But conversation is the basic unit of drama. Drama deals in the currency of characterization; we do not attend a stage play to see a wide variety of special effects, death-defying stunts, bank robberies, or car chases. We go to see a group of actors defining and exploring the human condition within the parameters set by the playwright.

While the action in a stage play may be physical—ranging from the Shakespearean swordplay of *Hamlet* to the life-and-death games of *Sleuth*—such activities are secondary to the dramatic underpinnings of the play as they relate to story, theme, and character. In many cases, the action of a play can be purely emotional in nature. In other cases, what action is present is not always easily definable. Beckett's *Waiting for Godot*, with some interludes, is primarily about two people waiting in the desert for someone named Godot—who never arrives. In the end, they are a little more desperate, somewhat more desolate, but they decide that they will continue to wait. They are essentially unchanged. Yet the play remains a fascinating, convoluted work that takes the audience through a series of verbal and existential mazes, finally depositing them right back where everything started.

These, then are the creative considerations that you must labor over before beginning to write your play. The next step is to examine some of the purely practical difficulties confronting the playwright that can affect the act of dramatic creation.

The Craft of the Stage Play

If a newly written play is to go no further than the typewriter carriage or the desk drawer or that already stuffed-to-the-limit box at the bottom of the closet, then there's really no need to concern oneself with the physical requirements of live theater. If, however, the eventual goal of writing is production, then it's always a good idea to pay attention to some of the theatrical conventions. These can be divided into three parts: Considerations of structure, performance, and staging.

Structure

Somewhere along the line, someone discovered that audiences have an aversion to sitting in cramped theater seats for two or more hours straight, without the chance to stand up, stretch, and walk around a bit. In addition, a play may call for several changes in story time that necessitate altering the stage, the set, and the costumes, a time-consuming process during which the audience is left literally in the dark.

To avoid these situations the playwright may either create a one-act play that is too brief to result in a general insurrection, or a multi-act play that has one or two intermissions built into its structure. Each of these presents different advantages and drawbacks.

The one-act play is theater in its sparest form. Because of its limited length—usually anywhere from twenty-five to as long as forty-five or even sixty minutes—it has little room for digression. Like a short story, it must contain only the most essential elements. It must tell its story, illustrate its characters, present its theme, and get out quickly. In most instances, the action presented is continuous, with few—if any—changes in story time. It also puts a premium on telling the story with one set, a proviso that makes a lot of sense when you consider a set change can take as long as a quarter hour. Looked at with a scriptwriter's sense of priorities, this is one fourth of the total time available to you as a playwright to tell your story, and in most instances, that quarter hour would be put to better use in moving your story forward than in moving furniture.

Because of its brevity, it's virtually impossible to cram a complex, many-layered plot into a one-act play. There simply isn't the time to develop it properly. As a result, most one-act plays present straightforward stories, emphasize the "slice of life" school of dramaturgy, or are primarily character pieces. Israel Horowitz's *The Line* is a one-act play that illustrates the interactions of a group of very different people while they're waiting in a line for a very long time. It is a play produced frequently by colleges and universities because it's a brilliant example of what a writer can do with a brief play, a minimum of props, and a collection of performers who are not averse to tossing, tumbling, falling, shouting, and generally making just a whole lot of noise. Other one-act plays that say a lot with a little include William Saroyan's *Hello Out There* and Luigi Pirandello's *The Man with the Flower in His Mouth*.

The multi-act play allows the writer to explore situations, themes, and characters in far greater detail than is possible in a one-act play. Multi-act plays consist of either two or three acts. Both run approximately the same length in real time, roughly two hours (or a little longer). A two-act play has one intermission of fifteen or twenty minutes, meaning that the two acts run about fifty minutes apiece. A very intense drama may be divided into two acts to sustain the tension for as long as possible at one stretch. A three-act play has two fifteen-minute intermissions, which thereby limits each act to thirty or thirty-five minutes. A clear majority of light dramas and nearly every comic play is of the three-act variety.

Whether using a two-act or three-act play format, it's a good idea to outline your play briefly before writing it. (An extensive treatment isn't usually necessary unless you're considering a *very* complex play.) You should be careful to keep the flow of the play moving, and layer in the small dramatic hooks or mini-climaxes evenly throughout the play, each act ending on a high note of tension or humor. Each small climax should build organically upon the one preceding it, cresting in the inevitable final climax of the play. It is necessary to layer evenly to avoid the problem of a finished play with a first and third act that are pure dynamite, but a second act that could put an insomniac into a coma.

It's also a good idea to use these natural breaks in structure to facilitate changes in story time and/or setting. An intermission gives the stage crew sufficient time to change the set without breaking the attention of the audience. In addition, when the audience returns from the intermission, they—like the characters—have had a little interlude, and can better accept the idea that time has elapsed in the story line. A change in story time that does not require a change in setting can be done through the intercession of an intermission, or may be integrated into the act by using a simple blackout to signal the transition in time. To further highlight the illusion of a transition, it's often a good idea to have different cast members onstage before the blackout and after the blackout, or have the same characters doing different things in different parts of the room.

It's also helpful to remember that the program the audience receives prior to the curtain going up (or sideways) will explain how much time has transpired at each break, if any, and whether or not any transitions will be taking place during an act. This saves the playwright the heartbreak of having a character come out at the beginning of a new act, pat his chest, look around at the other characters and say, "Well, well—so it's been two weeks, has it? My, how time *does* fly."

Probably one of the greatest benefits of the three-act format is the immediate structuring that it gives to a play. Act one generally contains the information and dialogue needed to establish the characters, the situation, the goal(s), and the means that the characters intend to use in accomplishing their desires. Act two contains the complications and the actual steps taken toward reaching the set goals. Act three resolves the question—they either do or do not accomplish their task—and explores the consequences, if any.

For the writer just starting out in the theater, it's often wise to start with one-acts and work your way up from there. Not only will this give you the experience of working with characters in a limited dramatic format and learning the basic techniques of theater, but—as we'll see later in the section on marketing—you have a far better chance of getting a one-act play produced and responded to by a critical audience than you do a full-length play that has not benefited from production experience on your part.

The Performers

One of the biggest adjustments in mindset a scriptwriter makes when writing a stage play concerns performers' bodies. You must train your ear to hear what your characters are saying *and* train your mind's eye to see what they are doing while they are speaking.

Example: In a film, you have two characters out on a boat, talking. That's the only action in the scene. But it is not a static scene, because the director can cut from one performer's face to the other, go from a tight shot to a long shot, pan the surrounding scenery, and shoot over one or the other actor's shoulder. This turns an otherwise static conversation into a very active part of the film.

You cannot, however, do this sort of thing on the stage. The actors are simply *there*, and it is up to you to find something for them to do while they're speaking. To have huge portions of your script comprised *only* of dialogue without the benefit of physical action is effectively to strap the performer to a chair, or reduce him to aimlessly wandering around the room. Both of these options are boring.

Waiting for Godot emerges, once again, as an excellent example of dealing with performers caught in a potentially static situation. There are large blocks of the play that consist of the two main characters talking and simply waiting. But they are by no means inactive. They rush from one side of the stage to the other, scanning the horizon; they check and exchange hats; they check their shoes for pebbles; they hit one another. Thanks to Beckett's forethought, *Godot* is not only a fascinating, thought-provoking play, it is also a play that demands considerable physical effort on the part of the performers, a factor that further enhances the overall effect of the play.

One device that many new playwrights fall back on is called, informally, The Alcoholism Syndrome. It works like this: Every time a new character enters the room, character A fixes him or her a drink and continues to prepare new drinks whenever anyone runs out. This gives the performer a chance to walk around a bit and *do* something while the plot is being unveiled. At least, that's the rationale. There are several problems with this, though. First of all, the sight of drinks passing from one person to another becomes rather tedious after a while. Second, this can be carried accidentally to ludicrous extremes. I once looked over a script and, after counting each drink the author forced the characters to consume, concluded that they all should have passed out in the middle of the second act. Finally, some consideration should be paid to the poor actors. Each time you see a character drink what passes for whiskey, he is actually drinking tepid, unsweetened tea that has probably been sitting there for hours. Imagine how *you* would feel after drinking stuff like that night after night, week after week.

Often, the problem is rooted in the fact that the playwright looks exclusively to dialogue to advance the plot, while viewing physical actions and mannerisms as something separate from the plot, something to be tossed in upon occasion to keep the audience from dozing off at a crucial moment. Nothing could be farther from the truth. The body of the actor as it moves through space and the words the actor speaks are *not* separate. They both must work together to advance the plot by emphasizing one of the most essential elements *of* plotting—characterization. Remember, no one does anything without a reason, and that reason is directly related to who that person is, how he sees the world, and his relationship to that world. All these character elements are demonstrated by what the characters say and how they behave. This requires that attention be paid to the little details, and that you truly know your characters.

Take, for instance, a very poor character given a moment's shelter in the home of a very *rich* character. No doubt the poor character will be struck by the interior of the house, and wander wide-eyed from painting to sculpture to the Ming vase on a pedestal over by the door. It's a simple character-based action, but then it snowballs. It leads to new lines, such as the poor character asking if the painting by the mantel is *really* an original Picasso. How does the rich character respond? Does he ignore the trappings of his lifestyle in deference to the evening paper's headlines? Or does he accompany the poor character from one *objet d'art* to another, explaining in detail how each piece was acquired, and how much it cost? Either action tells the audience something about the character.

Good playwriting, like any other form of drama, is predicated upon the actions and reactions of characters, each with his or her own set of attitudes, goals, and personal history. Whenever a writer ends up in some trouble while writing a script, it can usually be traced back to characterization. So if your character is fanatically neat, have her constantly tidying up the place and telling other characters where they may and may not rest their feet. It's certainly more sensible than having that character mention, "You know, I'm a fanatically neat person. Does that surprise you?" Because if it *isn't* already apparent, and it *does* come as a surprise to audience and other characters alike, then frankly, somebody has goofed—and it's nearly always the writer.

Another problem that aspiring playwrights must work around is the ever-present possibility of having one or more dead characters sitting about onstage. By this, I do not mean a character who has just been shot, stabbed, garrotted, run through by a sword, or forced to listen to twelve straight hours of Rod McKuen. No, what I mean here is the character who for long periods of time has nothing whatsoever to say.

Example: Let's say you've written a scene for television or film in which three people are having a conversation. As it happens, though, two of the three do nearly all of the talking, while the third character looks on. While this is a less than optimal situation, it is not necessarily deadly. The director can do the scene largely in close-ups of the two people who *are* talking. In this way, although there is officially a dead character in the scene, the audience isn't as bothered as they might be because they don't *see* him.

But a dead character onstage is very definitely visible, even though he may wish he could vanish into the background or hide under a seat cushion.

Part of this problem is rooted in the fact that beginning scriptwriters often have a hard time handling scenes in which three or more characters are present simultaneously. Hence, a substantial number of plays by novice playwrights feature either *just* two characters, or manage to handle more characters by having one leave shortly before the other enters, so that even though the play may call for nine characters, there are never more than two (or at most three) characters onstage at the same time.

The solution to this comes in three parts. First, there's simple pragmatics—make sure that every character onstage has at least one or two lines per page of script. Second, go back to the roots of your story, to characterization: What would people like those in your play be likely to say given such a situation? Finally, study the dynamics of conversation. Ambrose Bierce once defined conversation as "A fair for the display of the minor mental commodities, each exhibitor being too intent upon the arrangement of his own wares to observe those of his neighbor." Although this may be just a little too cynical, it contains a grain of truth. During a conversation, we tend to listen to what the other person is saying until such time as the speaker hits upon a subject that we can relate to. Then, though we continue to listen to the speaker, we are already starting to frame our own verbal response. When an opening presents itself, we interject this observation, which then triggers off a similar response in someone else. It's also worth remembering that conversations are rarely cut and dried—in many instances, one person will talk over another, and a third person may start a comment, think better of it, and withdraw. The best examples of such artfully handled conversations can be found in Ayckbourn's *Norman Conquests*, Pinter's *Old Times*, and other plays by these two brilliant writers.

Action and reaction. It's the basic law of physical science and the physics of drama. It's also the key element in improvisation, which emphasizes one performer *actively listening* to the other performer, and then *actively responding* to something that the first person said. If you want to see the act of creative conversation taking place before your very eyes, find a local theater of club that features an improvisational troupe and attend a performance. You may even want to get together with a few friends, each picking a different role and occupation, and try it yourself. For that matter, a little experience onstage as an actor may prove beneficial to understanding the inner dynamics of acting.

Couldn't hurt.

Staging

The final greatest obstacle thrown into the path of beginning playwrights—staging—is actually divisible into two different parts: the set, including furniture and props, and the movements of the performers in relation to the set. Since we've already touched upon the subject of movement, we'll continue in that vein and examine the requirements of set design and direction last.

It's not uncommon for a writer, on attempting his or her first play, to suffer a kind of stage fright. Knowing that a character must be doing certain things, the question then becomes *where* shall they be when they are undertaking this certain action? Shall I have my character cross downstage or move upstage right? How does this affect the positioning of my other character? What *is* upstage and downstage?

Actually, it's not uncommon to get upstage, downstage, stage right, and stage left confused. We are spectators, members of an audience, are used to looking at a stage from that perspective. But stage directions are written for use by the performer, not the audience. As a consequence, everything is reversed. Whenever doubt enters the scene, always imagine yourself standing on the stage and looking out at the audience, with the entire stage on a slight incline, tilting downward as you approach the audience, then rising as you retreat backward.

For slightly easier reference, the following diagram is offered.

Rear Curtain

Upstage Right	Upstage Center	Upstage Left
Right	Center	Left
Downstage Right	Downstage Center	Downstage Left

The Audience

Often, this confusion results from misinterpretation of the phrase, "She upstaged him." This can be taken to mean that by moving in front of him, she went upstage. But the correct interpretation of this is that, through her sudden move, she forced him into the upstage area, and therefore into lesser visual prominence.

Once you've finally memorized the diagram, the best thing to do is put the information in the back of your mind and forget it, calling out the spe-

cific stage directions—known as *blocking*— only when absolutely necessary. As it turns out, overly specific blocking not only is not required, but
frequently is unwanted.

When you're writing a script, and you want a character to move downstage right, there's a reason for it. The character doesn't just reach the indicated spot, hit his mark and stand there, doing nothing. (Unless, of
course, you've written a surreal, existentialist, or other kind of metaphysical play in which, for instance, each part of the stage represents something. Your concern as a writer is to tell the characters what to do and
where to go to accomplish that task. Therefore, a character crosses to the
desk and picks up a gun, or goes to the French windows and opens them,
or answers a knock at the front door. If you've established the approximate location of each part of the set—the desk, the windows, the door—
then you don't *need* to dwell on specific blocking indications. In nearly
every important instance, you need only describe what the character is
doing. If you find yourself doing a lot of blocking, seriously ask yourself if
it's all *really* necessary. Nine times out of ten, it won't be.

In addition, an author's attempts at blocking are frequently unwanted
by the director. From a director's point of view, the author should only be
concerned with the specific actions and movements that are necessary to
advance the story. The subtle little physical relationships between the
actors, the way they face one another, the way they stand or walk or gesture or talk—all these are within the exclusive province of the director.
The blocking can vary depending on the preferences of the director, the
size and shape of the stage, the actors themselves, and a variety of other
factors. The director may choose to adapt the play to a theater-in-the-
round format (in which case downstage right is whatever corner of the
arena he *decides* is downstage right), may opt for the characters to play a
scene nude, or have them hold a conversation while sitting in stiff-
backed wooden chairs facing *away* from one another.

The task of a director is to interpret your script, contributing to it those
physical touches that will—in the director's estimation—highlight certain aspects of the play and make the entire dramatic presentation a fluid,
living thing. This is why a play can vary greatly in pacing and delivery
when handled by two different directors who have conflicting attitudes
toward what makes good drama.

The other area in which a playwright has some degree of input is in the
creation of the set required by the play. The first part of any playscript is a
description of the arena in which the action will take place—a bedroom,
a den, a prison cell, or what have you. In describing this location, it's
sometimes possible to get carried away, writing in little details that
would look nice, but that don't really have anything to do with the story,
or that don't help to create the specific mood of the play. Chekov put the
situation in the proper perspective when he remarked, "If there is a gun

on the wall at the beginning of act one, then you'd best be sure that the gun has been fired by the end of act two." Just as your story should be spare and to the point, so too should the props and sets that you require.

In describing the set, you should write out what pieces of furniture and props are necessary, the period of time they should represent, the condition of said items, and where they are in relation to one another, using the stage directions as required to get your point across. If lighting is an essential element to creating the correct mood, you should describe the kind you want—dim, moody, suggestive of night, bright and glaring, slightly gold, or deeply blue. Beyond that, the set designer will come up with whatever else is easily available to help set the scene, and the lighting director will create a subtle effect to also highlight the play.

One very practical reason for the sparsity has to do with budgets. You can call for an extensive number and variety of props, but if the theater hasn't the money to purchase them, the shop to make them, or the clout to borrow them, then some of these props will have to be dispensed with, and it's better to state right up front which are necessary by virtue of their relation to the story than have someone make a mistake and not order an essential article. The same applies to lighting, if the theater has only a fixed lighting system; or costumes, if they are period costumes that are far too expensive to acquire.

Not infrequently, some compromise may be called for. A long, dark dress may be substituted for an 1880 house dress, or a plunger painted black with two black cans and a string may have to suffice for a telephone circa 1918. It's possible that the entire play could be staged using large boxes covered with black cloth, bunched together in groups and in forms that suggest a table, or a bed, or a set of chairs.

As a rule, you should try whenever possible not to make a given prop or effect the linchpin of your play, because that sets it out of the reach of those theaters that might want to produce your play, but simply don't have the facilities or the budget to do so.

There's the story of a director at a small theater who was given an extraordinarily fine script by a new playwright. The problem, however, was that the script called for the presence of an elephant onstage during all of act two. "But what does an elephant have to do with the story?" the director asked.

"Nothing," the playwright said enthusiastically. "But wouldn't it look great?"

Enough said. We proceed.

Since the portion of your script that contains staging information also includes a thumbnail description of your characters, be sure to make your descriptions as brief, to the point, and generalized as possible. It's not necessary to spell out the character's hair color, the way his eyes flash in the sunlight, the way her nose perks up just a little at the end. The best person for the role, in the director's estimate, may have hair of some color other than that which you have visualized, or may vary in some other way. But that's not important. All that is important is that the director have a rough idea of what the character is like at the beginning of your script. The rest of the character's personality will emerge through dialogue and action.

Bearing in mind all these points about movement, scene description, and staging, let's take a look at an excellent example of a spare opening, one that contains all the information that is important to the director, and that does not get lost in a maze of complex stage directions. The following excerpt comes from the first page of *Table Manners* by Alan Ayckbourn, a part of the *Norman Conquests* trilogy.

> The dining room. Saturday 6 p.m. A fine evening—sun streams through the large windows of the room. A solid table and four chairs. A sideboard. A window seat and a couple of additional upright chairs. The room is large and high-ceilinged and like the rest of this Victorian vicarage-type building, badly needs redecorating.
>
> ANNIE in baggy sweater, jeans and raffia slippers enters with a flower vase of water. She thumps this down in the middle of the table, picks up the roses which lie beside it and drops them into the vase. She gives the whole lot a final shake and that, as far as she's concerned, concludes her flower arrangement. She is moving to the sideboard, about to lay the table when SARAH enters. She wears a light summer coat and dress. She is breathless.

And that's the extent of it. It is, if anything, almost a simple inventory. It specifies what furniture is needed, what props (the vase and flowers), the type of clothing worn by the characters, the specific room, day and time. This gives the director the freedom to place the actors and the furniture anywhere he thinks would work best for that particular theater. Further, in this play, it doesn't matter so much what the characters look like as how they relate to one another, and that is something that develops slowly, within the play itself.

Should there be any specific requirements in terms of age, build, and appearance that the characters should conform to, then it is usually a good idea to write them up together on a separate page and include it in with the body of your script, a process we'll examine shortly.

Which brings us, at last, to the culmination of all our work so far.

The Playscript

You've decided upon your story, you know the characters as intimately as possible, you've roughly outlined your play in terms of what should happen during each act, and you are now ready to sit down behind the typewriter and begin writing and assembling your script. The only remaining questions are what does a script look like, what should be included in it, and in what order?

We'll take them one at a time, moving from the first page of your playscript to the last.

The first and most obvious requirement is your title page. This is typed in precisely the same way as the title page for a motion picture script. The only difference is that instead of typing "An Original Screenplay by" you type "A One-Act Play by," "A Play in Two Acts by," or "A Play in Three Acts by," with your name following directly below.

The very next page is the play breakdown, which appears in this order: At 75 picas, 4 lines from the top of the page, is the page number, Roman numeral i. Four lines farther down the page, at 8 lines, the title of the play is typed in all caps, underlined, and centered on the page.

Four lines below the title, at 20 picas, typed in all caps, are the words ACT ONE. A series of ellipses move across the page to 45 picas, where you describe the day and date of act one. This is done for each subsequent act, triple-spacing between each line. If the acts are broken up by time jumps in story time, then this is also indicated. If act one is divided into two scenes, then the first line of the page breakdown reads ACT ONE: Scene One, followed by the series of ellipses. ACT ONE: Scene Two appears two lines beneath the first line. In some cases, retyping ACT ONE may be unnecessary, in which case the words Scene Two are typed directly beneath the words Scene One.

At the bottom of the page, an inch from the end of the page, the approximate running time of the play is typed between 20 and 70 picas.

When completed, your play breakdown should look like this (See Fig. 35.):

The next page (Roman numeral ii) contains the information concerning your characters. The words *Cast of Characters* appear centered on the page, 8 lines from the top. Four lines farther down, you type the NAMES of each character in all caps, with a brief description of that character following. This information should be approximately centered on the page, using the longest line as a marker. The descriptions can be quite simple, as in this case:

GEORGE, a heavy-set man in his thirties.
JANE, his sister.
FRANK, his best friend.

Or they can be quite elaborate, spilling out to a maximum of 15 to 70 picas:

GEORGE, a somber-looking, overweight man in his thirties, prematurely balding, with a slight limp.

JANE, his spinster sister, a thin, bespectacled woman who looks much older than her years.

FRANK, a thin, happy-go-lucky fellow with a broad face and a hearty laugh.

Should the scene description be elaborate, it is often a good idea to sep-

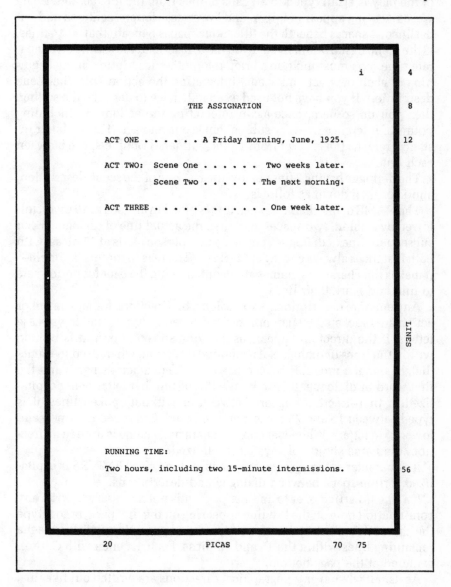

```
                                                    i        4


                    THE ASSIGNATION                          8


   ACT ONE . . . . . . A Friday morning, June, 1925.         12

   ACT TWO:  Scene One . . . . . . Two weeks later.
             Scene Two . . . . . . The next morning.

   ACT THREE . . . . . . . . . . . One week later.




                                                          LINES










   RUNNING TIME:
   Two hours, including two 15-minute intermissions.        56



        20                  PICAS                   70   75
```

Fig. 35

arate it from the text of the play itself and put the detailed information up front (page *iii*). In this case, *The Setting* is written in upper- and lower-case letters, and underlined in the center of the page, 8 lines from the top. The body of your description begins 4 lines farther down, between 15 and 75 picas, with the first line indented five spaces.

The actual playscript itself begins next, on Arabic numeral 1. The title of the play is again typed in all caps 8 lines from the top, centered. The words *Act One* appear in upper- and lower-case letters, centered and underlined, 2 spaces beneath the title. Four spaces beneath that, at 14 lines, is the scene description. Even if you have described the setting on a separate page, you must include a brief, referential description at the beginning of each new act and scene, integrating the action with the scene description. If you have not used a separate page to describe the setting, then you do so here, once again integrating the action and including points of reference in every subsequent scene and act. (For the latter instance, refer to the excerpt from *Table Manners*.) Double-space between each line.

The dialogue begins 2 lines below the last line of the scene description, and is broken down as follows:

The NAME of the character speaking is typed in all caps at 10 picas, followed by a colon, two spaces, and then the actual line of dialogue. Each subsequent line of dialogue spoken by that person starts at 15 picas, with both instances always ending at 75 picas. (The reason for this is simple— it makes the characters' names stand out, making it easier for performers to find and mark their lines.)

Any emotive descriptions, expressions, or directions for movement or action are bracketed by parentheses and typed in upper- and lower-case letters. If the direction appears as part of a speaking part, it is written within the lines of dialogue. An emotive direction, when used to immediately signal a mood, is placed between the character's name and the first word of dialogue. It is written without the first letter being capitalized. If the direction appears between or without spoken lines, it is typed between 15 and 75 picas, parenthesized, and typed in upper- and lower-case letters. Whenever another character's name is used in a direction, the name should always be capitalized.

If a character enters a room, the name and the word ENTERS is capitalized. Triple-space between dialogue and descriptions.

If a line is carried over to another page, it is not necessary to write any continuation note on the last line appearing on the first page, or to retype the character's name at the start of the second page. You simply type the remaining lines within the 15 and 75 picas. Each act ends with *Curtain* centered at the page bottom.

As usual, whenever typographical directions are written out like this, they tend to sound more confusing than they really are. To illustrate this, we'll look at a few pages that use these typographical specifications.

Since we have pretty well covered what the first page of act one looks like, we'll take it from the first page of act two of a play which, for our purposes, we shall call *The Assignation*. (See Fig. 36 through 40.)

The foregoing was written with the intention of bringing out certain contextual points, and—assuming that I've done my work properly—these are the elements that the preceding scene should have highlighted:

The action is outlined without using elaborate stage directions.

The action that does take place—running to the window, slamming the window, popping in and out of the room—is plot-specific, meaning that it is intended either to advance the story (the glance out the window that tips Fenwood off) or reveal the nature of our characters (Fenwood's nervousness in popping in and out).

The action described does not preclude any input by the director. For instance, in the section of dialogue where Jack warns Fenwood that he has three seconds to start making sense, the director can indicate for that line to be given from across the room, while Jack points a threatening finger. If, however, the director wanted to get a little more physical, he could have Jack grab Fenwood by his lapels, delivering the line nose-to-nose. This leaves the writer in control of the story, and gives the director substantial latitude in interpreting the mood and pace of the play.

The syntax, sentence structure, phrases and implied mannerisms are all written with the intent of sounding uniquely British, an attempt that—to refer back to the need for doing one's homework—necessitates a familiarity with English diction, currency, slang, and so forth.

Something of the plot structure is also intimated here. The implication is that act one set up the circumstances of the date, let Fenwood mention his encounter with "the girl on the ship," and established Jack as the dominant social personality. Act two will, from all appearances, be the culmination of that scheme—the date will take place, and given the meeting's lackluster start, it's doubtful that it will be pleasant. Act three, then, will probably be aimed at tying up all the loose strings in the relationship(s) that may or may not bloom among the participants.

And that, when you come right down to it, is all that's really involved in playwriting. You just have to be able to sustain it for long periods of time. Using the format demonstrated here, you should write approximately 90 pages in the case of a three-act play (30 pages per act), 100 to 105 pages for a two-act play (50 to 52 pages per act), or 20 to 50 pages in the case of a one-act play.

When you have finished writing your play, you should either read it aloud to yourself or find someone willing to read through it with you. In doing so, it's important to time the play (each page should equal about a minute when performed), and discover if there are any lines that are just impossible or generally difficult to say.

At this point, if your script seems pretty solid, your next step is to make one or more photocopies of the manuscript. It's also a good idea to make up a stiff cover sheet for the manuscript, similar to the one described in the chapter on screenwriting. The difference here is that it needn't be nearly so elaborate. The purpose of a cover sheet for a play is to make it stand out from other plays that may be stacked up around it, and to protect the manuscript from undue damage. In most cases, you can simply

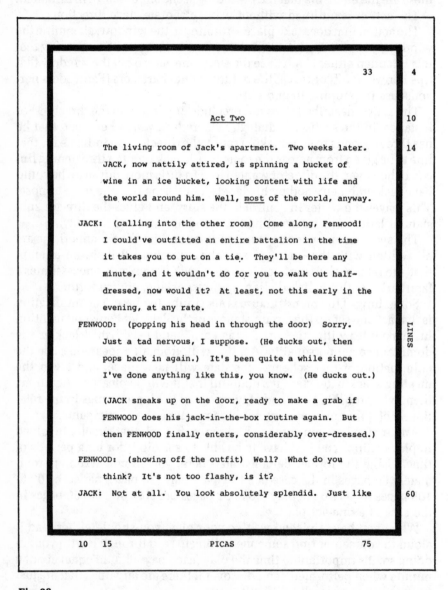

Fig. 36

type the title of your play in all caps on the page, usually in the center, or use pressure-sensitive letters for the same purpose. The cover sheet is then photocopied onto 60-pound colored stock, with a backing sheet of the same stock.

When your manuscript has been copied, punch three holes along the left margin, and fasten the pages together with 1-inch brass paper fasteners.

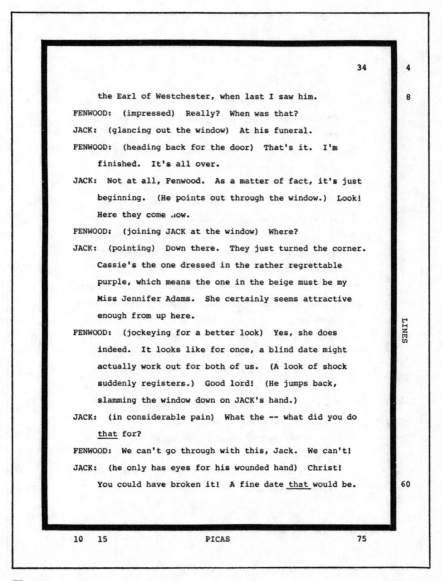

```
                                                    34        4

                                                              8
           the Earl of Westchester, when last I saw him.
    FENWOOD:  (impressed)  Really?  When was that?
    JACK:  (glancing out the window)  At his funeral.
    FENWOOD:  (heading back for the door)  That's it.  I'm
           finished.  It's all over.
    JACK:  Not at all, Fenwood.  As a matter of fact, it's just
           beginning.  (He points out through the window.)  Look!
           Here they come now.
    FENWOOD:  (joining JACK at the window)  Where?
    JACK:  (pointing)  Down there.  They just turned the corner.
           Cassie's the one dressed in the rather regrettable
           purple, which means the one in the beige must be my
           Miss Jennifer Adams.  She certainly seems attractive
           enough from up here.
    FENWOOD:  (jockeying for a better look)  Yes, she does
           indeed.  It looks like for once, a blind date might     LINES
           actually work out for both of us.  (A look of shock
           suddenly registers.)  Good lord!  (He jumps back,
           slamming the window down on JACK's hand.)
    JACK:  (in considerable pain)  What the -- what did you do
           that for?
    FENWOOD:  We can't go through with this, Jack.  We can't!
    JACK:  (he only has eyes for his wounded hand)  Christ!
           You could have broken it!  A fine date that would be.   60


          10   15            PICAS                      75
```

Fig. 37

Then, at last, you have your completed playscript in hand and ready for production. The question, though, is what does one do with a play once it's finished?

Marketing the Stage Play

What steps are taken in marketing a play depend entirely upon the type of play—one-act or multi-act—you've written.

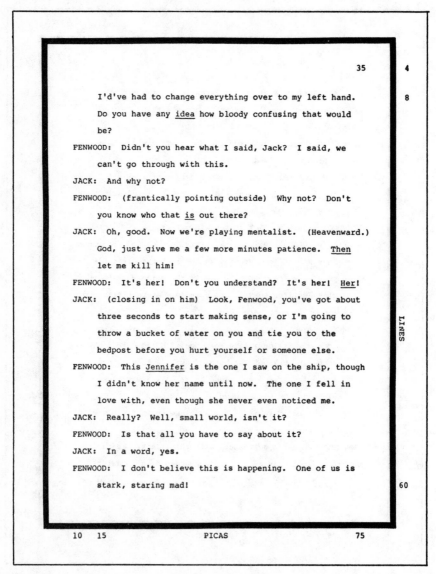

Fig. 38

In most respects, the marketing approach for a one-act play is probably the most flexible, both in terms of production and publication. To start with, contact the dramatic arts departments of your local colleges and universities. Most college-level schools—including junior colleges—that have such departments invariably have directing classes as part of their theater arts curriculum. As it happens, the only way to learn how to direct is by following the same technique used when learning how to

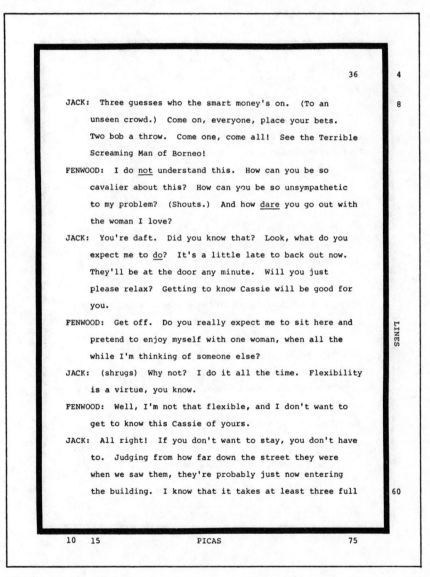

```
                                                    36        4

      JACK:   Three guesses who the smart money's on.  (To an          8

              unseen crowd.)  Come on, everyone, place your bets.

              Two bob a throw.  Come one, come all!  See the Terrible

              Screaming Man of Borneo!

      FENWOOD:  I do not understand this.  How can you be so

                cavalier about this?  How can you be so unsympathetic

                to my problem?  (Shouts.)  And how dare you go out with

                the woman I love?

      JACK:   You're daft.  Did you know that?  Look, what do you

              expect me to do?  It's a little late to back out now.

              They'll be at the door any minute.  Will you just

              please relax?  Getting to know Cassie will be good for

              you.

      FENWOOD:  Get off.  Do you really expect me to sit here and

                pretend to enjoy myself with one woman, when all the

                while I'm thinking of someone else?

      JACK:   (shrugs)  Why not?  I do it all the time.  Flexibility

              is a virtue, you know.

      FENWOOD:  Well, I'm not that flexible, and I don't want to

                get to know this Cassie of yours.

      JACK:   All right!  If you don't want to stay, you don't have

              to.  Judging from how far down the street they were

              when we saw them, they're probably just now entering

              the building.  I know that it takes at least three full   60


      10   15                 PICAS                      75
```

LINES

Fig. 39

write—you *do* it. Because it would simply cost too much and take up too much time to assign each directing student a different full-length play, most colleges compensate by assigning directors the task of directing three or more one-act plays during a given semester. This frequently results in a new one-act play being produced on the college campus at least once or possibly twice a week during the academic year.

Many of these one-act plays have been written by established authors

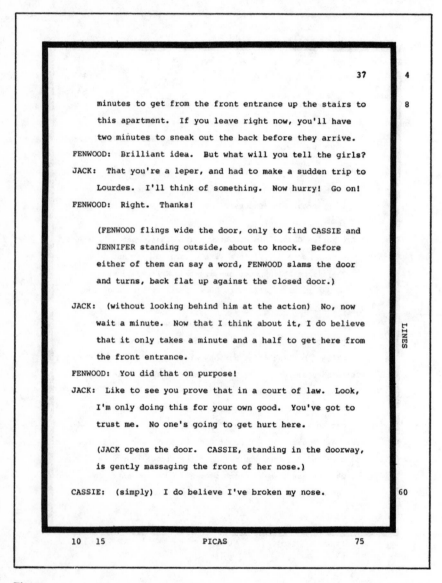

```
                                                        37        4

          minutes to get from the front entrance up the stairs to    8
          this apartment.  If you leave right now, you'll have
          two minutes to sneak out the back before they arrive.
    FENWOOD:  Brilliant idea.  But what will you tell the girls?
    JACK:  That you're a leper, and had to make a sudden trip to
          Lourdes.  I'll think of something.  Now hurry!  Go on!
    FENWOOD:  Right.  Thanks!

          (FENWOOD flings wide the door, only to find CASSIE and
          JENNIFER standing outside, about to knock.  Before
          either of them can say a word, FENWOOD slams the door
          and turns, back flat up against the closed door.)

    JACK:  (without looking behind him at the action)  No, now
          wait a minute.  Now that I think about it, I do believe
          that it only takes a minute and a half to get here from
          the front entrance.
    FENWOOD:  You did that on purpose!
    JACK:  Like to see you prove that in a court of law.  Look,
          I'm only doing this for your own good.  You've got to
          trust me.  No one's going to get hurt here.

          (JACK opens the door.  CASSIE, standing in the doorway,
          is gently massaging the front of her nose.)

    CASSIE:  (simply)  I do believe I've broken my nose.          60


    10    15              PICAS                      75
```

Fig. 40

and published in book form, mainly because they're easier to find. Many drama programs, however, encourage the students to use new works. Presenting an original play carries with it several substantial benefits. It allows the student director to work with the author; it puts the director in the position of having to fall back on his own ideas instead of simply copying past productions of a given play, a fact not lost on the instructors; a production of an original play from a local writer helps reinforce the college's interest in working with the community, the publicity that results is never a bad thing; and finally, should the play go on to be successful, meaning that it continues to get produced and eventually published, the published book—as a courtesy—usually lists where the play was first produced, which is, again, nice publicity for the college. The overall benefits of such a series of productions is so great, in fact, that many college drama departments require their directing students to exert every possible effort to make one of their three selected plays an original one-act by a new author.

What are the benefits of such a program to a playwright? First of all, it gets the play produced, which is itself something of an accomplishment. Ideally, it should permit the author to work with the director, and in the process actually see how a play takes shape after it leaves the writer's hands. (Some colleges permit only limited interaction between writer and director, though, fearing that the director might rely too much on the writer's vision. Such is life.) It lets the author witness the reaction of an impartial audience to the content and style of the play. Since most audience members will probably be drama students themselves, you can count on getting an informed, highly critical audience. If something in the play doesn't work, you'll know it *real* fast. This can give you an excellent picture of the play's strengths and weaknesses, which can be, respectively, maximized and eliminated in your rewrite.

Along with the benefits, however, there are also some potential drawbacks. For one thing, there's rarely any money involved. The idea here is that the production is its own reward, which if you stop to think about it for a minute, is really a pretty fair assessment.

You should also be prepared, should you go this route, to separate the play from the performers and/or the director. In most instances, these students are, themselves, still learning their craft, and it could very well be that their combined efforts may not be equal to the quality of the play. (In remembering this, also bear in mind that it *can* work the other way around.) So if something doesn't work in the performance, ask yourself if the problem is the written word or the delivery, and act accordingly when the time comes for a rewrite. For this approach, the following steps are in order: First, find out which colleges in your area have one-act directing programs. You then have the option of either calling the department chairperson directly, or putting your request into a query letter.

(My own experience has been that a brief, straightforward telephone inquiry is preferred.) Explain to the chairperson that you are a playwright, you have recently completed a one-act play that doesn't require extensive set or production-oriented budgets, and, if the department is open to original one-acts, you would like to submit the play to the director's program with the clear understanding that no royalties will be required. This last stipulation, by the way, also ensures that the copyright stays in your name. Be certain to find out what the parameters are within which a playwright is permitted to work with the director.

Should the door for a submission open up, package your script and send it off to the department head. Enclose a brief letter that restates the main points of your conversation, and offers a promise of support and assistance to the director should any be desired and permitted.

When your play arrives, an announcement will be made to the directing students that an original play is available to anyone who wants to do it. It's possible that after going from one director to another, no one might want to direct it. But this should not be taken as a statement about the quality of the play. It could very well be that it just didn't excite that particular group of aspiring directors. If this is the case, and you really believe in the play, let it remain in the department's hands until the following semester, when a new group comes in. The odds are good that if the play has any quality whatsoever, someone will want to direct it.

Since no money is being paid, and there is often no direct connection between the theater arts departments of different colleges, there is nothing wrong with submitting the play to a number of different departments. This only increases your chance of seeing your play produced. When one of the departments decides to produce the play, you can then either yank the script from the others, or allow them to produce it as well. Whether you do or do not tell them that some other college is going to, or already has, produced the play is something only you can decide. The odds are that if you don't tell them, they probably won't find out. And in many instances, it won't make any difference.

If there aren't any colleges in your area with such a program, or if you simply prefer a production in a less academic environment, your attention should shift to your community theaters.

A community theater can produce a one-act play in several ways. There is, for instance, what's known as a "showcase" production. It runs for one to three nights—usually over a weekend—and consists of several one-act plays by local playwrights, which may be bannered to the local public as "An Evening of One-Acts" or suchlike. The plays are often selected on the basis of how they differ in style, approach, theme, and content. These productions are often limited to the smaller or medium-sized community theaters, and are built up into theatrical events. Both the theater and the playwrights benefit from such a production. An event of this type generates publicity, which in turn brings in audiences, which theaters need in order to survive. In addition, the theater can usually be confident that the brief run will enjoy at least a modest success. Those who aren't attracted by the event status will probably come because they happen to know the playwright or someone in the cast.

If the theme or approach of your play happens to coincide with a full-length play that the theater is planning to produce, it's altogether possible your play could be presented as a "warmup" for the main feature. This possibility is further increased if the full-length play is relatively brief.

Finally, if you live in a town with an experimental theater, or a large town that has a substantial, theater-going community, other possibilities open up. One local theater may have an after-theater-theater program, presenting a one-act play in the evening hours as an optional follow-up to a full-length play. In many cases, plays chosen for this program are experimental, or just a little too bawdy for the general public, so they are presented under a separate heading altogether. In areas where the theater-going community is large, some theaters may offer a lunchtime theater program, presenting one-acts or, in some instances, improvisational performances at little or no cost, staged in the middle of the day.

Depending upon the fiscal condition of the theater and their policy toward new playwrights, there may or may not be any payment. Some theaters set aside a certain percentage of the receipts from the last performance to be divided between the playwrights and, on occasion, the performers. (Note: Nearly 90 percent of all small community theaters pay little or nothing to their performers. In some cases, the amount paid may amount to nothing more than carfare. Usually, the actors are people who hold daytime jobs, but who *want* to act, if only to gain the experience they need to move on to better-paying acting jobs. Always be as nice to starving actors as your artistic integrity and patience will permit—they live just as close to the edge—if not closer—than writers do.)

As with a college production, the greatest benefit to the writer is the production itself. But there are other advantages as well. Your play will be seen by the general public, rather than by a specialized group of students. Their reactions may be just a little more representative of other potential audiences as a result. It also gives you as a playwright more exposure to your community, establishing you in their minds as a talent to be reckoned with. Finally, there is every chance in the world that a production at a local theater will be reviewed by a community newspaper, and even though there are times when *every* playwright is convinced that the reviewer must have attended some other play than the one you wrote, reviews are desperately important. They are critical evaluations of your work by someone who sees a *lot* of theater, and who is, presumably, educated in the art and craft of live drama. If the review is negative, it would be expedient to closely examine the portions of the play the reviewer took exception to. If the reviewer had a point, change that section. If not, don't change a word. If the review is complimentary, use it as a means of locating and reinforcing the strongest points of your play. In addition, a good review will be of great help in getting your play produced elsewhere, or in getting it published.

Publication and production outside your community are the last outlets for the one-act play. Neither should be attempted unless your play has first been produced by someone—a college or small community theater—or unless you're absolutely convinced about the quality of your play. In either event, your first step should be to consult the very latest edition of *Writer's Market*, which contains a comprehensive listing of those interested in publishing or producing original one-act plays, a list which is—and this is vital—updated annually.

Some notes on both of these avenues:

It's very, very difficult, if not almost impossible, to get a one-act play published in book form, particularly if it hasn't been produced at least once. As a rule, most outlets for published plays are magazines that deal with the subject of drama. Some magazines feature one-act plays infrequently, and others regularly publish a new one-act as part of their format. There are also quarterly publications and other magazines that publish nothing but one-act plays. Some of these copyright the play in their own name, others copyright the work in the name of the author; most pay something to the author, and some make special provisions for royalties. The key benefit in having your play published is exposure. The only people who subscribe to such publications are those who are actively interested in drama and have at least a passing interest in reading and producing new plays.

A considerable number of theatrical organizations throughout the United States produce one-act plays. Some will take scripts that have not been produced at all in any workshop or showcase performances, while others prefer a script that has gone through these steps. Small theaters, community theaters, theater clubs and repertory companies that accept new material are listed in *Writer's Market*, along with their current needs and preferences. Some of these theaters pay no royalties at all; others pay anywhere from 5 percent to 25 percent royalties, or offer a single, specific sum for each performance, a dollar amount ranging from $10 to $100 or more each time the play is staged. When going through the current listings, it's important to find a target theater whose orientation is similar to the approach of your play. It would be fruitless, for instance, to send a surreal existentialist play to a dinner theater, or to send a lighthearted comedy to an experimental theater that specializes in socially relevant productions.

Whenever submitting a play to an outside producer, it's always a good idea to include in your query letter anything that uniquely qualifies you to write the play, and of course, enclose a self-addressed, stamped envelope if you ever expect to see your script again. The waiting period following submission can be anywhere from two weeks to six months or more, depending upon the size of the theater, the backlog of scripts, and the possibility that the theater only operates during certain seasons.

Marketing the Full-length Play

Contests and outside productions are also a very big part of selling your full-length, multi-act playscript, and the steps outlined for the one-act play apply equally to these.

One variance comes in the form of different publication possibilities. Because a full-length play is simply too long for a magazine to handle, it must be published in book form. The publishers who are open to new works fall under two categories.

First, there are the playbook publishers who specialize in children's plays exclusively. There are also those who handle only plays for junior and high school productions, religious-themed productions, and so on. These markets are probably the easiest to crack, and the ones most open to unproduced scripts. Writers interested in the juvenile market should be sure to include all the elements of plot, story, and characterization, because children can be the toughest critics of all. Most publishers in this area offer a royalty contract of 5 percent to 10 percent of the book rights, 15 percent to 25 percent of performance rights, and generally copyright the play in the author's name. Under common-law copyright laws, the play remains in the author's name indefinitely. Once produced, though, you should take the steps to formally copyright the work, securing the forms from the US copyright office. Some theaters insist on the play being formally copyrighted prior to production.

Publishers of contemporary, adult plays for the community and legitimate theater market are often more selective of the plays they publish. There are also fewer of these around, which makes the market even more restrictive. Because of the risks of publishing an untested play in book form, a terrific financial undertaking, most publishers prefer to see a play that has been produced to good reviews at least once.

If the play has been produced earlier, and seems like a good investment, a majority of established publishers will agree to a royalty contract such as that outlined above. If it hasn't, many of these publishers may only agree to publish the play provided they pay for it through an outright purchase. This minimizes their risk by cutting down on any money they have to pay out after the publication. *All* the royalties, both for performance and publication, belong to them. In time, even a barely adequate play, under this arrangement, will at least recoup the initial expenditures.

But . . . if the play goes on to be a considerable success, you don't get a penny of the resultant money. And *that* is why it's so essential to have your play produced at least once at any of the theaters available through the published listings, or at a local community theater.

Therefore, you should contact each of your community theaters by telephone and find out which of them are open to new playwrights with original scripts. Your best bet is with the middle-sized theater group, or an experimental theater. Many such theaters provide different kinds of outlets for original scripts. If the play is good enough and the budget permits, they can go ahead with a full-fledged production. As a rule, it will probably not be quite as elaborate as the staging of a well-known play. The budget for props and other equipment may be less, and the play may run for only three weeks instead of the usual five or six, but the important thing is the production itself. Again, depending on the theater's finances, there may or may not be any payment to the author.

There are other outlets besides a complete, extended production. A limited showcase production may be staged for one weekend, using the stage setting for another ongoing play. More and more theaters now are conducting "play discovery projects," in which new plays are solicited and staged in a readers' theater format. This eliminates props, costumes, and blocking, and instead relies on the verbal interpretive skills of the actors.

It is preferable, overall, to exert every possible effort in securing a local production before taking your play "on the road," so to speak. This gives you the opportunity to work with the cast, see the play come together, and work out all the bugs before sending it to an outside theater. Remember, being a locally based playwright carries with it certain inherent advantages. Every theater likes to look at itself as a valid part of the community, responsive to the theatrical talents within that community. So even though two equally acceptable scripts may arrive in the hands of the theater's artistic manager, or producing director, or what-have-you, one from a local resident and one from another city or state, the local resident will *always* have the inside track. Mind you, though, that's when all things are equal—the ultimate question comes down to which is the *better* script, if either.

Finally, many community theaters hold contests in which area playwrights are invited to contribute a full-length play written around a certain theme—a play based on the history of the community, or that utilizes a dramatic device not often seen in contemporary playwriting, such as the classic melodrama. If you feel comfortable with the requirements, then you might be well-advised to enter the competition. If not, keep the theater in mind for future submissions of original plays, because the contest is an indication of the theater's openness to new material.

All of which pretty much sums up the state of the contemporary marketplace for original works by new playwrights. The question now, however, is what can be expected in coming years?

Forthcoming Attractions in the Theater

For the early part of the history of American theater, most—if not *all*—of the plays produced were by European or English playwrights. Then, gradually, American playwrights began to develop their own voices. Their works contained the scope of much of American culture. It was a process of *defining* what American theater was, and in that process, of discovering who we as a people were, and are.

The late seventies and the eighties are shaping up as a redirection of that process of definition. Or, more precisely perhaps, a *refinement*. The emphasis has moved from the multinational to the national, and now to the local. A sense of regionalism has arisen in American theater, with the development of plays that are distinctly New York, Hollywood, Texan, or even Oregonian in flavor. They take the monolithic block that is called *American Culture* and slice it into very thin segments, so that we can see through it and, by understanding a part of it, better come to understand the whole.

With this continuing emphasis on communities, it seems likely that the interest of local theaters in playwrights from their area will not only persist, but grow. The eighties, from all indications, will continue to put a premium on the discovery of new playwrights.

Nor is this emphasis only centered about regionalism. There is a growing demand for plays that deal with ethnic issues, with social issues, with the lives of women. Women! Along with the feminist revolution of the sixties, theatergoers discovered that women not only can act, but can also write, and they have their own stories to tell. For centuries, half the population has spoken with a muted voice, or been interpreted through the words of men. This is changing, and it seems certain that just as minorities of all types have entered the world of playwriting and staked a claim of their own, so too will women playwrights be a vital force in American Theater.

Which is not to say, however, that all plays and all playwrights should aim for stratification by region or ethnic background or sex. The greatest plays of all are those that are universal, that speak to all people of matters not confined to any one group—love, war, happiness and the quest for meaning in life.

The eighties and the years beyond will probably not be any simpler than the years preceding them. If anything, they will be more complex. The quest to find out who we are will continue, and theater has always been a very big part of that quest. It mirrors people. It says, "This is who we are today, and how the world looks to us today." New voices who contribute to that vision of ourselves and the world will always be needed.

Evidence of this can be found in the fact that although the economy of the seventies and eighties has become more difficult to deal with, more and more community theaters have arisen, and though still struggling, persist. There are no new or shattering developments in technology that will propel theater and playwrights into a golden era of opportunity. But neither is there anything sufficient to stop an art form that has been around for thousands of years. Theater has never been dependent upon technology. It is, and will be, as it has always been—some words, a flat patch of ground to stand upon, someone to move and give life to the words, and the unending story of human beings trying to live in the world in the face of adversity, death, joy, love, and loneliness and somehow come through it with dignity, courage, and a belief in the greatness of the human being singular.

APPENDIX ONE

Glossary of Visual Terminology
For Television and Film

The world of television and film scripting has its own unique language, and it is essential that anyone aspiring to write for these media fully understand this language. A knowledge of production terminology enables the scriptwriter to visualize the concept under construction in very specific terms and, equally as important, to communicate that concept in a way that can be immediately understood by anyone who reads the script.

The following is a list of the visual terms used most frequently in television and film production.

Camera Directions

Background (B.G.): The area farthest from the lens of the camera that is still within clear visible range. This term is used to convey something happening away from the primary action. For example: "As Bob and Kathy speak, an elephant moves across the stage in the B.G."

Close shot: An indication for the camera to close in on a certain action, usually to emphasize the action and the way it relates to the plot. "As Robert drives, we see Fred removing a gun from his belt in a CLOSE SHOT."

Close-up: An indication for the camera to close in on an actor's expression: often just the face, other times including the whole head. A call for a close-up is indicated by the abbreviation CU, and takes place whenever a dramatic moment needs to be emphasized, or when you want to dwell on a character's reaction to an incident in your script. "Sherwood opens the box and finds a bomb inside. CU on Sherwood's reaction." (To clarify the difference between a close-up and a close shot, a close shot used in this scene would be handled thus: "Sherwood opens the box and finds a bomb inside. CLOSE SHOT on the bomb's timer ticking away the seconds.")

Exterior (EXT): A notation establishing that the action taking place is shot *outside* something—an office, a building, a spaceship. The notation EXT is used at the beginning of a scene along with the scene number (if needed), and a notation of time of day. "EXT. HOTEL-PARKING LOT-DAY."

Extreme close-up (ECU): Similar in intention to a basic close-up, but more intense, with only the eyes and possibly a nose visible in the shot.

Frame: That portion of the scene visible to the camera and framed by its lens. (Think of it as a picture frame surrounding a portrait.) "As smoke rises from the manhole, Rick enters the frame."

Interior (INT): Similar to *Exterior* in purpose. Used to establish that the action being described takes place inside something. "INT. SUBMARINE-CONTROL ROOM-NIGHT."

Long shot: An indication for the camera to be placed some distance from its subject(s). "In a LONG SHOT, Jeremy and Betty walk on the beach at sunset."

Medium shot: The happy medium between a close and a long shot. In most cases, you do not need to signal such a shot, since most camerawork is done in medium shots anyway. It is generally used to return the camera's perspective to normal after a close or long shot. "We return to a MEDIUM SHOT of Jeremy and Betty as they walk past a sign reading 'Beach Closed.' "

Pan: An indication for the camera to move in a steady horizontal line across the scene. "The camera PANS the faces of the mourners."

Shot: Same as *Frame.*

Stock footage: This tells the director that the scene can be realized using material already on film and in the camera from previous episodes. Many exteriors and car-driving sequences are stored on stock footage, and plugged into a program whenever a similar scene is required, thereby saving the expense of reshooting the location all over again. "The ship steams away into the distance. STOCK FOOTAGE."

Swish-pan: Similar to a pan, but faster, with more dizzying effects. Frequently used to connote rapidity of movement.

Zoom: An indication for the camera to move from a long to a close or medium shot in the same take, "zooming" in on the subject. "Shooting over John's shoulder, the camera ZOOMS IN on the front window of the bank across the street."

Special Effects Shots

Aerial shot: An indication that the scene is to be shot from a great height, usually from a helicopter or airplane.

Crane shot: A camera shooting from a less dramatic height, in this case from a movable crane that can move from a face-on shot to a perspective looking down on the action.

Freeze-frame: A term used mostly in videotape, this means literally freezing the action onscreen. (Freeze-frames are widely used at the conclusion of situation comedies, with the end credits rolling over the frozen scene.)

Hand-held camera: This is a device used to increase the "you-are-there" sensation. The cameraman walks toward the scene with the camera hand-held instead of on wheels and this gives the finished film a jerky, documentary feel that also follows the rhythm of actual footsteps. You often see this effect in detective mysteries—the camera is used to represent the point of view of a burglar about to break into someone's house. This would be written as, "EXT. HOUSE-THIEF'S P.O.V.—CAMERA HAND-HELD."

Insert: Any momentary aside or diversion from the body of the script, very much like a parenthetical statement in prose writing. If, during your scene, there is a man holding a box, and you want to go to a close-up on the label of that box, you write: "INSERT: CU ON THE LABEL ON THE BOX." You describe what's on the label, and then, to return to the body of the action, you simply write "BACK TO SCENE" 2 spaces below your insert.

Pixillation: A computerized process that omits two out of three frames of action, thereby creating a surreal, jumpy look. The effect is similar to that associated with a flashing strobe light at a discotheque. (Also used in film animation.)

Point of view (P.O.V.): This informs the reader that the scene is being filmed from the perspective of one of the characters. For an example of this, see *Hand-held camera.*

Series of shots: A montage of camera shots of different locations connected to create a certain impression—say, a father looking for his lost daughter. This would be written as, "SERIES OF SHOTS: EXT. LOCATIONS-DAY AND NIGHT-SHOPS, STORES, OFFICES," followed by, on the next line, "Father goes from store to store, asking patrons if they have seen his daughter." This is a time-saving device, and is usually shot without sound; a musical soundtrack might accompany the action.

Split-screen shot: This means just what it says—the frame is split down the middle, with each side displaying an action taking place at a different location. This is often used to show both sides of a telephone conversation. "INT. SPLIT-SCREEN—JOHN AND MARSHA ON THE TELEPHONE."

Slow motion: Slowing the action down in order to heighten the moment or—in parodies—to ridicule it.

Superimpose: To place one image over another.

Tracking shot: When your characters are walking along the beach, and the camera stays right beside them all the way—this is a tracking shot. The name came about because on rough or uneven terrain—such as a beach—wooden tracks are set down for the camera to roll upon.

Transitions

Blackout: An immediate darkening of the screen that does not signal the end of the script. Blackouts are frequently used in comedy sketches to signal the end of the sketch.

Cut to: The most common transition of all: To cut to one scene from another means that the transition is immediate, without break or blackout or fancy camerawork in between.

Dissolve: This device moves us from one location to another by superimposing the first few seconds of the next scene over the last few seconds of the preceding one.

Fade-in: An indication that the script is now beginning. The term fade-in is used only once, at the very start of the manuscript.

Fade-out: Also used only once, this signals the conclusion of the script.

Intercutting: Signals important things happening in two distant locations at the same time. This means that the camera will cut back and forth from one location to the other during the scene. When you have established your primary scene, and come to the location you want to cut back and forth from, you simply write the scene indication and description as you would otherwise, and follow it with, "Camera INTERCUTS between the two scenes."

Match cut: Let's say your character is reading about a grand opening at a new bank. The opening is announced in a newspaper headline, and the scene you want to cut to is of a banner draped over the front of the bank bearing the same words, in the same typestyle, with one overlapping the other as in a dissolve. This is called a match cut, meaning that one element in the second scene is identical in some fashion to an element of the same visual size in the preceding scene.

Solarization: The opposite of a blackout. The scene fills with light so that, eventually, nothing is visible but the light.

APPENDIX TWO

Sample Release Forms

In nearly every instance, a film, radio, or television producer will specifically ask that a release form be signed by the person submitting a script for his or her examination, and that the release be included with the script.

To facilitate this process a bit, two separate release forms are presented here for your use and convenience. The first is a short-form release generally favored by most television producers. The second is a somewhat longer release that can be used in a variety of circumstances, for television, film, and radio.

If desired, you can simply white out the page numbers and other identifying marks that these pages contain and photocopy the forms as printed. Otherwise, you can just retype them and photocopy them onto 8½x11 pages.

Whenever you approach a producer, be sure to mention that you possess a standard release form, but that if there is one preferred by his production company, to please forward it along to you. When mailing your script, be sure to write the words RELEASE FORM ENCLOSED on the envelope to avoid having the package sent back unopened.

PROGRAM MATERIAL RELEASE FORM: TELEVISION

_____, 19_____

Title and/or Theme of Material Submitted Hereunder: _____

Gentlemen:

I am today submitting to you certain program material, the title and/or theme of which is indicated above (which material is hereinafter referred to as the "program material"), upon the following express understanding and conditions.

1. I acknowledge that I have requested permission to disclose to you and to carry on certain discussions and negotiations with you in connection with such program material.

2. I agree that I am voluntarily disclosing such program material to you at my request. I understand that you shall have no obligation to me in any respect whatsoever with regard to such material until each of us has executed a written agreement, which by its terms and provisions will be the only contract between us.

3. I agree that any discussions we may have with respect to such program material shall not constitute any agreement expressed or implied as to the purchase or use of any of such program material which I am hereby disclosing to you either orally or in writing.

4. If such material submitted hereunder is not new or novel, or was not originated by me, or has not been reduced to concrete form, or if because other persons including your employees have heretofore submitted or hereafter submit similar or identical program material which you have the right to use, then I agree that you shall not be liable to me for the use of such program material and you shall not be obligated in any respect whatsoever to compensate me for such use by you.

5. I further agree that if you hereafter produce or distribute a television program or programs based upon the same general idea, theme, or situation, and/or having the same setting or background and/or taking place in the same geographical area or period of history as the said program material, then, unless you have substantially copied the expression and development of such idea, theme or situation, including the characters and story line thereof, as herewith or hereafter submitted to you by me in writing, you shall have no obligation or liability to me of any kind or character by reason of the production or distribution of such program(s), nor shall you be obligated to compensate me in connection therewith.

6. You agree that if you use any legally protectible portion of said program, provided it has not been obtained by you from, or independently created by, another source, you will pay me an amount that is comparable to the compensation normally paid by you for similar material or an amount equal to the fair market value thereof as of the date of this agreement, whichever is greater.

I acknowledge that but for my agreement to the above terms and conditions, you would not accede to my request to receive and consider the said program material that I am submitting to you herewith.

Very truly yours,

_____

_____

_____

EVALUATION AGREEMENT

Gentlemen:

I am submitting to you herewith the following material (hereinafter referred to as "said Material").

TITLE: _____

FORM OF MATERIAL

Synopsis   Screenplay   Radioplay
Treatment   Telescript   Other:_____
                                       _____

PRINCIPAL CHARACTERS:_____

_____

BRIEF SUMMARY OF THEME OR PLOT: _____

_____

_____

WGA REGISTRATION NO.:_____ NO. OF PAGES: _____

1. I request that you read and evaluate said material, and you hereby agree to do so, and you agree to advise me of your decision with respect to the material.

2. I warrant that I am the sole owner and author of said material, that I have the exclusive right and authority to submit the same to you upon the terms and conditions stated herein; and that all of the important features of said material are summarized herein. I will indemnify you of and from any and all claims, loss or liability that may be asserted against you or incurred by you, at any time, in connection with said material, or any use thereof.

3. I agree that nothing in this agreement nor the fact of my submission of said material to you shall be deemed to place you in any different position than anyone else to whom I have not submitted said material.

4. I understand that as a general rule you purchase literary properties through the established channels in the industry and not through a submission such as this. I recognize that you have access to and/or may create or have created literary materials and ideas which may be similar or identical to said material in theme, idea, plot, format or other respects. I agree that I will not be entitled to any compensation because of the use by you of any such similar or identical material which may have been independently created by you or may have come to you from any other independent source. I understand that no confidential relationship is established by my submitting the material to you hereunder.

5. You agree that if you use any legally protectible portion of said material, provided it has not been obtained by you from, or independently created by, another source, you will pay me an amount that is comparable to the compensation normally paid by you for similar material or an amount equal to the fair market value thereof as of the date of this agreement, whichever is greater. If we are unable to agree as to said amount, or in the event of any dispute concerning any alleged use of said material or with reference to this agreement, such dispute will be submitted to arbitration.

6. I have retained at least one copy of said material, and I hereby release you of

and from any and all liability for loss of, or damage to, the copies of said material submitted to you hereunder.

7. I enter into this agreement with the express understanding that you agree to read and evaluate said material in express reliance upon this agreement and my covenants, representatives and warranties contained herein, and that in the absence of such an agreement, you would not read or evaluate said material.

8. I hereby state that I have read and understand this agreement and that no oral representatives of any kind have been made to me, and that this agreement states our entire understanding with reference to the subject matter hereof. Any modification or waiver of any of the provisions of this agreement must be made in writing and signed by both of us.

9. If more than one party signs this agreement as submittor, the reference to "I" or "me" through this agreement shall apply to each party jointly and severally.

Very truly yours,

_____

Address

_____

Signature

_____

City and State

_____

Print Name

_____

Telephone Number

Accepted and Agreed to by

_____

Signature

APPENDIX THREE

Index of Producers, TV and Film

A large part of selling a screenplay or telescript to a producer is finding the production company in the first place. To cut down on some of the legwork, a compendium of the most long-lived and respected production companies follows. When sending an inquiry or script off to a television production company for a continuing series, always be sure to specify the producer and the series. When addressing an inquiry for a screenplay, head the letter with the name (if available) of the studio story editor.

Key: (F) Motion picture company exclusively.
(T) Television company exclusively.
(F/T) Produces both television and film programs.

ABC Pictures, Inc., 2040 Avenue of the Stars, Los Angeles, California 90067. (213) 557-7777. (T)

ABC Television, New York Headquarters, 101 West 67th Street, New York, New York 10023. (212) 581-7777. (T)

Irwin Allen Productions, Inc., 4000 Warner Boulevard, Burbank, California 91522. (213) 954-6000. (F/T)

American International Pictures, 9038 Wilshire Boulevard, Beverly Hills, California 90211. (213) 278-8118. (F)

The Samuel Z. Arkoff Company, 9200 Sunset Boulevard, Penthouse 3, Los Angeles, California 90069. (213) 278-7600. (F)

Allied Artists Pictures Corporation, 9255 Sunset Boulevard, Los Angeles, California 90069. (213) 278-7162. (F)'

Avco Embassy Pictures Corporation, 956 Seward Avenue, Los Angeles, California 90038. (213) 460-7200. (F)

Bob Banner Associates, Inc., 8687 Melrose Avenue, Suite M-20, Los Angeles, California 90069. (213) 657-6800. (F/T)

Steven J. Cannell Productions, 5451 Marathon Street, Los Angeles, California 90038. (213) 465-5800. (T)

Capitol Pictures, Inc., 1438 Gower Street, Los Angeles, California 90028. (213) 467-7726. (F)

CBS Television, Studio Center, 4024 Radford Avenue, Studio City, California 91604. (213) 760-5000. (T)

Columbia Pictures, Columbia Plaza, Burbank, California 91505. (213) 954-6000. (F)

Columbia Pictures Television (Screen Gems), Columbia Plaza, Burbank, California 91505. (213)954-6000. (T)

Francis Ford Coppola, 1040 North Las Palmas Avenue, Los Angeles, California 90038. (213)463-7191. (F)

Crown International Pictures, 292 South La Cienega Boulevard, Beverly Hills, California 90211. (213)657-6700. (F)

Dan Curtis Productions, 5451 Marathon Street, Los Angeles, California 90038. (213)468-5000. (T)

Dino DeLaurentiis Corporation, 202 North Canon Drive, Beverly Hills, California 90210. (213)550-8700. (F)

Disney Productions, 500 South Buena Vista Street, Burbank, California 91521. (213)840-1000. (F/T)

EMI Productions, 4024 Radford Avenue, Studio City, California 91604. (213)760-5000. (F/T)

Filmways, Inc., 2049 Century Park East, Suite 3500, Los Angeles, California 90067. (213)557-8700. (F)

First Artists, 4000 Warner Boulevard, Burbank, California 91522. (213)843-6000. (F)

Four D Productions, 1438 North Gower Street, Los Angeles, California 90038. (213)557-7777. (T)

Chuck Fries Productions, 4024 Radford Avenue, Studio City, California 91604. (213)760-5000. (F/T)

Golden West Television, 5800 Sunset Boulevard, Los Angeles, California 90028. (213)560-5500. (T)

Goodson-Todman Productions, 6430 Sunset Boulevard, Los Angeles, California 90028. (213)464-4300. (T)

Merv Griffin Productions, 1541 North Vine Street, Los Angeles, California 90028. (213)461-4701. (T)

Hanna-Barbera Productions, Inc., 3400 Cahuenga Boulevard, West, Los Angeles, California 90068. (213)851-5000. (T)

The Komack Company, 4000 Warner Boulevard, Burbank, California 91522. (213)954-6000. (T)

Krofft Entertainment, Inc., 7200 Vineland Avenue, Sun Valley, California 91352. (213)875-3250. (T)

Glen Larsen Productions, 100 Universal City Plaza, Universal City, California 91608. (213)985-4321. (T)

Lorimar Productions, 10202 West Washington Boulevard, Culver City, California 90230. (213)836-3000. (F/T)

LucasFilm Ltd., 3855 Lankershim Boulevard, North Hollywood, California 91604. (213)760-3800. (F)

Marble Arch Productions, 4024 Radford Avenue, Building 2, Studio City, California 91604. (213)760-6200. (F/T)

Mark VII Productions, 1041 North Formosa Avenue, Los Angeles, California 90046. (213)650-2492. (T)

Garry Marshall Productions, 5451 Marathon Street, Los Angeles, California 90038. (213)468-5000. (T)

MCA-Television, 100 Universal City Plaza, Universal City, California 91608. (213)985-4321. (T)

Meadowlane Enterprises, 15201 Burbank Boulevard, Suite B, Van Nuys, California 91411. (213)988-3830. (T)

Bert Metcalf, 10201 West Pico Boulevard, Los Angeles, California 90064. (213)277-2211. (T)

Metro-Goldwyn-Mayer, 10202 West Washington Boulevard, Culver City, California 90230. (213)836-3000. (F/T)

Mary Tyler Moore (MTM) Enterprises, 4024 Radford Avenue, Studio City, California 91604. (213)760-5000. (T)

NBC Television, 3000 West Alameda Boulevard, Burbank, California 91523. (213)840-4444. (T)

New World Pictures, Inc., 11600 San Vicente, Los Angeles, California 90049. (213)820-6733. (F)

NRW Company, 8500 Wilshire Boulevard, Suite 515, Beverly Hills, California 90211. (213)657-0585. (T)

Orion Pictures Company, 4000 Warner Boulevard, Burbank, California 91522. (213)954-6000. (F)

Paramount Pictures/TV, Inc., 5451 Marathon Street, Los Angeles, California 90038. (213)468-5000. (F/T)

Playboy Productions, 8560 Sunset Boulevard, Los Angeles, California 90069. (213)659-4080. (F)

Poly Gram Pictures, 8255 Sunset Boulevard, Los Angeles, California 90046. (213)650-4300. (F)

Quinn Martin Productions, Ltd., 1041 North Formosa Avenue, Los Angeles, California 90046. (213)650-2653. (T)

Rastar Films, Inc., 300 Colgems Square, Burbank, California 91505. (213)954-6000. (F)

George Schlatter Productions, 8321 Beverly Boulevard, Los Angeles, California 90048. (213)655-1400. (T)

Screen Gems, Inc., Columbia Plaza, Burbank, California 91505. (213)954-6000. (T)

Melvin Simon Productions, 260 S. Beverly Drive, Beverly Hills, California 90212. (213)273-5450. (F)

Spelling-Goldberg Productions, 10201 West Pico Boulevard, Los Angeles, California 90064. (213)277-2211. (T)

Tandem Productions/T.A.T. Communications Company, 5746 Sunset Boulevard, Los Angeles, California 90069. (213)462-7111. (T)

Twentieth Century-Fox Film Corporation/TV Productions, 10201 West Pico Boulevard, Los Angeles, California 90064. (213)277-2211. (F/T)

Universal City Studios, Inc., 100 Universal City Plaza, Universal City, California 91608. (213)985-4321. (F/T)

Viacom Productions, 4024 Radford Avenue, Studio City, California 91604. (213)760-5000. (T)

Warner Brothers, Inc., 4000 Warner Boulevard, Burbank, California 91522. (213)954-6000. (F/T)

Witt-Thomas-Harris Productions, 1438 North Gower Street, Los Angeles, California 90028. (213)464-1333. (T)

Zoetrope Studios, 1040 North Las Palmas Avenue, Los Angeles, California 90038. (213)463-7191. (F)

Note: Many production companies share studio space, or are divisions of the same parent company, and therefore can be found at the same street address.

APPENDIX FOUR

Index of Literary Agents and How to Get One

There's an old Hollywood cliché that states, "It's impossible to get an agent until you've reached a point in your career when you no longer need one." Like most clichés, this one is largely inaccurate, although it does contain a grain or two of truth, to wit: An agent only makes 10 percent of what his or her client(s) earn. That is the primary, and in many cases the exclusive, source of an agent's income. If a writer is a little crazy to think that he can make a living by tic-tacking out blackonwhite figments of a far-flung imagination, consider how much *crazier* someone else has got to be in thinking he can make a living off 10 percent of the other person's income.

It's a dirty job, but somebody's got to do it.

There is a lot of craziness in being an agent. In an effort to minimize that craziness—and in the process save a bit on long-running therapy—agents only take on clients who they genuinely believe have the talent to be successful scriptwriters. Agents do not accept charity cases. Period. So an agent is careful, selecting writers from one of two groups: those who've been making a living scriptwriting, and those who've not yet sold anything but have the native talent and drive to become successful.

There is absolutely *no* truth to the rumor that agents aren't interested in acquiring new scriptwriters. Their interest may vary across time, depending upon how many clients they are currently handling, but the interest is there. Why? Because the roster of clients is always changing. Agents and writers share one characteristic with the shark—as soon as they stop moving, they die. A writer may start with one agent, enjoy some success, then at the expiration of the contract move on to a bigger agent.

Or the writer may give up writing, or *want* to stay with the first agent, but get lured away by a major agency, presumably by the bigger agent's dangling a candy cane out the rear seat of a Packard.

Some writers change agents like others change socks, and if an agent doesn't have at least a few new talents on tap to fill the gap with, then the real estate profession will find itself with yet another practitioner.

It's the simple law of supply and demand—the writer supplies the scripts, and the agent demands whatever he or she humanly can without being run out of town on a rail. (There's a new theory of economics in there, somewhere.)

So . . . agents need writers. Writers need agents. How do the two sides come together? The first step is to *find* an agent. A good, reliable, legitimate agent who does not happen to share any of the other characteristics of the shark except the need to keep moving. The problem is that there are literally hundreds of agents in the Los Angeles area *alone*. Some of them work out of lavish offices, some package stars and directors as well as writers, some are small but try very hard, and some have offices built into the rear of a Ford station wagon, or that go in and out with the tide in Santa Monica. Where do you start?

Well, you want an agent who's been around for a while, an agent who specializes in the marketing of scripts. There are, after all, a lot of very good literary agents who can sell a book in two minutes, but who simply don't or can't handle scripts. And finally, you want an agent who is bound to certain standards in terms of the amount of money they can charge a writer, and the services they can provide in exchange.

What you are looking for, then, is an agent who is a signator to the Writers Guild of America Artists Managers' Basic Agreement. Not only does this usually guarantee that the agency is legitimate and respected, but it also has long-term advantages. Let's say, for the moment, that you sign with a non-Guild signator, and by gosh, he makes a sale for you. You then join the Writers Guild. The problem, though, is that writers can only be represented by Guild signatories after they join the Guild. Which simply means that the writer must now change agencies, a move that can be painful for both parties.

Where can you find a list of such agencies? Well, there is an extensive index of agencies that have signed the WGA agreement at the end of this appendix. An updated list is published every few years by the Guild itself, and a copy can be obtained for $2 or so (contact the WGA for the latest price). But the agencies listed here have all been in business for many years, and will probably continue to exist happily for many more.

With this list in hand, the next step is to contact an agent. One option here is to wait until, using the techniques detailed in this book, you have made your first sale. You then pick almost any of the listed agencies and tell them you've made a sale, and want continued representation and/or for them to come in and do the actual negotiations, after which a contract will be signed.

Now you need not wait until you've sold something. But you do have to have something in hand: a script. You've got to have completed at least one, and preferably more, full-length film or television scripts. This is the only basis upon which an agent can determine whether or not to accept you as a client. If you approach an agent with the statement that you are *interested* in doing some scripts, and that you will do one at some time in the future, or that your're considering one now, but that you want to have an agent first, you'll get a rather rude response. Under those circumstances, an agent doesn't even want to know you *exist*.

"Nothing bugs me more than the person who calls and says, 'I'd like to be a scriptwriter, and I've got a lot of good ideas, but I'd really rather not bother actually writing the script until I've got an agent first,' as though an agent were a guarantee of success," one agent told me. "The *only* guarantee of success is talent combined with persistence, and I can generally be certain that if someone comes at me with that kind of attitude, he hasn't got either of those qualities. Writing is *work*, just like anything else. There are no magic formulas, no miracles. If someone doesn't have the wherewithal to put together a script *before* I take him on as a client, the odds are good that he never *will* put together anything even remotely acceptable."

It therefore becomes apparent that in the world of scriptwriting, no matter what part of that world is being discussed, the words have to come first.

Onward.

Using the creative techniques pointed out in this book combined with your own talent and imagination, you have written a couple of scripts. Your next step is to write one of the agents listed in this appendix and inquire about the possibility of representation. Explain that you have written a complete script which is available for examination by the agent, and which is also capable of being marketed. If you have a background in other areas of writing, from playwriting to newspaper reporting, be sure to include them. If not, the less said the better. Briefly spell out what your goals are as a writer, and emphasize what kinds of scripts you are most interested in writing. This is a very important addition, because not all agents handle the same areas. Some prefer to work only with feature films or television movies, while others work closely with the producers of episodic television. Many, though, do cover both areas. State in closing that if the agent would be interested in looking at the script, you would be happy to send it along at his or her convenience. If the agency is not fully booked up with clients, you will probably get a positive response. After that, it's all up to the quality of the script.

If the script looks good, and the agent sees in you a person of considerable talent and potential, you will probably be contacted by telephone or mail, and the agent will want to know a little more about you. At least, that's the expressed reason. In many cases, the agent wants to see how the two of you will get along, if you are open to advice and suggestions, how you react to criticism, and so forth. Scriptwriting can be a temperamental business, and so a client-agent relationship is built predominantly upon mutual respect and trust. Although this should probably go without saying, the incidence of such occurrences makes it necessary: Never, ever mislead an agent or do anything to endanger the mutual trust of that relationship. Once shattered, it's almost impossible to reconstruct.

If all the signs are right, and each party understands exactly what is expected by the other party, then a contract will be sent to you. Actually, you will get three separate contracts, all identical, each signed by yourself and the agent. One copy is for your records, a second copy stays with the agent, and the third copy is filed with the Guild. Attached to the contract is a huge, bulky document called a "Rider W" which explains in detail the principles of the Basic Agreement, so that both parties know precisely what their rights and responsibilities are.

All contracts used by the Guild signatories, such as that provided here, are exactly the same. If you decide to go with a non-Guild signator, or if you do get a contract that differs from a standard agent-client agreement, check it against the one provided below for any unusual loopholes.

CLIENT-AGENT CONTRACT

1. I hereby employ you as my sole and exclusive literary agent for a period of _____ (not to exceed 7 years) from date hereof to negotiate contracts for the rendition of my professional services as a writer, or otherwise, in the fields of motion pictures, legitimate stage, radio broadcasting, television, and other fields of entertainment.

2. You hereby agree to advise and counsel me in the development and advancement of my professional career and to use reasonable efforts to procure employment and to negotiate for me, as aforesaid.

3. As compensation for your said services agreed to be rendered hereunder, I hereby agree to pay you a sum equal to ten percent (10%) of all moneys or things of value as and when received by me, directly or indirectly, as compensation for my professional services rendered or agreed to be rendered during the term hereof under contracts, or any extensions, renewals, modifications or substitutions thereof, entered into or negotiated during the term hereof and to pay the same to you thereafter for so long a time as I receive compensation on any such contracts, extensions, options or renewals of said contracts. It is expressly understood that to be entitled to continue to receive the payment of compensation on the aforementioned contracts after the termination of this agreement you shall remain obligated to serve me and to perform obligations with respect to said employment contracts or to extensions or renewals of said contracts or to any employment requiring my services on which such compensation is based.

4. I hereby agree that you may render your services to others during the term hereof.

5. In the event that I do not obtain a bona fide offer of employment from a responsible employer during a period of time in excess of four (4) consecutive months, during all of which said time I shall be ready, able, willing and available to accept employment, either party hereto shall have the right to terminate this contract by notice in writing to that effect sent to the other by registered or certified mail.

6. Controversies arising between us under the provisions of the California Labor Code relating to artists' managers and under the rules and regulations for the enforcement thereof shall be referred to the Labor Commission of the State of California, as provided in Section 1700.44 of the California Labor Code.

7. In the event that you shall collect from me a fee or expenses for obtaining employment for me, and I shall fail to procure such employment or shall fail to be paid for such employment you shall, upon demand therefore, repay to me the fee and the expenses so collected. Unless repayment thereof is made within forty-eight (48) hours after demand therefore, you shall pay to me an additional sum equal to the amount of the fee as provided in Section 1700.40 of the California Labor Code.

8. This instrument constitutes the entire agreement between us and no statement, promises or inducement made by any party hereto which is not contained herein shall be binding or valid and this contract may not be enlarged, modified or altered, except in writing by both the parties hereto; and provided further, that any substantial changes in this contract must first be approved by the Labor Commissioner.

9. You hereby agree to deliver to me an executed exact copy of this contract.
Dated _____

AGREED TO AND ACCEPTED BY:

_____   _____
Talent Agency   Name of Artist

_____   _____
Address   Address

_____   _____
City and State   City and State

_____
Social Security Number

Most agent-client contracts are signed for an initial period of one to two years, after which the contract must be renewed. One positive element of this contract is the four-month escape clause. Should the agent possess salable scripts, but fail to sell them or secure other employment for you as a writer at a minimum level of $10,000, you can discharge the agent. This is particularly helpful when dealing with an agent who is not shopping your scripts around as much as possible. If the agent *is* exerting every possible effort, however, and something just hasn't clicked yet, you would be well advised to wait a while longer, perhaps as long as nine months or so. The benefit to the agent here is that if you as a writer fail to provide anything, or anything that is marketable, the agent can terminate the contract and move on to more rewarding clients.

Once you've secured representation, you should attempt to pick the agent's brain as much as you can without becoming an irritation. A good agent will provide a list of producers he or she has worked with before and can sell to again; can instruct you in the best way to "pitch" your particular idea; can tell you what is currently hottest in the marketplace; and can direct your energies into the areas where you stand the greatest chance of succeeding.

Although it's possible to go it alone (over 90 percent of all my script sales have been done without the benefit of an agent, although I do have one now—actually two, one on the East Coast and one on the West Coast), a good agent can be a powerful ally. To assist in the process of selecting an agent, this list is offered. Those agencies marked by an asterisk are those that tend to be the most receptive to new writers. Those marked by (P) are packagers, those who handle actors, writers and directors. (For more on the role of packagers, see the chapter on screenwriting.)

Act 48 Management, 1501 Broadway, #1713, New York, New York 10036. (212) 354-4250. (*)

Adams, Ray & Rosenberg, 9200 Sunset Boulevard, Los Angeles, California 90069. (213) 278-3000. (*P)

Agency for Artists, 9200 Sunset Boulevard, #531, Los Angeles, California 90069. (213) 278-6243.

Agency for the Performing Arts, 9000 Sunset Boulevard, #315, Los Angeles, California 90069.(*)

Arcara, Bauman & Hiller, 9220 Sunset Boulevard, Los Angeles, California 90069. (213) 271-5601.

The Artists Agency, 190 North Canon Drive, Beverly Hills, California 90210. (213) 278-3200. (*)

Artists Career Management, 9157 Sunset Boulevard, Los Angeles, California 90069. (213) 278-9157.

Barr/Wilder and Associates, 8721 Sunset Boulevard, #205, Los Angeles, California 90069. (213) 652-7994. (*)

The Barskin Agency, 8730 Sunset Boulevard, Los Angeles, California 90069. (213) 985-2992.

Ron Bernstein Agency, Inc., 200 West 58th Street, New York, New York 10019. (212) 759-9647.

William Blake Agency, 1888 Century Park East, Los Angeles, California 90067. (213) 274-0321.

Harry Bloom Agency, 9460 Wilshire Boulevard, #425, Beverly Hills, California 90212. (213) 550-8087.

J. Michael Bloom, Ltd., 400 Madison Avenue, 20th Floor, New York, New York 10017. (212) 832-6900.

Bulbman Agency, P.O. Box 1317, Sparks, Nevada 89431. (702) 329-5913.

The Calder Agency, 8749 Sunset Boulevard, Los Angeles, California 90069. (213) 652-3380.

The Cambridge Company, 9000 Sunset Boulevard, Los Angeles, California 90069. (213) 666-1920.

William Carroll Agency, 2321 West Olive Avenue, Burbank, California 91501. (213) 848-9948. (*)

Polly Connell and Associates, 4605 Lankershim Boulevard, North Hollywood, California 91602. (213) 985-6266. (*)

Contemporary-Korman Artists, Ltd., 132 Lasky Drive, Beverly Hills, California 90212. (213) 278-8250.

Ben Conway and Associates, 999 North Doheny Drive, Los Angeles, California 90069. (213) 271-8133.

Werner Cosay & Associates, 9744 Wilshire Boulevard, #310, Beverly Hills, California 90212. (213) 550-1535.

Creative Artists Agency, 1888 Century Park East, Los Angeles, California 90067. (213) 277-4545. (P)

John Crosby and Associates, 9046 Sunset Boulevard, Los Angeles, California 90069. (213) 278-5121.

Dade/Rosen Associates, 999 North Doheny Drive, #102, Los Angeles, California 90069. (213) 278-7077.

Diamond Artists Ltd., 9200 Sunset Boulevard, #909, Los Angeles, California 90069. (213) 278-8146. (*)

Eisenbach-Greene-Duchow, Inc., 760 North La Cienega Boulevard, Los Angeles, California 90069. (213) 659-3420. (*P)

FCA Agency, 1800 Century Park East, Los Angeles, California 90067. (213) 277-8422.

William Felber Agency, 2126 Cahuenga Boulevard, Hollywood, California 90068. (213) 466-7629. (*)

Carol Ferrell Agency, 9034 Sunset Boulevard, #214, Los Angeles, California 90069. (213) 273-7511. (*)

Jack Fields & Associates, 9255 Sunset Boulevard, #1105, Los Angeles, California 90069. (213) 278-1333.

Film Artists Management Enterprises, 8278 Sunset Boulevard, Los Angeles, California 90046. (213) 656-7590.

Sy Fischer Company Agency, Inc., 10100 Santa Monica Boulevard, #2440, Los Angeles, California 90067. (213) 557-0388. (P)

Kurt Frings Agency, Inc., 9440 Santa Monica Boulevard, Beverly Hills, California 90210. (213) 274-8881.

Phil Gersh Agency, Inc., 222 North Canon Drive, Beverly Hills, California 90210. (213) 274-6611.

J. Carter Gibson Agency, 9000 Sunset Boulevard, Los Angeles, California 90069. (213) 274-8813. (*)

Goldfarb/Lewis Agency, 8733 Sunset Boulevard, Los Angeles, California 90069. (213) 659-5955. (*)

Goldin, Dennis, Karg and Associates, 470 South San Vicente Boulevard, Los Angeles, California 90048. (213) 651-1700. (*)

The Ivan Green Agency, 1888 Century Park East,#908, Los Angeles, California 90067. (213) 277-1541. (*)

Maxine Groffsky Literary Agency, 2 Fifth Avenue, New York, New York 10011. (212) 677-2720.

Grossman-Stalmaster Agency, 8730 Sunset Boulevard, #405, Los Angeles, California 90069. (213) 657-3040.

Marquita Hall, 5705 Meldon Drive, Louisville, Kentucky 40216. (502) 447-2099. (*)

Reece Halsey Agency, 8733 Sunset Boulevard, Los Angeles, California 90069. (213) 652-2409. (*)

Mitchell J. Hamilburg Agency, 292 South La Cienega Boulevard, Beverly Hills, California 90211. (213) 657-1501.

Robert G. Hussong Agency, 8271 Melrose Avenue, Los Angeles, California 90046.

International Creative Management (ICM), 8899 Beverly Boulevard, Los Angeles, California 90048. (213) 550-4000. (P)

International Creative Management (ICM), 40 West 57th Street, New York, New York 10019. (212) 556-5600. (P)

Merrily Kane Agency, 9171 Wilshire Boulevard, #507, Beverly Hills, California 90210. (213) 550-8874.

King, Archer, Ltd., 777 Seventh Avenue, New York, New York 10019. (212) 581-8513. (*)

Howard King Agency, Inc., 6362 Hollywood Boulevard, #320, Los Angeles, California 90028. (213) 462-1745. (*)

The Kingsley Corporation, 112 Barnsbee Lane, Coventry, Connecticut 06238. (203) 742-9575. (*)

The Paul Kohner-Michael Levy Agency, 9169 Sunset Boulevard, Los Angeles, California 90069. (213) 550-1060. (P)

Otto R. Kozak Agency, 1089 West Park Avenue, Long Beach, New York 11561. (516) 889-4370.

John LaRocca & Associates, 3907 West Alameda Avenue, Burbank, California 91505. (213) 841-0031.

Irving Paul Lazar Agency, 211 South Beverly Drive, Suite 100, Beverly Hills, California 90212. (213) 275-6153.

Llewellyn Company, 142-41 41st Avenue, Flushing, New York 11355. (212) 353-8276.

Lovell & Associates, 1350 North Highland Avenue, #24, Los Angeles, California 90028. (213) 462-1672. (*)

Major Talent Agency, 12301 Wilshire Boulevard, Los Angeles, California 90025. (213) 820-5841. (P)

Raya Markson Literary Agency, 1888 Century Park East, Los Angeles, California 90067. (213) 552-2083. (*)

Harold Matson Co., Inc., 22 East 40th Street, New York, New York 10016. (212) 679-4490.

Memminger Artists, Ltd., 4321 Colfax Avenue, Studio City, California 91604. (213) 980-4449.

George Michaud Agency, 4950 Densmore, #1, Encino, California 91436. (213) 981-6680. (*)

William Morris Agency, Inc., 151 El Camino, Beverly Hills, California 90212. (213) 274-7451. (P)

William Morris Agency, Inc., 1350 Avenue of the Americas, New York, New York 10019. (212) 586-5100. (P)

Marvin Moss Inc., 9200 Sunset Boulevard, Los Angeles, California 90069. (213) 274-8483. (P)

The Pickman Company, Inc., 9025 Wilshire Boulevard, #303, Beverly Hills, California 90211. (213) 273-8273.

Lynn Pleshette Agency, 2643 Creston Drive, Hollywood, California 90068. (213) 465-0428.

The Guy Prescott Agency, 8920 Wonderland Avenue, Los Angeles, California 90046. (213) 656-1963. (*)

Progressive Artists Agency, 400 South Beverly Drive, Beverly Hills, California 90210. (213) 553-8561.

Raper Enterprises Agency, 9441 Wilshire Boulevard, #620D, Beverly Hills, California 90212. (213) 273-7704.

Robinson-Weintraub Associates, Inc., 554 South San Vicente Boulevard, Los Angeles, California 90048. (213) 653-5802.

Sandy Roth Ruben, 9418 Wilshire Boulevard, Beverly Hills, California 90212. (213) 271-7209.

The Sackheim Agency, 9301 Wilshire Boulevard, #203, Beverly Hills, California 90210. (213) 276-3151.

Irving Salkow Agency, 9350 Wilshire Boulevard, #203, Beverly Hills, California 90210. (213)276-3141.

SBK Associates, 11 Chamberlain, Waltham, Massachusetts 02154. (617) 894-4037. (*)

John W. Schallert Agency, 9350 Wilshire Boulevard, Beverly Hills, California 90212. (213) 276-2044.

The Irv Schechter Company, 404 North Roxbury Drive, Beverly Hills, California 90210. (213) 278-8070.

Don Schwartz & Associates, 8721 Sunset Boulevard, Los Angeles, California 90069. (213) 657-8910. (*)

Shapiro-Lichtman, Inc., 2049 Century Park East, #1320, Los Angeles, California 90067. (213) 557-2244. (*)

Jerome Siegel Associates, 8733 Sunset Boulevard, Los Angeles, California 90069. (213) 652-6033.

Susan Smith & Associates, 9869 Santa Monica Boulevard, Beverly Hills, California 90212. (213) 277-8464.

STE Representation, Ltd., 211 S. Beverly Drive, #201, Beverly Hills, California 90212. (213) 550-3982.

Stiefel Office, Ltd., 8899 Beverly Boulevard, Los Angeles, California 90048. (213) 550-4000.

H.N. Swanson, Inc., 8523 Sunset Boulevard, Los Angeles, California 90069. (213) 652-5385. (*)

Talent Enterprises Agency, 1607 North El Centro, Suite 2, Los Angeles, California 90028. (213) 462-0913.

Trejos Literary Agency, 18235 Avalon Boulevard, Carson, California 90746. (213) 538-2945. (*)

Twentieth Century Artists, 13273 Ventura Boulevard, Studio City, California 91604. (213) 990-8580.

The Ufland Agency, 190 North Canon Drive, Beverly Hills, California 90210. (213) 273-9441. (P)

Lew Weitzman & Associates, Inc., 9171 Wilshire Boulevard, Beverly Hills, California 90210. (213) 278-5562.

Francine Witkin Agency, 6430 Sunset Boulevard, #1010-B, Hollywood, California 90028. (213) 461-3726. (*)

Ted Witzer Agency, 1900 Avenue of the Stars, #2850, Los Angeles, California 90067. (213) 552-9251.

Wormser, Heldfond & Joseph, Inc., 1717 North Highland Avenue, Hollywood, California 90028. (213) 466-9111. (*)

Sylvia Wosk Agency, 439 South La Cienega Boulevard, Los Angeles, California 90048. (213) 274-8063.

Writers & Artists Agency, 450 Roxbury Drive, Beverly Hills, California 90210. (213) 550-8030. (P)

Ziegler, Diskant, Inc., 9255 Sunset Boulevard, Los Angeles, California 90069. (213) 278-0070. (P)

APPENDIX FIVE

The Writers Guild of America

The history of the Writers Guild of America can be traced back to 1912, when the Authors Guild was formed to protect the vested and creative interests of novelists, short story writers, nonfiction writers and others. A few years later, the Authors Guild merged with the Dramatists Guild and began the Authors League. By 1921, with the arrival of motion pictures, some of the League's members formed a social organization called the Screen Writers Guild, which functioned informally as a branch of the League. It soon became apparent, however, that more than a social organization was needed: A protective association to safeguard the rights and economic prospects of screenwriters became the goal. In 1936 the SWG reincorporated as an affiliate of the Authors League, and the 1937 U.S. Supreme Court decision upholding the National Labor Relations Act gave the SWG the right to act as a collective bargaining agent for screenwriters.

After the first collectively bargained contract was signed in 1942, the SWG—flushed with victory but hopelessly disorganized and torn by internal dissension—went on to assist in the creation of a Radio Writers Guild in 1947, and a Television Writers Group in 1950.

In time, though, the collective bargaining structure became top-heavy and too compartmentalized, leading to confusion and duplication of effort. So, starting in the 1950s, meetings were held in New York between the leaders of the Authors Guild, the Dramatists Guild, the Television Writers Group, the Radio Writers Guild, and the Screen Writers Guild in the hope of figuring some way or other out of the organizational quicksand they had found themselves in.

The Writers Guild of America, founded in 1954, was the solution to the problem. One single agency would act as the bargaining force for all the professional screen, radio, and television writers in the United States. Because the entertainment industry was divided so evenly between New York for television and the West Coast for motion pictures (at least, that was the case at the time), the Guild was divided in half, with the Mississippi River designated as the line between the two areas of jurisdiction. Thus, there now exist the Writers Guild of America, east, Inc., located at 27 West 48th Street, New York, New York 10036, (212) 575-5060, and the Writers Guild of America, west, Inc., at 8955 Beverly Boulevard, Los Angeles, California 90048, (213) 550-1000.

By the beginning of the 1980s the total membership of the WGA came to just under 7,000 with nearly 6,000 of these members located on the West Coast.

It is this relatively small group of writers that is responsible for virtually everything you see on television, in movie theaters, and hear on a majority of radiodrama series.

Anyone can become a current member of the Writers Guild after having sold at least one script to television, film, or radio as a non-Guild freelancer. (Which is precisely what this book is all about—providing the information to help make that one important sale.) After making that first sale—permissible under the Taft-Hartley Act, which permits any nonunion individual to take part in a union activity once—you can't make any further sales in that particular area without joining the Guild. The usual procedure is to use the money from that first sale and attend to the membership fees as soon as the check arrives in the mail.

Membership in the Guild is not automatic. When an application is submitted, the work you undertook is evaluated and confirmed. Then an initiation fee of $500 is required, after which you are charged dues of $10 per quarter, and 1 to 1½ percent of all your earnings within Guild jurisdiction. (All three figures subject to change.)

Membership in the Guild promises neither success nor Ultimate Happiness. The WGA does not actively find work for any of its writers, and it makes no pretensions to being a school for scriptwriters.

The most important thing that the Guild *does* do is to allow you to continue to work as a scriptwriter for the media. Virtually every major and independent film producer, all of the television networks, and many radio networks are signatories to the Guild, promising that they will not employ non-Guild members on any basis other than that permissible under the Taft-Hartley Act.

In addition, the Guild oversees all contracts, arbitrates and assures proper listings of writing credit, provides a registration service open to Guild members and other writers, handles all contracts with agents, publishes a newsletter with marketing information and other material useful to a scriptwriter, provides a forum for meeting other writers, producers, and directors on a social basis, provides a credit union, oversees a group insurance plan and a pension plan, operates a film society, organizes committees that support freedom of expression, and emphasizes the importance of a steady supply of material from freelance and minority writers.

There are other benefits as well, not all of which are entirely tangible. Being a member of the Writers Guild means that you are recognized as a professional within the entertainment field. You have gone forever past the appellation of "amateur." Once a member of the Guild, it becomes remarkably easier to get an agent, which by itself is an advantage well worth the price of membership.

One benefit that any writer may derive from the Guild has to do with its script registration activities. If you have written a particularly marketable script, registration with the Guild will protect you against plagiarism, if it becomes necessary to determine who actually wrote the earliest version of that particular script. Scripts for radio, television and motion pictures can be registered by sending one copy of the script and $10 (if you are a member of the Guild the fee is $4) to the the Writers Guild of America, west, Script Registration Office, 8955 Beverly Boulevard, Los Angeles California 90048. A registration number will be sent to you when the script is received. This number should appear in the lower left-hand corner of the title page, thus: WGAw Registration #_____.

A current television market list—excerpted from the Guild newsletter—can be obtained by sending $2 to the same address.

The Writers Guild of America operates in affiliation with the Association of Canadian Television and Radio Artists (ACTRA), at 105 Carlton Street, Toronto, Canada M5B 1M2, (416) 363-6335; the Writers' Guild of Great Britain (WGGB), 430 Edgware Road, London, England W2 1EH, (01)723-8074; and the Australian Writers' Guild, at 197 Blues Point Road, North Sydney, NSW, Australia 2060, 922-3856.

INDEX

About the Author

J. Michael Straczynski has worked in every facet of the entertainment industry. He has published more than 150 articles on film, theater, radio, and television in such publications as the *Los Angeles Times*, *San Diego Magazine*, *Writer's Digest* Magazine, the *Daily Californian*, and others.

For the electronic media, Straczynski has written scripts that have been produced for television and by such radiodrama producers as *Alien Worlds* and the Mutual Radio Network. He has also produced and directed his own and others' radiodrama scripts, and for more than two years was the resident theater and film critic for San Diego's KSDO Newsradio.

For the theater, Straczynski has written more than a dozen produced plays that have been staged at community, legitimate, dinner, and children's theaters across the United States. Several of his plays have also been published in book form, one of which has been performed over 100 times.

Straczynski has written several screenplays under contract for the motion picture industry.

A member of the Writers Guild of America, west, Straczynski has taught writing at San Diego State University and Grossmont College in El Cajon, California, conducted seminars in scriptwriting through Airstage Radiodrama Productions, San Diego, for which he was artistic director and—following publication of this book—the Hollywood Script Writing Institute. Forthcoming are several new motion picture screenplays—one an independently produced suspense film and a CBS television movie based on his recently completed novel *Shattered Glass*, the others under contract and slated for production—several episodic telescripts and a new three-act play.

Other Writer's Digest Books

General Writing Books
Writer's Market, $17.95
Beginning Writer's Answer Book, edited by Polking, et al $9.95
How to Get Started in Writing, by Peggy Teeters $10.95
Law and the Writer, edited by Polking and Meranus (paper) $7.95
Make Every Word Count, by Gary Provost (paper) $6.95
Treasury of Tips for Writers, edited by Marvin Weisbord (paper) $6.95
Writer's Resource Guide, 488 pp. $12.95

Magazine/News Writing
Complete Guide to Marketing Magazine Articles, by Duane Newcomb $9.95
Craft of Interviewing, by John Brady $9.95
Magazine Writing: The Inside Angle, by Art Spikol $12.95
Magazine Writing Today, by Jerome E. Kelley $10.95
Newsthinking: The Secret of Great Newswriting, by Bob Baker $11.95
1001 Article Ideas, by Frank A. Dickson $10.95
Stalking the Feature Story, by William Ruehlmann $9.95
Write On Target, by Connie Emerson $12.95
Writing and Selling Non-Fiction, by Hayes B. Jacobs $12.95

Fiction Writing
Fiction Writer's Market, edited by Fredette and Brady $16.95
Creating Short Fiction, by Damon Knight $11.95
Handbook of Short Story Writing, by Dickson and Smythe (paper) $6.95
How to Write Best-Selling Fiction, by Dean R. Koontz $13.95
How to Write Short Stories that Sell, by Louise Boggess $9.95
One Way to Write Your Novel, by Dick Perry (paper) $6.95
Secrets of Successful Fiction, by Robert Newton Peck $8.95
Writing the Novel: From Plot to Print, by Lawrence Block $10.95

Special Interest Writing Books
Cartoonist's & Gag Writer's Handbook, by Jack Markow (paper) $9.95
Children's Picture Book: How to Write It, How to Sell It, by Ellen E.M. Roberts $17.95
Complete Book of Scriptwriting, by J. Michael Straczynski $14.95
Confession Writer's Handbook, by Florence K. Palmer. Revised by Marguerite McClain $9.95
Guide to Greeting Card Writing, edited by Larry Sandman $10.95
Guide to Writing History, by Doris Ricker Marston $9.95
How to Write and Sell Your Personal Experiences, by Lois Duncan $10.95
How to Write "How-To" Books and Articles, by Raymond Hull (paper) $8.95
Mystery Writer's Handbook, edited by Lawrence Treat (paper) $8.95
The Poet and the Poem, Revised edition by Judson Jerome $13.95
Poet's Handbook, by Judson Jerome $11.95
Sell Copy, by Webster Kuswa $11.95
Successful Outdoor Writing, by Jack Samson $11.95
TV Scriptwriter's Handbook, by Alfred Brenner $12.95
Travel Writer's Handbook, by Louise Purwin Zobel $13.95
Writing and Selling Science Fiction, by Science Fiction Writers of America (paper) $7.95
Writing for Children & Teenagers, by Lee Wyndham. Revised by Arnold Madison $10.95
Writing for Regional Publications, by Brian Vachon $11.95
Writing to Inspire, by Gentz, Roddy, et al $14.95

The Writing Business
Complete Handbook for Freelance Writers, by Kay Cassill $14.95
How to Be a Successful Housewife/Writer, by Elaine Fantle Shimberg $10.95

How You Can Make $20,000 a Year Writing, by Nancy Hanson (paper) $6.95
Jobs For Writers, edited by Kirk Polking $11.95
Profitable Part-time/Full-time Freelancing, by Clair Rees $10.95
**The Writer's Survival Guide: How to Cope with Rejection, Success and 99 Other
Hang-Ups of the Writing Life**, by Jean and Veryl Rosenbaum $12.95

To order directly from the publisher, include $1.50 postage and handling for
1 book and 50¢ for each additional book. Allow 30 days for delivery.

Writer's Digest Books, Department B
9933 Alliance Road, Cincinnati OH 45242
Prices subject to change without notice.